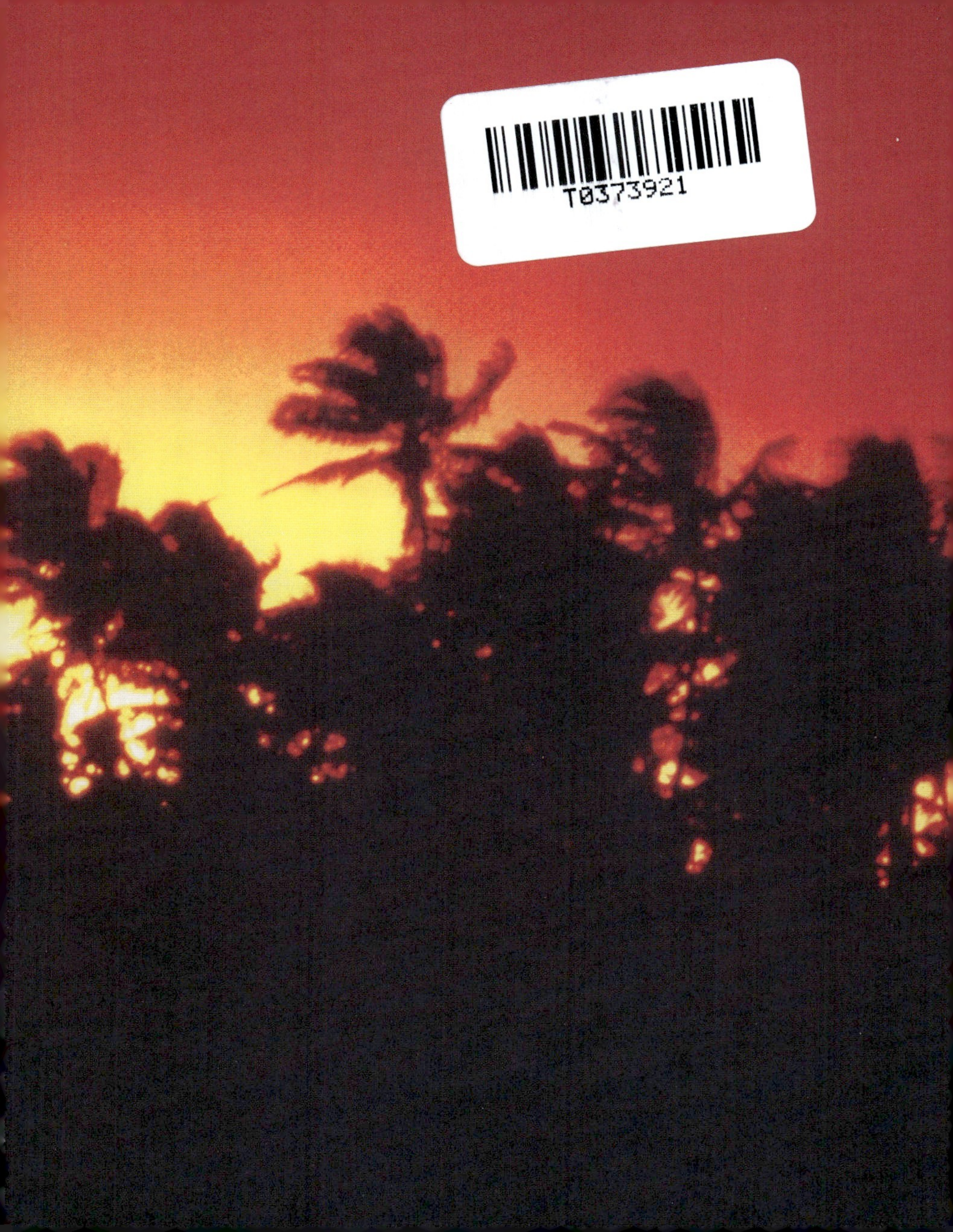

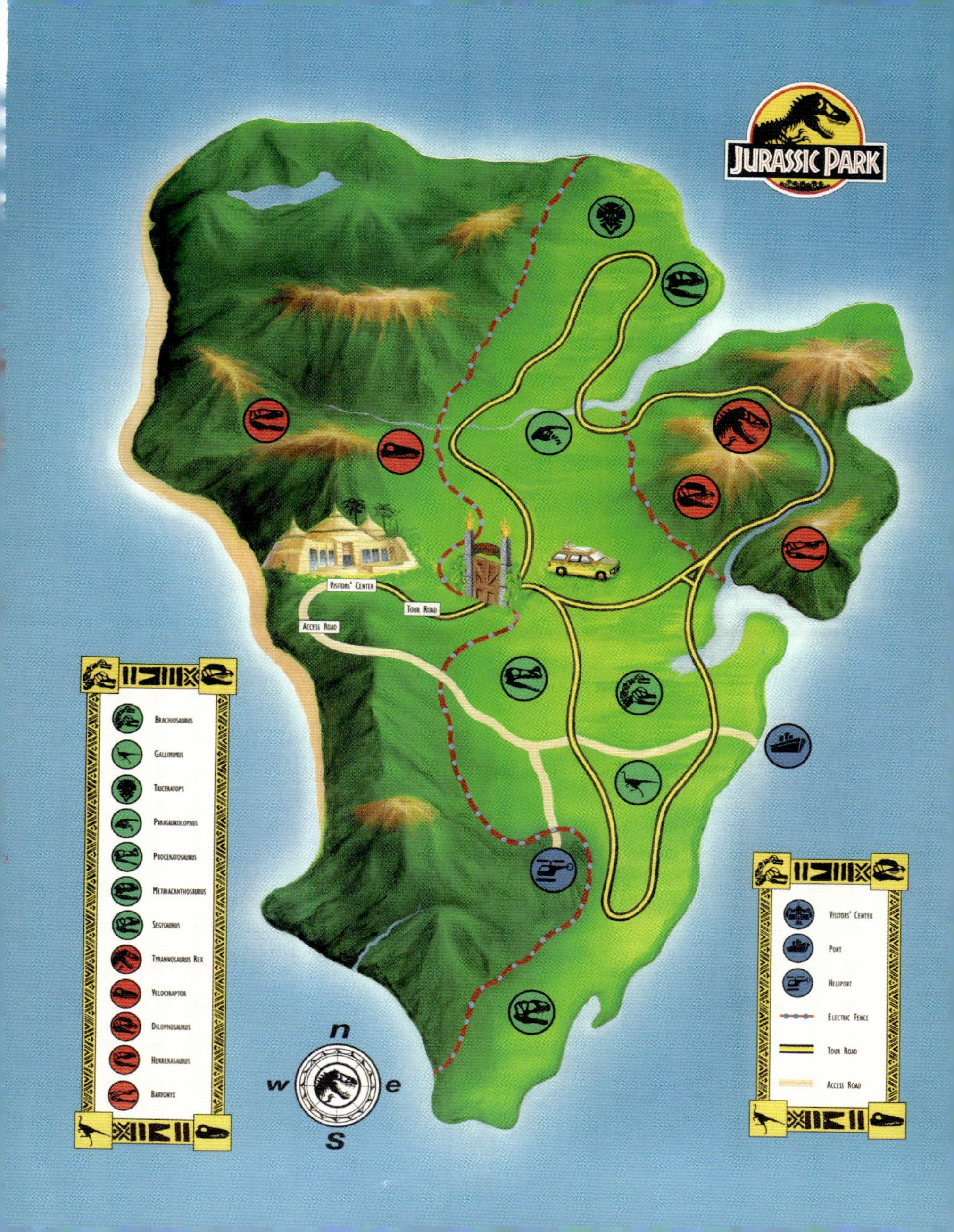
Jurassic Park
Visitors' Center
Tour Road
Access Road
Brachiosaurus
Gallimimus
Triceratops
Parasaurolophus
Proceratosaurus
Metriacanthosaurus
Segisaurus
Tyrannosaurus Rex
Velociraptor
Dilophosaurus
Herrerasaurus
Baryonyx
n
w
e
s
Visitors' Center
Port
Heliport
Electric Fence
Tour Road
Access Road

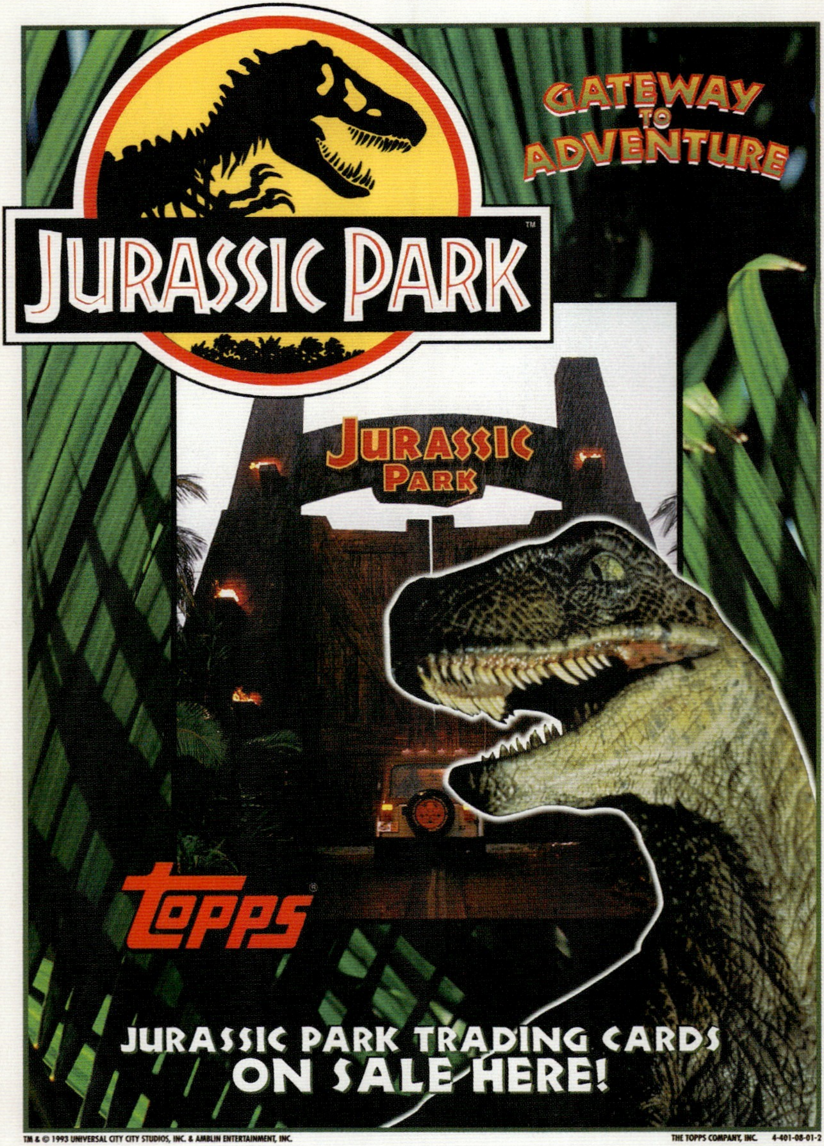
JURASSIC PARK™
GATEWAY TO ADVENTURE
JURASSIC PARK
Topps®
JURASSIC PARK TRADING CARDS
ON SALE HERE!

THE ORIGINAL TOPPS TRADING CARD SERIES

Introduction and Commentary by Gary Gerani
Afterword by Chip Kidd

Abrams ComicArts, New York

I dedicate this book to my loving parents, John and Jean Gerani. And to one particular Christmas morning, December 1959, when I found my first set of plastic dinosaurs under the tree. Who says true love doesn't last forever?

Special thanks to Ira Friedman at Topps; Kristin Conte, Barb Layman, Michael Moccio, and Susan Weber at NBC/Universal; and Marty Grosser at *Previews*. At Abrams, thanks to Jessica Gotz, Charles Kochman, and Jody Mosley (editorial); Liam Flanagan and Brenda Angelilli (design); Mary O'Mara and Maggie Rothfus (managing editorial); and Alison Gervais (production). And thanks to Geoff Spear (photography) and Chip Kidd (afterword).

Editor: Jessica Gotz
Project Manager: Charles Kochman
Designer: Liam Flanagan
Managing Editor: Mary O'Mara
Production Manager: Alison Gervais

Library of Congress Cataloging Number
2021941271

ISBN 978-1-4197-5241-4

Universal press kit for *Jurassic Park* courtesy of Charles Kochman
Images courtesy of Chip Kidd: 380, 383
All other photography by Geoff Spear, shot in New York City on April 21, 2021

Front endpaper: detail, Universal press kit folder, 1993
Page 1: Promotional map from Universal press kit for *Jurassic Park*, 1993
Page 2: *Jurassic Park* Topps promotional poster, 1993
Page 6: Promotional newspaper from Universal press kit for *Jurassic Park*, 1993

Cover design by Liam Flanagan
Case photography by Geoff Spear

Published in 2022 by Abrams ComicArts®, an imprint of ABRAMS. All rights reserved.

Printed and bound in China
10 9 8 7 6 5 4 3 2 1

Abrams ComicArts books are available at special discounts when purchased in quantity for premiums and promotions as well as fundraising or educational use. Special editions can also be created to specification. For details, contact specialsales@abramsbooks.com or the address below.

Abrams ComicArts® is a registered trademark of Harry N. Abrams, Inc.

ABRAMS The Art of Books
195 Broadway, New York, NY 10007
abramsbooks.com

Topps presents JURASSIC PARK

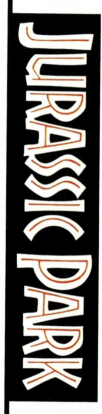

JURASSIC NEWS

VOLUME 1 ISSUE 1   FEBRUARY 1993

FROM THE DESK OF JOHN HAMMOND

It gives me great pleasure to share the good news that ten years of laboratory research on Isla Nublar have made it possible for me to provide an experience so astonishing that it will capture the imagination of the entire world!

Thanks to the efforts of our high-tech, real estate and entertainment divisions, Jurassic Park will be the world's most advanced amusement park and a once-in-a-lifetime experience for each of its visitors.

All of us at InGen look forward to the day when we will open the gates and invite you and your family to share the lost world of our prehistoric past.

We look forward to meeting you.

JOHN HAMMOND

INTRODUCING JURASSIC PARK
160 MILLION YEARS IN THE MAKING

Artist's conception of Jurassic Park, the world's most spectacular theme park.

When the gates of JURASSIC PARK open in June 1993, visitors will gain entry to a world we have never seen before, a melding of scientific discovery and visual imagination: grand in its scope and diversity of life, a complete universe.

Imagine you are one of the first visitors to the park. You arrive as a child would, free of preconceptions and ready for anything. Your adventure is about to begin.

Entering the gates of the park, your senses are overwhelmed by the world that surrounds you: the sounds, the smells, even the feel of the earth is curiously different. Somewhere in the distance, you hear the movement of huge animals – the ground shakes with their passing. You are a stranger in an alien world.

You look into the night sky, at stars whose light was born long before humans ever existed; born when a different race of beings walked the planet – swift, powerful animals, rulers of the earth for 160 million years. Like those ancient stars, the Jurassic has left only faint traces of itself – fossils, footprints, relics of blood cells encased in amber. A time capsule that has remained closed for countless millennia.

Now the time capsule has been opened, and man and dinosaurs, the two rulers of the earth, will meet for the first time in JURASSIC PARK.

John Hammond, Chief Executive Officer of Hammond Development Corporation and InGen Inc., has announced that construction has begun on "the world's most spectacular theme park," a celebration of prehistoric wonders and modern technology.

The billion dollar complex, to be built on a twenty-two square mile island, will take visitors on a unique journey into the age of dinosaurs, which ended 65 million years ago. The park will also feature a four-star resort hotel, retail, dining and entertainment facilities, and an innovative transportation plan.

Located one hundred miles off the west coast

(continued on back)

THE PAST COMES ALIVE... WITH A VENGEANCE!

BY GARY GERANI

Kids and dinosaurs. It's a special relationship.

It was with yours truly. Something about these amazing-looking animals hooked me big-time when I was a youngster, which was decades before Steven Spielberg's blockbuster film, based on Michael Crichton's equally successful book, popularized them. Maybe it's because they resembled dragons and the kind of cool, scarifying monsters I'd seen in movies and comic books. Their massive jaws, towering size, and nasty spiked appendages were about as awesome as you can get. For me, a trip to the American Museum of Natural History in New York City was like visiting Disneyland, only without the crowds. And I found these prehistoric giants, even in fossilized skeleton form, to be a heck of a lot more compelling.

Companies that manufactured entertainment products for children began to realize the enormous sales potential of dinosaur-themed items. Just about everyone in my generation grew up with those nifty Marx playset figures, first manufactured during the 1950s. A plastic model kit re-creating the New York museum's famed *Tyrannosaurus* exhibit was also a big hit with

us kids. Not so much with our ever-patient dads, of course, who were often tasked with gluing these multi-pieced models together. And then there was every kid's favorite gas station, Sinclair. Starting with its *Brontosaurus* logo, this company offered dinosaur imagery everywhere, not to mention some supercool inflatable dino toys. Sinclair's contributions to the 1964 World's Fair were remarkable life-size dinosaur statues that, once seen, are never forgotten.

During the Eisenhower era and beyond, Topps and other trading-card companies dallied with dinosaurs in a number of penny and nickel products. A company called Nu-Cards created a set in 1961 that boasted beautiful public domain paintings (printed in tinted black and white). These cards included the work of several celebrated paleo-artists, among them the legendary Charles Knight, whose work I would see on display at the American Museum of Natural History.

Always wildly photogenic, dinosaurs would often pop up in humorous card or sticker products, and sometimes as guest stars in movie-themed products. Fans could delight in seeing the Eighth Wonder of the World square off against his *Tyrannosaurus* opponent in the *King Kong* trading-card set issued by Topps in 1965. It was based on the classic 1933 movie that became a monster hit on early television. Disney jumped into the prehistoric parade with a 1985 adventure movie called *Baby: Secret of the Lost Legend*, which Topps also tied into. And then, later in the '80s, Topps released a pair of popular prehistoric-themed products: The first was a wild and crazy fiction card series called *Dinosaurs Attack!*, which reworked the company's infamous *Mars Attacks* formula with *Garbage Pail Kids*–like satirical flavoring. The second was *Dino Toys with Candy Eggs*, which offered scrumptious little treats and mini-dinosaur figures to go with them. As the ultimate homage to my childhood obsession, I made sure our little toy dinosaurs used the same colors that the classic Marx versions employed back in the day.

This leads me to *Jurassic Park*, finally, and the reinvention of the science-fiction movie genre with a groundbreaking special effects technique that was nothing short of jaw-dropping. Computer generated imagery (CGI) provided sophisticated special effects that were so naturalistic and fluid that the approach instantly eclipsed stop-motion animation (which was, up until that point, the go-to cinematic method of bringing fantastic creatures to life). Although frame-by-frame animation made movies like *King Kong* and Ray Harryhausen's later creations exciting classics, there was always a certain jerkiness to the creatures' move-ments, a built-in flaw known as strobing.

CGI smoothed out that anomaly, dazzling viewers with living, moving animals that simply looked real. Special effects for the movies would never be the same, with CGI opening up an infinite number of creative possibilities.

But before there was a movie with dazzling effects in 1993, there was Michael Crichton's 1990 novel, which was a national bestseller. And before the book, a sudden, unexpected resurgence of interest in dinosaurs across the board, something of an unexpected fad that began in the early '80s. Over at Topps, we New Product developers were generally quite good at sniffing out trends of the moment. It didn't take long for us to catch wind of all this renewed dino interest. As mentioned, the painted card set *Dinosaurs Attack!* and the candy product *Dino Toys* were our two big contributions to dinosaur hysteria during this lively period. Remarkably, I was told that Michael Crichton himself was a fan of the Topps *Dinosaurs Attack!* cards. Proud as we are of the pulpy sci-fi premise dreamed up for *Dinosaurs Attack!* (a mishap in space creates a time-warping anomaly), Crichton's idea to bring these wondrous animals back to life was one of the most brilliant and believable notions ever imagined for a story of this kind. Just use a prehistoric mosquito trapped in amber to genetically re-create living dinosaurs like the ones this insect originally drew blood from. That's so simple and logical, how can it not work? And what could possibly go wrong?

In the early '90s, before the *Jurassic Park* novel was published, the galleys for Crichton's new opus were circulated to

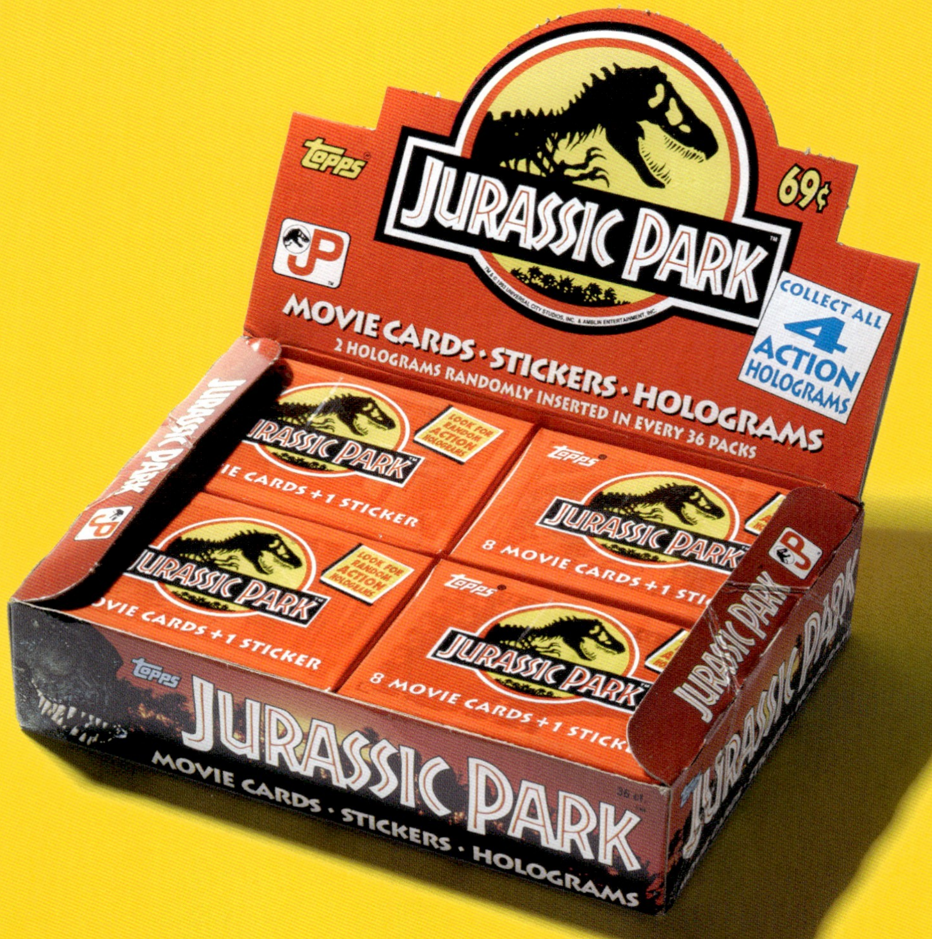

Topps
69¢
JURASSIC PARK
JP
MOVIE CARDS • STICKERS • HOLOGRAMS
2 HOLOGRAMS RANDOMLY INSERTED IN EVERY 36 PACKS
COLLECT ALL 4 ACTION HOLOGRAMS
8 MOVIE CARDS +1 STICKER
LOOK FOR RANDOM ACTION HOLOGRAMS

Jurassic Park trading card display box, 1993

major film studios. Steven Spielberg had already snapped up the rights, although *Gremlins* director Joe Dante had also expressed interest. (Ironically, Dante had just optioned *Dinosaurs Attacks!* and was planning a big-budget movie for Warner Bros., a project that never came to fruition.)

In no time, the synergy between the *Jurassic Park* novel's release and the upcoming Steven Spielberg movie began generating a great deal of excitement. The big question on everybody's mind was how these new-age dinosaurs were going to be brought to life. Before the groundbreaking CGI techniques were put into play, stop-motion was indeed attempted for a sequence of special-effects tests. Phil Tippett was the FX veteran behind this approach to dino motion, and he produced some impressive results. About ten years earlier, Industrial Light & Magic, George Lucas's visual effects company, brought the titular beast of *Dragonslayer* to life in the same fashion, dazzling audiences with some of the smoothest stop-motion ever presented in a movie.

Advanced computer technology had already produced movie magic in films such as James Cameron's *The Abyss* and *Terminator 2*, and Tim Burton's *Batman Returns* (the latter giving us an army of waddling, booby-trapped penguins!). But now it was being used for something that truly called for digital perfection, as all eyes would be scrutinizing Spielberg's front-and-center behemoths for signs of imperfection and artificiality. Before long a lucky blurring of realities provided *Jurassic Park* with a promotional asset no other movie has had, before or since. Dr. John Hammond used

a miraculous process to give prehistoric creatures new life in Crichton's story; Steven Spielberg was giving them new life on film, through an equally miraculous process. It pretty much added up to, "They've found a way to bring dinosaurs back to life!" so just about everyone on the planet *had* to eventually experience this movie. Once information about the film was out, word of mouth (in these pre-internet days) bolstered the marketing, taking on a life of its own.

In the midst of all this, the Topps Company was doing its usual candy-counter thing, creating both original novelty products for young buyers and tying in with movie studios for licensed opportunities. Hollywood studios would let us know what they were developing for release, and their licensing division would send us scripts, photos, and other promotional materials in the hopes of making a deal. *Jurassic Park* was no exception. As with most Spielberg projects, Topps had already learned of the movie while it was in preproduction. (Ever since *Close Encounters of the Third Kind*, Topps had allied itself with just about all of Spielberg's endeavors.) Although, coincidentally, we had gotten very close to our own dinosaur property being made into a multimillion-dollar movie, the potential for enormous profits promised by a new Spielberg-Crichton adventure simply couldn't be ignored.

I had been a Brooklyn boy my entire life. But in 1989, while Steven Spielberg was developing *Jurassic Park* and a little pirate movie called *Hook*, I moved from the East Coast to Southern California—Sherman Oaks to be exact. In the right place to pursue my screenwriting ambitions (a side career that started in 1988 with my horror

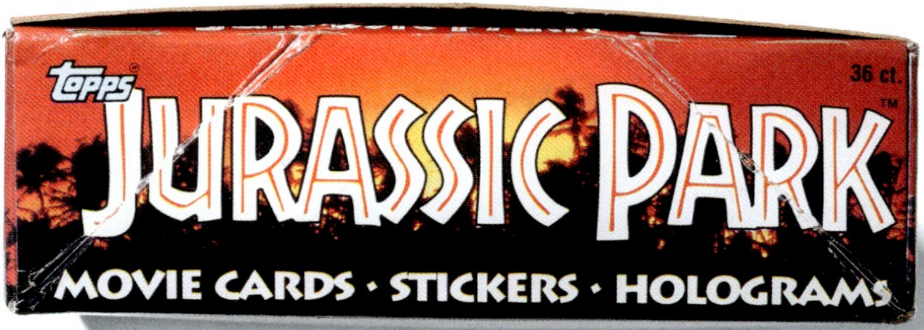
Topps
36 ct.
JURASSIC PARK
TM
MOVIE CARDS · STICKERS · HOLOGRAMS

film *Pumpkinhead*), I was also able to take Topps with me. Most of my creative duties involved trips to the film studios, and, ever since *Star Wars* hit in 1977, the company had been flying me to Hollywood on a regular basis. So having a representative out in LA to permanently gather materials, in addition to writing and editing trading-card products, made sense. I was still able to draw/fax pencil designs of card borders, and regular visits to Topps headquarters in New York a few times a year guaranteed that business would continue as usual.

It was my job to write and edit the inevitable Topps card sets based on *Jurassic Park* and *Hook*, and living in LA, I spent time at the studios for both of Spielberg's upcoming projects. Even as I was selecting photographic images of Robin Williams in an elf costume and Dustin Hoffman making like a pre–Johnny Depp pirate, Denise Durham at Amblin was sharing some amazing *Jurassic Park* artwork with me. I spent half a day in their offices going through the most breathtaking storyboards I had ever seen. If the upcoming movie looked anything like these, I remember thinking, there was no doubt Spielberg's film would be a hit of gargantuan proportions.

Topps, being a reliable partner in these movie licensing deals, was entrusted with the screenplays for films we'd be adapting into trading cards. I honestly can't recall if they locked me in a room with the top-secret screenplay and I wrote extensive notes, or if I was given the script to take home so I could write the card copy. But either way, access to specific scene descriptions and exact dialogue was essential to doing this adaptation correctly.

Of course, we'd have no product at all without dinosaurs. Fortunately, the unique nature of the special effects created for *Jurassic Park* would result in some pretty impressive coverage. While the groundbreaking wonders of CGI got all the

Side panel from Topps trading card display box, 1993

MOVIE CARDS

hype, Stan Winston's life-size animatronic puppets were physically on the set, sharing the same scenes and the same space with all those scared-looking actors. Winston also fabricated rubber raptor costumes that were worn by skilled experts, including frequent *Alien* actor/creature-creator Tom Woodruff Jr. In the end, Spielberg would seamlessly blend live-action coverage and computer imagery.

As is usual for someone who does what I do, I was taken to a room and shown hundreds of breathtaking color photos that covered all of the scenes in the movie—on-set dinosaurs included. I then made a

selection based on what I knew Topps's overall needs were. Beyond the trading card and sticker set, our primary products, Topps had signed on to do a souvenir magazine, comic books, and some cool candy containers (the *T. rex* and a raptor hatching from oversized eggs). I'd be involved with all of these in one capacity or another, particularly the magazine, which I'd write and edit. But my main concerns, as always, were our primary products, the trading cards and stickers.

Our first task was breaking the card set down into chapters—individual sections dedicated to one specific theme or another. I based this idea on a book's traditional table of contents, and it seemed to elevate the proceedings, suggesting greater detail and density. It was logically placed on the

Side panel from Topps trading card display box, 1993

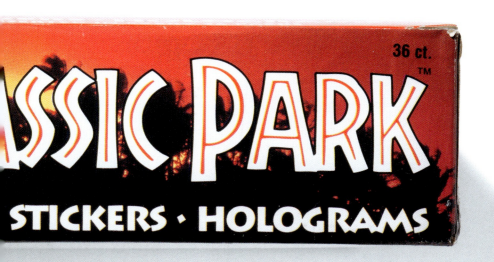

36 ct.

™

SSIC PARK

STICKERS · HOLOGRAMS

back of our Title Card. We'd been doing more sophisticated card sets for a few years at this point, as the ones created expressly for the discriminating comics market required a more focused, fan-centric treatment. A movie like *Jurassic Park* appealed to both worlds, and our product benefitted from this relatively grown-up, yet still mainstream, handling.

Throughout most of the '70s, when Hollywood took only a casual interest in what its licensees did creatively with their properties, Topps would happily conjure up its own designs and graphics, often just dropping in a film's official logo. The famous *Star Wars* "red blast" in Series 1 was our own graphic, not Lucasfilm's. But gradually, movie studios began to exert greater control over the films they licensed, especially when

most were blossoming into blockbuster hits. So style guides were created by the studios for each movie, which were an invaluable explosion of graphics, typefaces, and all kinds of imagery their marketing and publicity teams wanted the movie to be associated with.

Fair enough . . . that made our jobs a little easier. The colors and patterns ultimately used for both the Series 1 and 2 card borders all came from the *Jurassic Park* style guide, as did the font for the captions. Our design differs slightly in the vertical cards, but it's essentially selling the same stylistic message. All of our subsets and stickers were designed in much the same way. Looking back at them now, I think these cards really benefit from this semi-impressionistic approach. They're almost miniature museum pieces, which seems appropriate given the film's subject matter.

After I selected the final images and wrote all the text, it was up to Topps to take this colorful product into final form. As always, veteran art department directors Ben Solomon and Ted Moskowitz supervised the job as it went through various stages of production. But it was the dedicated New Product Development (NPD) team that pulled the elements together after I delivered them—including department head Ira Friedman; creative director Len Brown; artist/designer Brad Kahlhamer; editors John Williams, Don Alan, and Matt Saunders; and others. NPD made all the style guide background selections for the cards, along with most of the other graphic choices. The wrapper was certainly simple enough (the *Jurassic Park* logo), and both it and the bright red box were designed horizontally . . . evoking the bent-over, scientifically accurate dinosaurs from the film.

The *Jurassic Park* trading cards performed quite well for Topps, and the various tie-in products we concocted pleased kids and collectors alike. Our cards and containers joined the ranks of other candy counter items with a dinosaur theme, and whetted everyone's appetite for the inevitable big-screen sequel. That came in the form of *Jurassic Park: The Lost World* in 1997, a much-anticipated movie that Topps also tied into. But that's another story for another book.

Gary Gerani, author of the *Star Wars* Topps series and *Planet of the Apes: The Original Topps Trading Card Series*, is a screenwriter, author, noted film and TV historian, and children's product developer. He is best known as the cowriter of the film *Pumpkinhead*; the author of the book *Fantastic Television*; and the creator, editor, and writer of literally hundreds of Topps trading card sets since 1972. He lives in California.

Opposite: *Jurassic Park* marketing one sheet, 2020

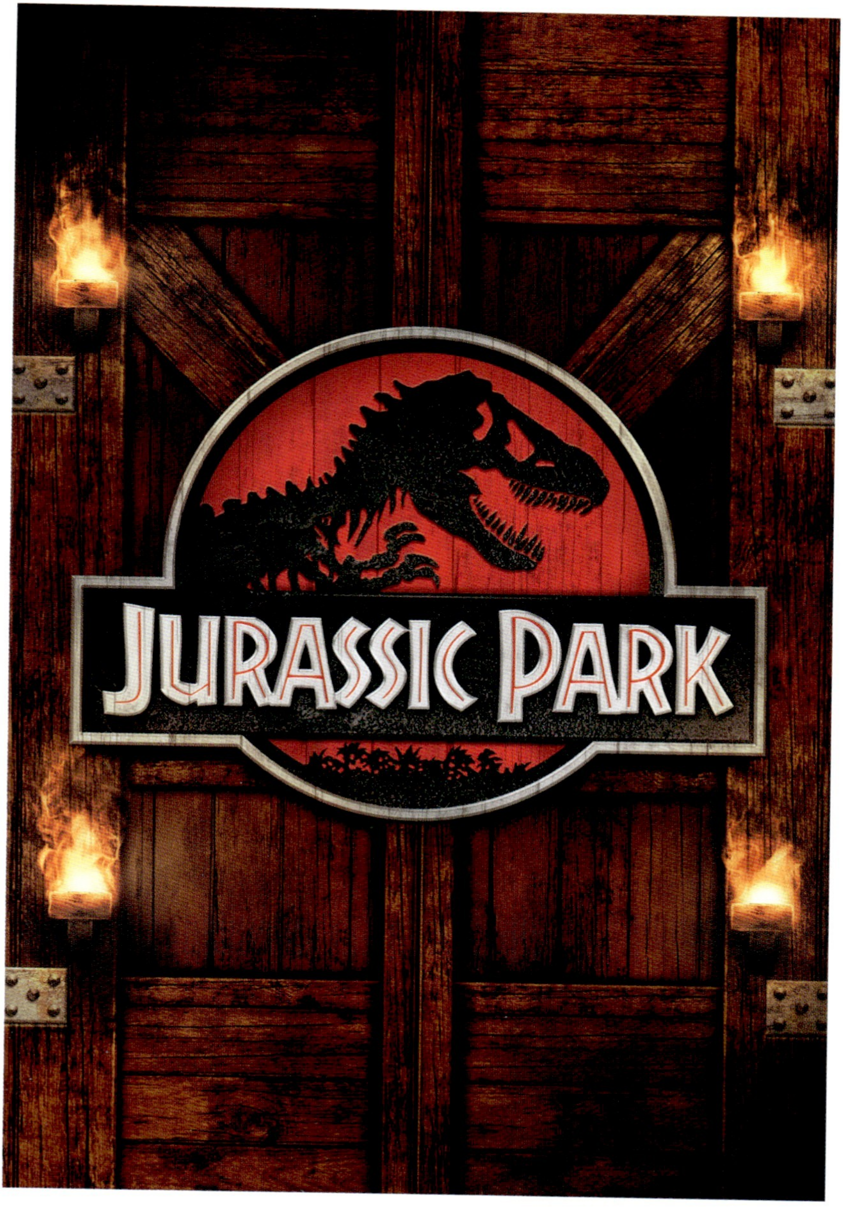
JURASSIC PARK

SERIES ONE

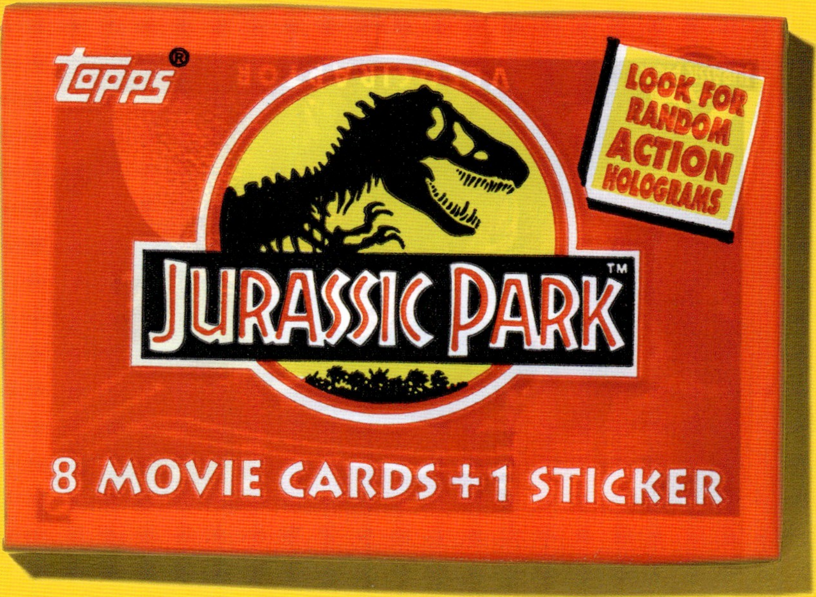
topps®
LOOK FOR RANDOM ACTION HOLOGRAMS
JURASSIC PARK™
8 MOVIE CARDS +1 STICKER

Topps presents JURASSIC PARK
The Trading Card Series

CARD NO.	CONTENTS
1	TITLE CARD
3-8	THE DINOSAURS — Photo/data coverage of the six major dinosaurs: Tyrannosaurus, Dilophosaurus, Velociraptor, Gallimimus, Triceratops, Brachiosaurus
9-11	THE PARK — Main Gate/Visitor Center, Park Explorers, Raptor Pen/Control Room
12-19	CAST OF CHARACTERS
20-70	STORYLINE
71	THE NOVEL BY MICHAEL CRITCHTON
72-75	THE MOVIE BY STEVEN SPIELBERG Behind-the-scenes
76-88	STAN WINSTON STUDIO SUB-SET: THE ART OF CRASH — Illustrations and exclusive commentary from the designer of JURASSIC PARK's dinosaurs

JURASSIC PARK

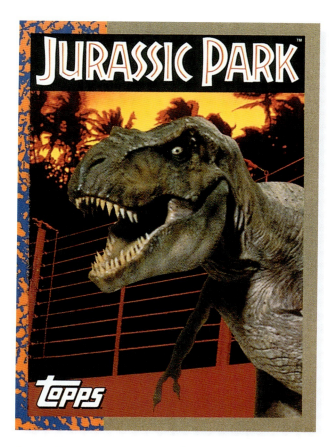

The Title Card concept, established by Topps in the very late 1970s to early '80s, was intended to function like the cover of a book. We took this to the next level by the time the '90s came along, with the flip side of the Title Card now providing a table of contents. Here, an exciting combination of the *T. rex* and some compound fence imagery gets things off to a roaring start.

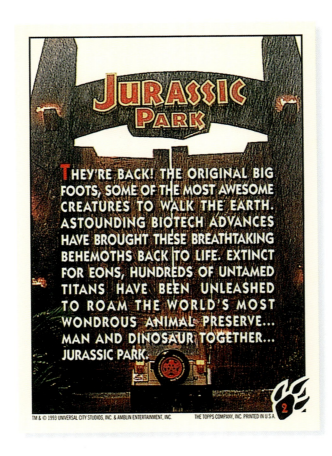

THEY'RE BACK! THE ORIGINAL BIG FOOTS, SOME OF THE MOST AWESOME CREATURES TO WALK THE EARTH. ASTOUNDING BIOTECH ADVANCES HAVE BROUGHT THESE BREATHTAKING BEHEMOTHS BACK TO LIFE. EXTINCT FOR EONS, HUNDREDS OF UNTAMED TITANS HAVE BEEN UNLEASHED TO ROAM THE WORLD'S MOST WONDROUS ANIMAL PRESERVE... MAN AND DINOSAUR TOGETHER... JURASSIC PARK.

TM & © 1993 UNIVERSAL CITY STUDIOS, INC. & AMBLIN ENTERTAINMENT, INC.   THE TOPPS COMPANY, INC. PRINTED IN U.S.A.

WELCOME TO
JURASSIC
PARK
JURASSIC PARK

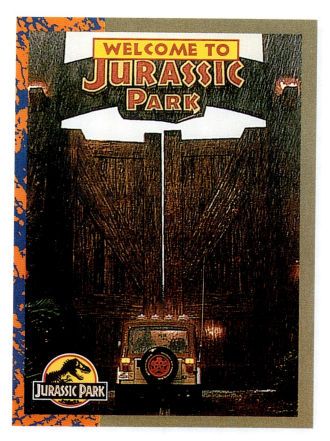

A distantly sinister "welcome" to the park where dreams come true—along with some especially terrifying nightmares. Simple but powerful text, presented in alarming uppercase, sets the stage for the story to come.

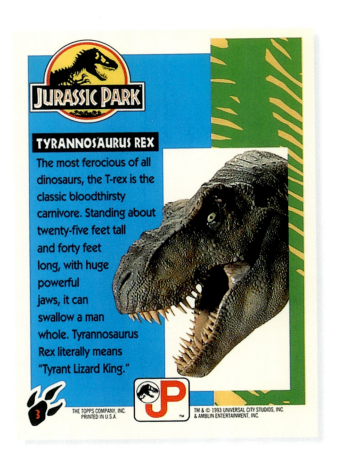

JURASSIC PARK
TYRANNOSAURUS REX
The most ferocious of all dinosaurs, the T-rex is the classic bloodthirsty carnivore. Standing about twenty-five feet tall and forty feet long, with huge powerful jaws, it can swallow a man whole. Tyrannosaurus Rex literally means "Tyrant Lizard King."
3
THE TOPPS COMPANY, INC.
PRINTED IN U.S.A.
JP
TM
TM & © 1993 UNIVERSAL CITY STUDIOS, INC.
& AMBLIN ENTERTAINMENT, INC.

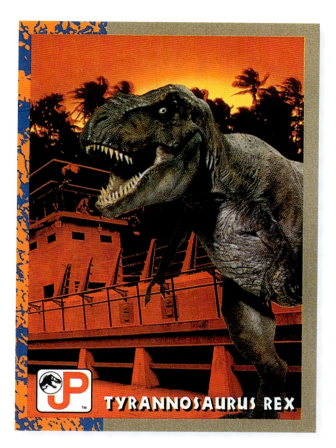

TYRANNOSAURUS REX

Our first subset introduces the true stars of *Jurassic Park*—the scientifically generated dinosaurs that dominate the movie. First up: the apex predator, the *Tyrannosaurus rex*.

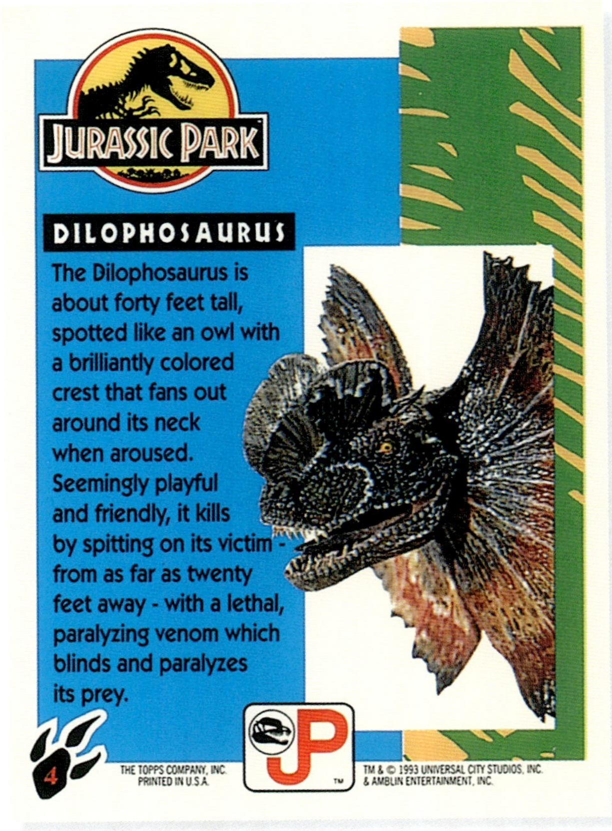
JURASSIC PARK
DILOPHOSAURUS
The Dilophosaurus is about forty feet tall, spotted like an owl with a brilliantly colored crest that fans out around its neck when aroused. Seemingly playful and friendly, it kills by spitting on its victim - from as far as twenty feet away - with a lethal, paralyzing venom which blinds and paralyzes its prey.
4
THE TOPPS COMPANY, INC.
PRINTED IN U.S.A.
JP
TM
TM & © 1993 UNIVERSAL CITY STUDIOS, INC.
& AMBLIN ENTERTAINMENT, INC.

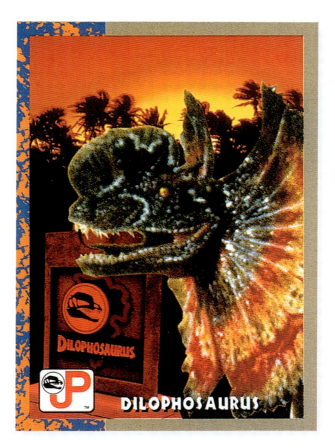

DILOPHOSAURUS

Given the astonishing number of different dinosaurs, *Jurassic Park* filmmakers chose to include a number of lesser-known species alongside the *T. rex*. The *Dilophosaurus*, or "Spitter," was an unusual-looking, colorful animal with a most peculiar method of nailing potential meals: it would paralyze prey by spewing deadly venom.

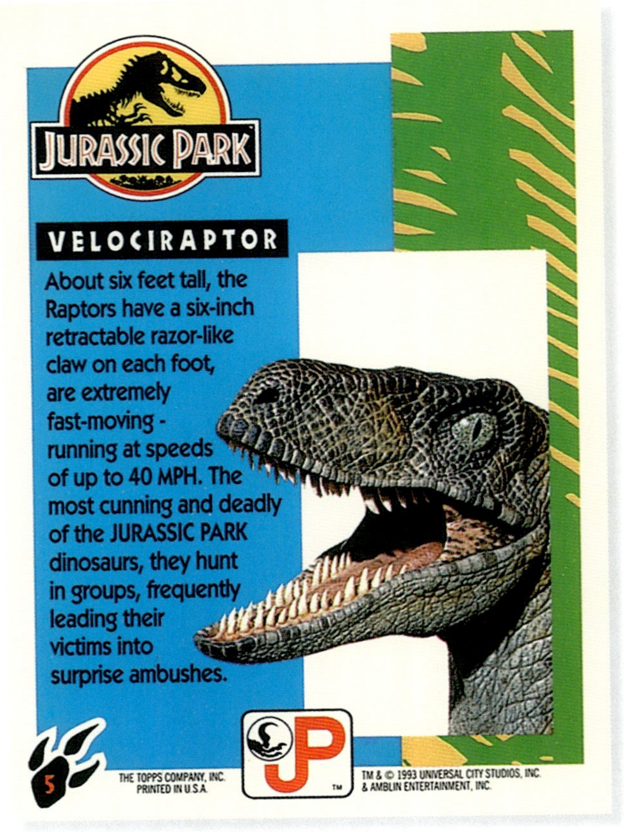
JURASSIC PARK
VELOCIRAPTOR
About six feet tall, the Raptors have a six-inch retractable razor-like claw on each foot, are extremely fast-moving - running at speeds of up to 40 MPH. The most cunning and deadly of the JURASSIC PARK dinosaurs, they hunt in groups, frequently leading their victims into surprise ambushes.
5
THE TOPPS COMPANY, INC. PRINTED IN U.S.A.
JP
TM & © 1993 UNIVERSAL CITY STUDIOS, INC. & AMBLIN ENTERTAINMENT, INC.

VELOCIRAPTOR

Going into this project, we were aware that the *Velociraptor*, or raptor, was designed to be the breakout dinosaur species of *Jurassic Park*. The combination of this animal's newness to the screen and the fact that it was similar in some ways to the man-sized monster from the film *Alien* gave the raptor an interesting edge over veteran movie dinosaurs like the *T. rex* and *Triceratops*.

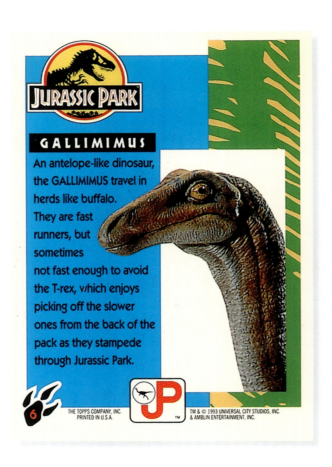

JURASSIC PARK

GALLIMIMUS

An antelope-like dinosaur, the GALLIMIMUS travel in herds like buffalo. They are fast runners, but sometimes not fast enough to avoid the T-rex, which enjoys picking off the slower ones from the back of the pack as they stampede through Jurassic Park.

6

THE TOPPS COMPANY, INC.
PRINTED IN U.S.A.

JP
™

TM & © 1993 UNIVERSAL CITY STUDIOS, INC.
& AMBLIN ENTERTAINMENT, INC.

DANGER
10,000
VOLTS
GALLIMIMUS

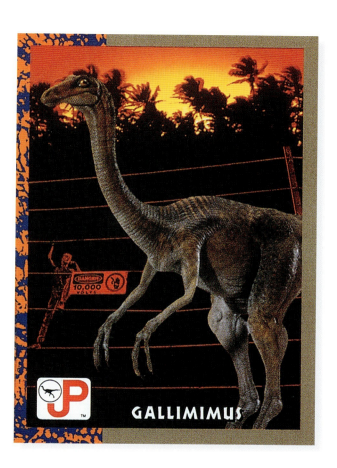

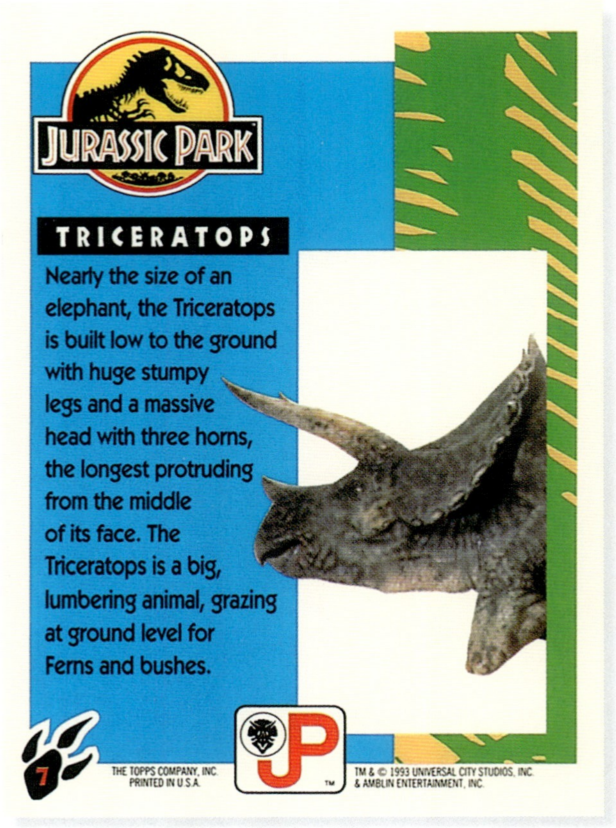
JURASSIC PARK
TRICERATOPS
Nearly the size of an elephant, the Triceratops is built low to the ground with huge stumpy legs and a massive head with three horns, the longest protruding from the middle of its face. The Triceratops is a big, lumbering animal, grazing at ground level for Ferns and bushes.
7
THE TOPPS COMPANY, INC. PRINTED IN U.S.A.
JP TM
TM & © 1993 UNIVERSAL CITY STUDIOS, INC. & AMBLIN ENTERTAINMENT, INC.

TRICERATOPS

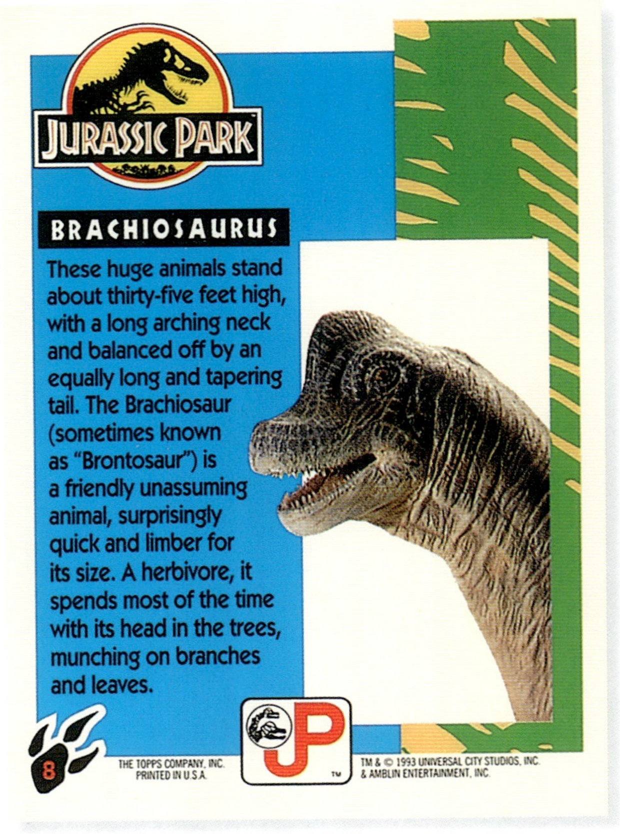
JURASSIC PARK
BRACHIOSAURUS
These huge animals stand about thirty-five feet high, with a long arching neck and balanced off by an equally long and tapering tail. The Brachiosaur (sometimes known as "Brontosaur") is a friendly unassuming animal, surprisingly quick and limber for its size. A herbivore, it spends most of the time with its head in the trees, munching on branches and leaves.
8
THE TOPPS COMPANY, INC.
PRINTED IN U.S.A.
JP
TM
TM & © 1993 UNIVERSAL CITY STUDIOS, INC.
& AMBLIN ENTERTAINMENT, INC.

BRACHIOSAURUS

For years, the enormous *Brachiosaurus* was considered a plant-eating animal that most scientists believed had a friendly disposition. The popular theory that it spent an inordinate amount of time underwater in order to support its enormous weight has been questioned by paleo-revisionists.

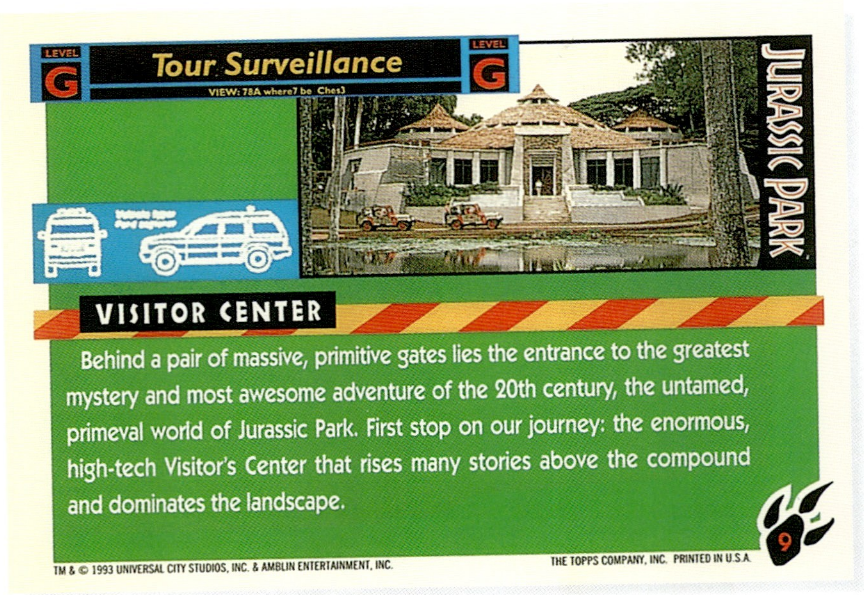
LEVEL G
Tour Surveillance
LEVEL G
VIEW: 78A where7 be Ches3
JURASSIC PARK
VISITOR CENTER
Behind a pair of massive, primitive gates lies the entrance to the greatest mystery and most awesome adventure of the 20th century, the untamed, primeval world of Jurassic Park. First stop on our journey: the enormous, high-tech Visitor's Center that rises many stories above the compound and dominates the landscape.
9
TM & © 1993 UNIVERSAL CITY STUDIOS, INC. & AMBLIN ENTERTAINMENT, INC.
THE TOPPS COMPANY, INC. PRINTED IN U.S.A.

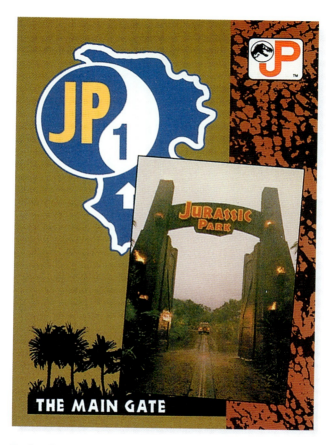

THE MAIN GATE

For the "Tour Surveillance" subset, we had a reduced photo sharing card space with a graphic of the Jurassic Park island icon. It made sense to start off with the Visitor's Center, which is where patrons would begin their excursion. Our front photo ushers us inside the park, while the back image depicts the center itself.

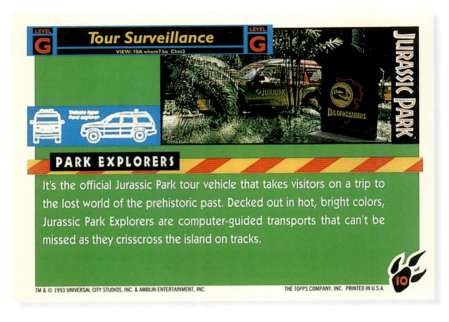

LEVEL G
Tour Surveillance
LEVEL G
JURASSIC PARK
JURASSIC
DILOPHOSAURUS
PARK EXPLORERS
It's the official Jurassic Park tour vehicle that takes visitors on a trip to the lost world of the prehistoric past. Decked out in hot, bright colors, Jurassic Park Explorers are computer-guided transports that can't be missed as they crisscross the island on tracks.
10
TM & © 1993 UNIVERSAL CITY STUDIOS, INC. & AMBLIN ENTERTAINMENT, INC.
THE TOPPS COMPANY, INC. PRINTED IN U.S.A.

JP
1
PARK EXPLORERS

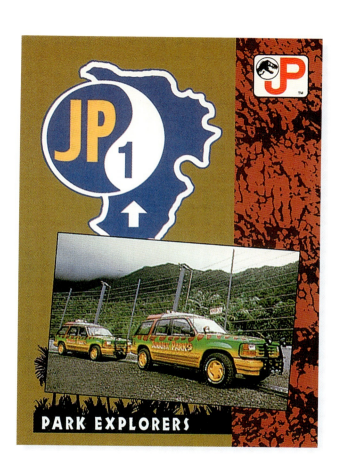

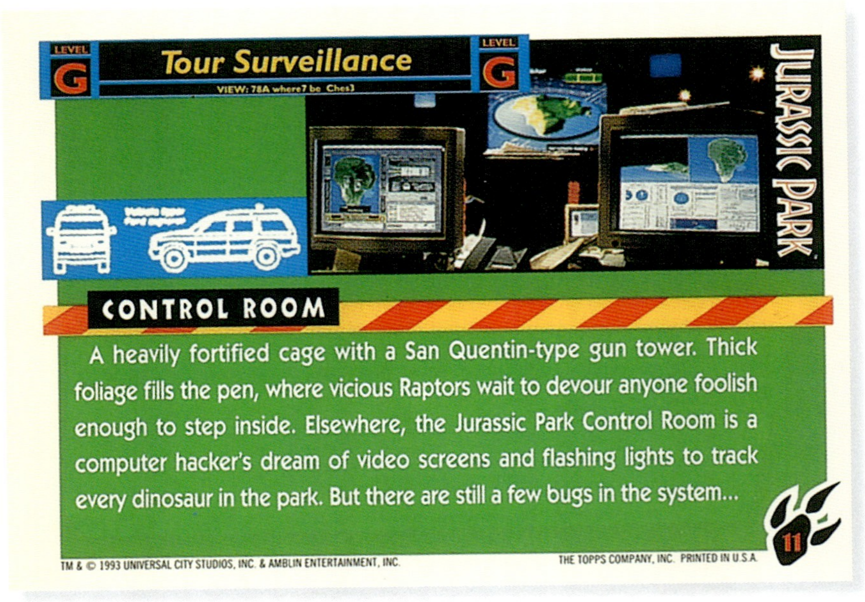
LEVEL G
Tour Surveillance
VIEW: 78A where7 be Ches3
LEVEL G
JURASSIC PARK
CONTROL ROOM
A heavily fortified cage with a San Quentin-type gun tower. Thick foliage fills the pen, where vicious Raptors wait to devour anyone foolish enough to step inside. Elsewhere, the Jurassic Park Control Room is a computer hacker's dream of video screens and flashing lights to track every dinosaur in the park. But there are still a few bugs in the system...
11
TM & © 1993 UNIVERSAL CITY STUDIOS, INC. & AMBLIN ENTERTAINMENT, INC.
THE TOPPS COMPANY, INC. PRINTED IN U.S.A.

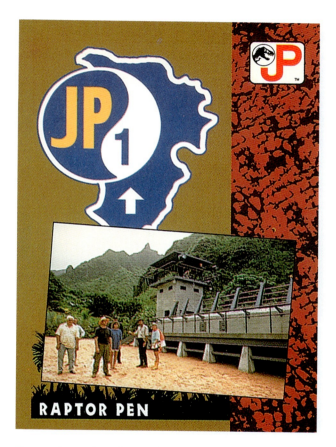

There are two captions, front and back, for this card. "Raptor Pen" covers what we're seeing on the front, while "Control Room" gives a view of computer screens and such. This is a little unusual, but both images serve the movie's setup.

SATTLER

Dr. Ellie Sattler (Laura Dern) is a palebotanist, late twenties, athletic looking. Ambitious and impatient, Dr. Sattler also has her domestic side - obviously in love with Grant, she wants to marry him and have children.

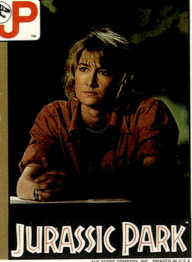

12

TM & © 1993 UNIVERSAL CITY STUDIOS, INC. & AMBLIN ENTERTAINMENT, INC.

THE TOPPS COMPANY, INC. PRINTED IN U.S.A.

JURASSIC PARK

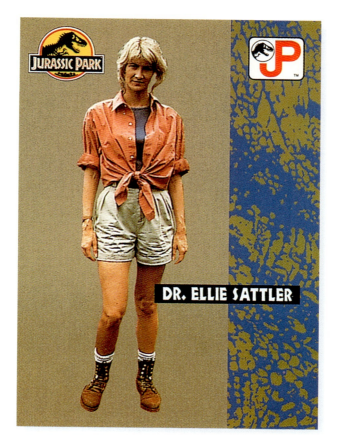

DR. ELLIE SATTLER

Actress Laura Dern was a superb choice to play Dr. Ellie Sattler, a smart, empathetic paleobotanist. She's also a potential love interest for the film's hero, Dr. Alan Grant.

HAMMOND
Forceful, energetic and sprightly, John Hammond (Sir Richard Attenborough) is the visionary entrepreneur who conceived and built Jurassic Park. Seventyish, he walks with a slight limp and cane which might only be for show.
JP
JURASSIC PARK
13
TM & © 1993 UNIVERSAL CITY STUDIOS, INC. & AMBLIN ENTERTAINMENT, INC.
THE TOPPS COMPANY, INC. PRINTED IN U.S.A.

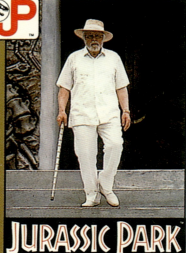

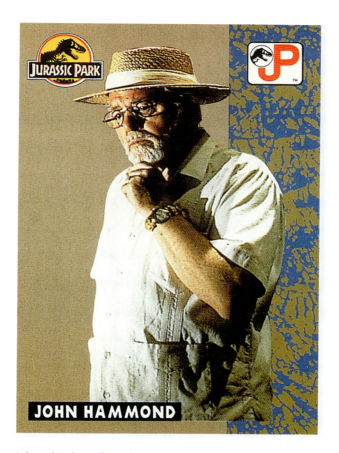

JOHN HAMMOND

I chose this photo of Dr. John Hammond because of the thoughtful look on actor Richard Attenborough's face. "Have I done the right thing?" would make an appropriate caption if this were a storyline card, summing up the essence of the well-intentioned, but ultimately guilt-ridden character.

TIM
Tim (Joseph Mazzello) is the nine year old grandson of John Hammond. Smart and a non-stop talker, he's also a major dinosaur enthusiast... and Dr. Grant is one of his heroes.
When Hammond invites Tim and sister Lex to visit the still-under-construction Jurassic Park, the boy is ecstatic. Little does he realize that soon he'll be menaced by the very creatures that have always captivated him.
14
JURASSIC PARK
TM & © 1993 UNIVERSAL CITY STUDIOS, INC. & AMBLIN ENTERTAINMENT, INC.
THE TOPPS COMPANY, INC. PRINTED IN U.S.A.

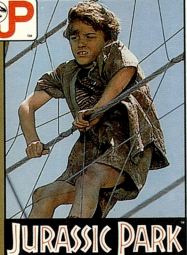

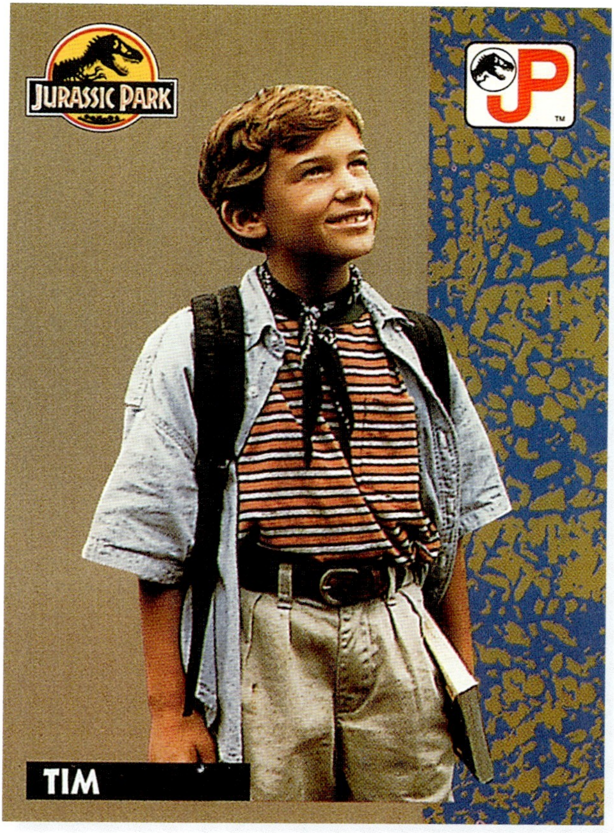
JURASSIC PARK
JP
TM
TIM

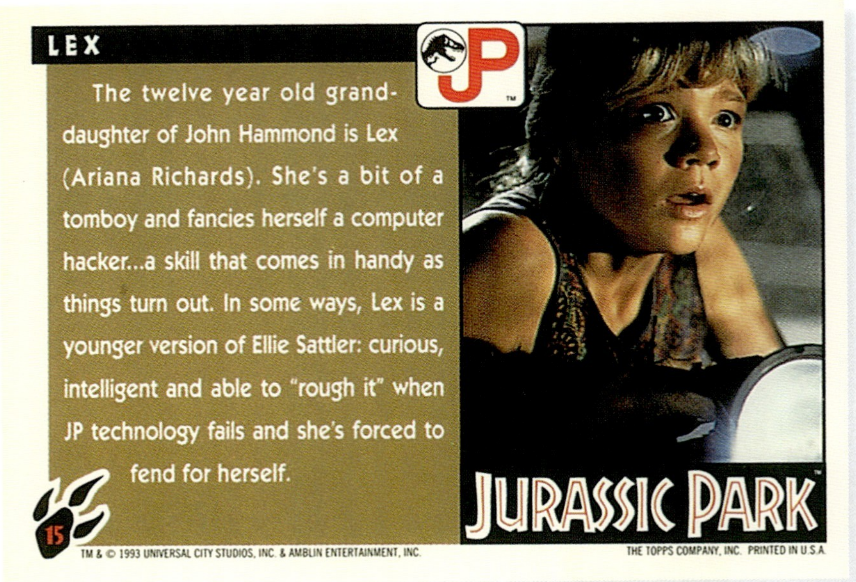
LEX
JP
The twelve year old grand-daughter of John Hammond is Lex (Ariana Richards). She's a bit of a tomboy and fancies herself a computer hacker...a skill that comes in handy as things turn out. In some ways, Lex is a younger version of Ellie Sattler: curious, intelligent and able to "rough it" when JP technology fails and she's forced to fend for herself.
15
JURASSIC PARK
TM & © 1993 UNIVERSAL CITY STUDIOS, INC. & AMBLIN ENTERTAINMENT, INC.
THE TOPPS COMPANY, INC. PRINTED IN U.S.A.

JURASSIC PARK
JP
LEX

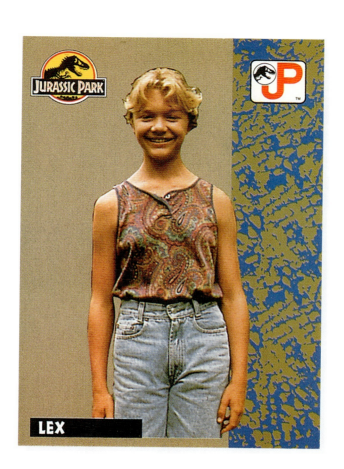

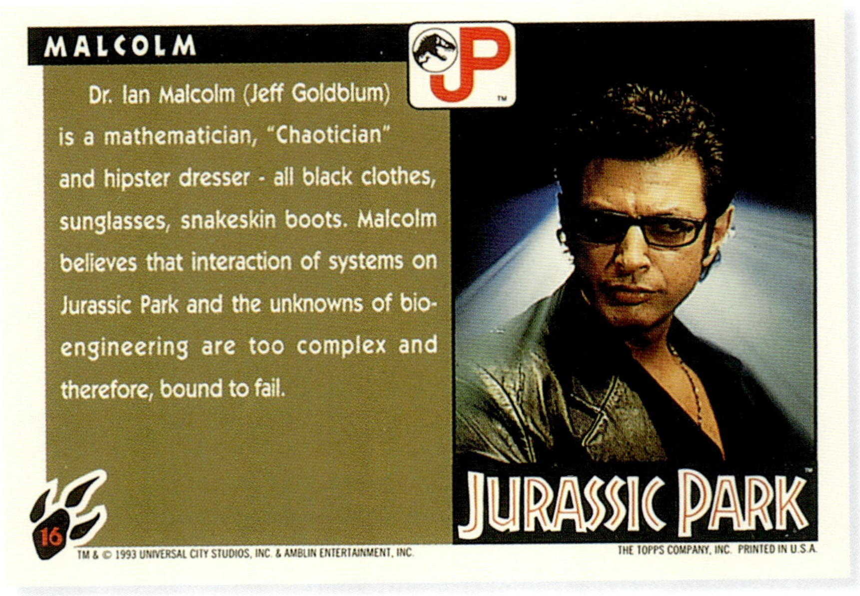
MALCOLM
Dr. Ian Malcolm (Jeff Goldblum) is a mathematician, "Chaotician" and hipster dresser - all black clothes, sunglasses, snakeskin boots. Malcolm believes that interaction of systems on Jurassic Park and the unknowns of bio-engineering are too complex and therefore, bound to fail.
JP
JURASSIC PARK
16
TM & © 1993 UNIVERSAL CITY STUDIOS, INC. & AMBLIN ENTERTAINMENT, INC.
THE TOPPS COMPANY, INC. PRINTED IN U.S.A.

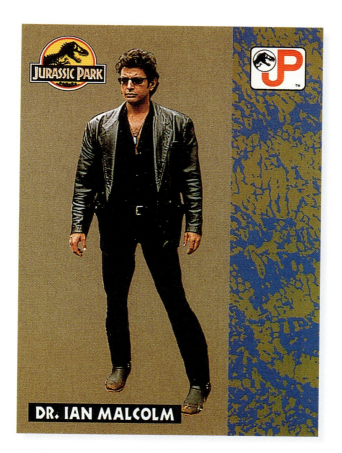

DR. IAN MALCOLM

Dr. Malcolm's sexy wardrobe helped define his cool nature, so this head-to-toe silhouette conveyed the personality of his character nicely. Jeff Goldblum was also perfectly cast, bringing his special brand of wry and dry humor to the part.

MULDOON
Jurassic Park's Game Warden is Robert Muldoon (Bob Peck). Muldoon's powerful and authoritative, fortyish, a British no-nonsense type. He has a fateful encounter with the Raptors in the jungle while trying to turn the park's power system back on.
JP
JURASSIC PARK
17
TM & © 1993 UNIVERSAL CITY STUDIOS, INC. & AMBLIN ENTERTAINMENT, INC.
THE TOPPS COMPANY, INC. PRINTED IN U.S.A.

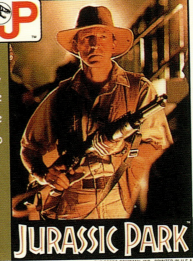

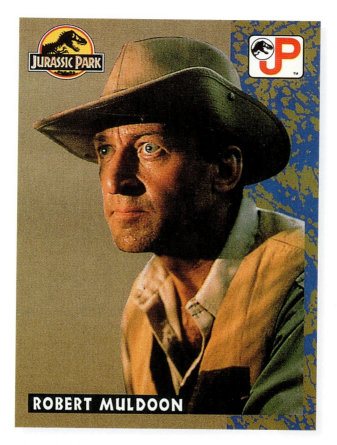

ROBERT MULDOON

I always liked the iconography of a classic big-game hunter on the track of dinosaurs. There's a certain doomed, Captain Ahab–like quality about characters of this nature, and actor Bob Peck seemed to capture that in his portrayal of game warden Robert Muldoon. The lighting on this portrait added some melodrama, resulting in a simple but absolutely beautiful trading card.

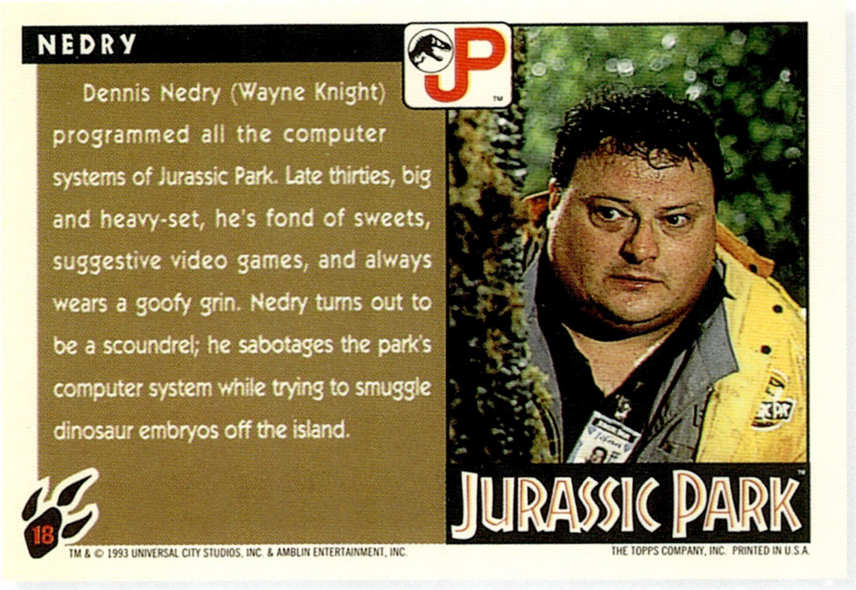
NEDRY
Dennis Nedry (Wayne Knight) programmed all the computer systems of Jurassic Park. Late thirties, big and heavy-set, he's fond of sweets, suggestive video games, and always wears a goofy grin. Nedry turns out to be a scoundrel; he sabotages the park's computer system while trying to smuggle dinosaur embryos off the island.
JP
JURASSIC PARK
18
TM & © 1993 UNIVERSAL CITY STUDIOS, INC. & AMBLIN ENTERTAINMENT, INC.
THE TOPPS COMPANY, INC. PRINTED IN U.S.A.

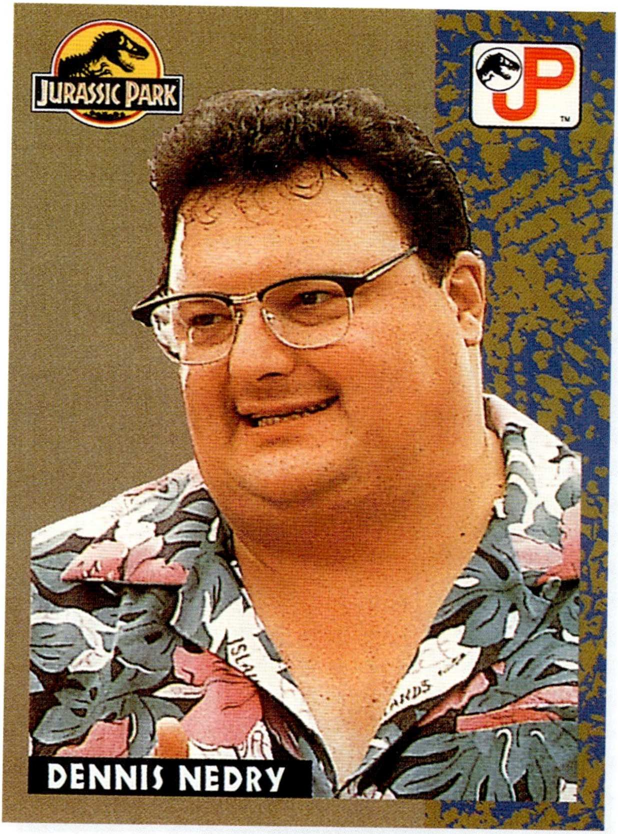
JURASSIC PARK
JP
TM
DENNIS NEDRY

GRANT
Paleontologist, thirtyish, intensely focused on his work, less so on his appearance...this is Dr. Alan Grant (Sam Neill). He's ragged looking and used to roughing it after long stretches in the dessert digging up dinosaur bones. Grant doesn't like kids which is a problem for his girlfriend/partner, Dr. Ellie Sattler.
JP
TM
JURASSIC PARK
TM
19
TM & © 1993 UNIVERSAL CITY STUDIOS, INC. & AMBLIN ENTERTAINMENT, INC.
THE TOPPS COMPANY, INC. PRINTED IN U.S.A.

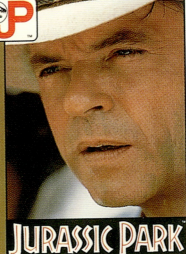

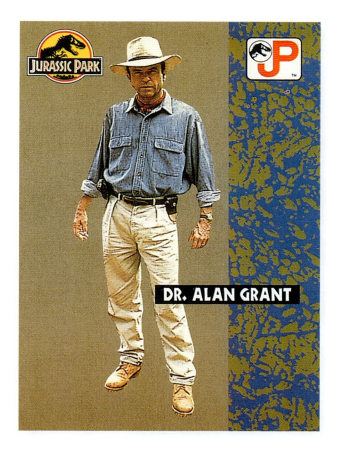

DR. ALAN GRANT

Why is Dr. Alan Grant, the lead character in this movie, played by Sam Neill, parked at the back of the character card bus? To be perfectly honest, I'm not exactly sure. Judging from my text, I was clearly building toward the Ellie Sattler card, which should have followed. And I believe it did, originally. Since trading cards are generally collected into nine-slot plastic sheets, we arrange subjects with that number in mind.

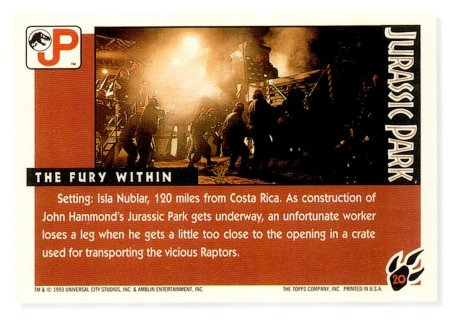

JP
JURASSIC PARK
THE FURY WITHIN
Setting: Isla Nublar, 120 miles from Costa Rica. As construction of John Hammond's Jurassic Park gets underway, an unfortunate worker loses a leg when he gets a little too close to the opening in a crate used for transporting the vicious Raptors.
20
TM & © 1993 UNIVERSAL CITY STUDIOS, INC. & AMBLIN ENTERTAINMENT, INC.
THE TOPPS COMPANY, INC. PRINTED IN U.S.A.

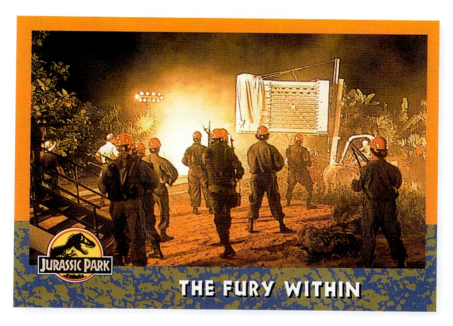

THE FURY WITHIN

I'm glad we were able to cover the film's portentous teaser sequence, which sets up the sinister, almost preternatural aspects of the raptors.

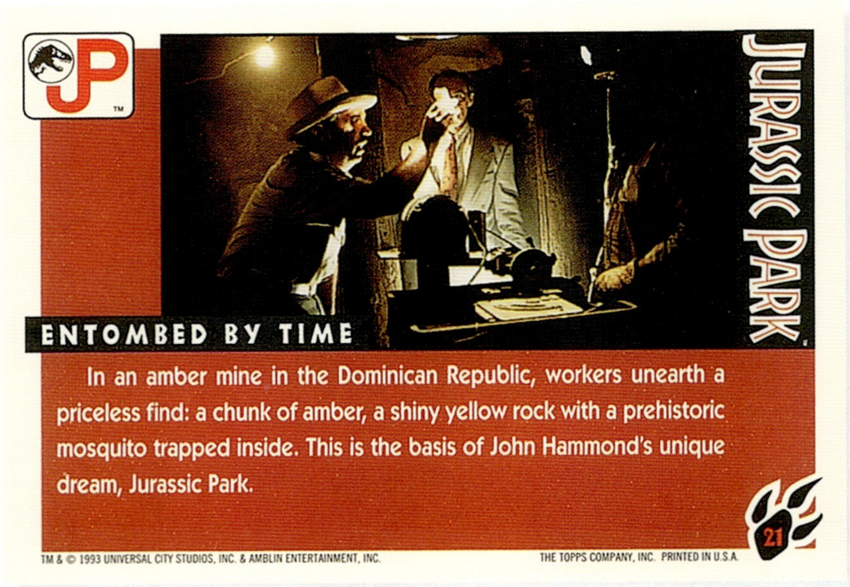
JP
JURASSIC PARK
ENTOMBED BY TIME
In an amber mine in the Dominican Republic, workers unearth a priceless find: a chunk of amber, a shiny yellow rock with a prehistoric mosquito trapped inside. This is the basis of John Hammond's unique dream, Jurassic Park.
21
TM & © 1993 UNIVERSAL CITY STUDIOS, INC. & AMBLIN ENTERTAINMENT, INC.
THE TOPPS COMPANY, INC. PRINTED IN U.S.A.

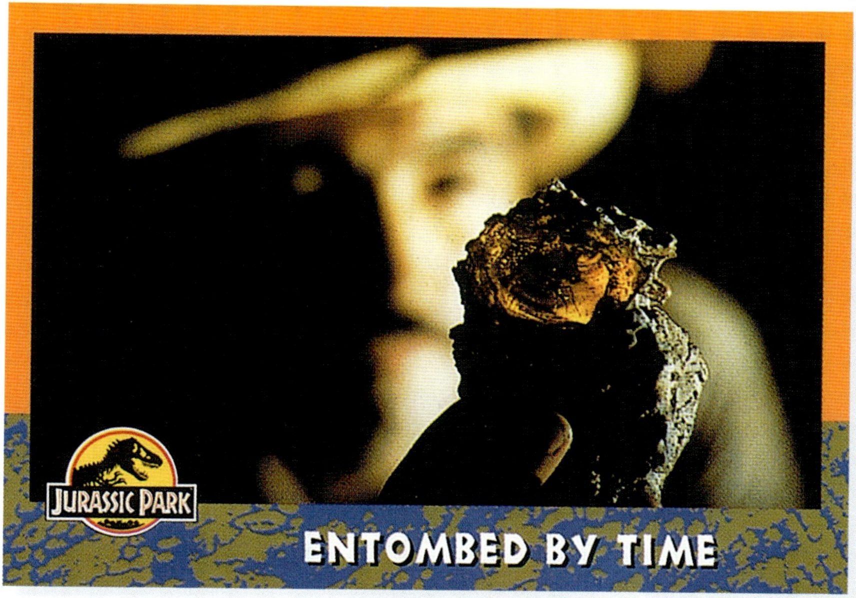
JURASSIC PARK
ENTOMBED BY TIME

This image of the mosquito trapped in amber was logically emphasized in *Jurassic Park*, with the background gawker blurred in the movie frame. Naturally, such an important moment required its own trading card . . . and here it is.

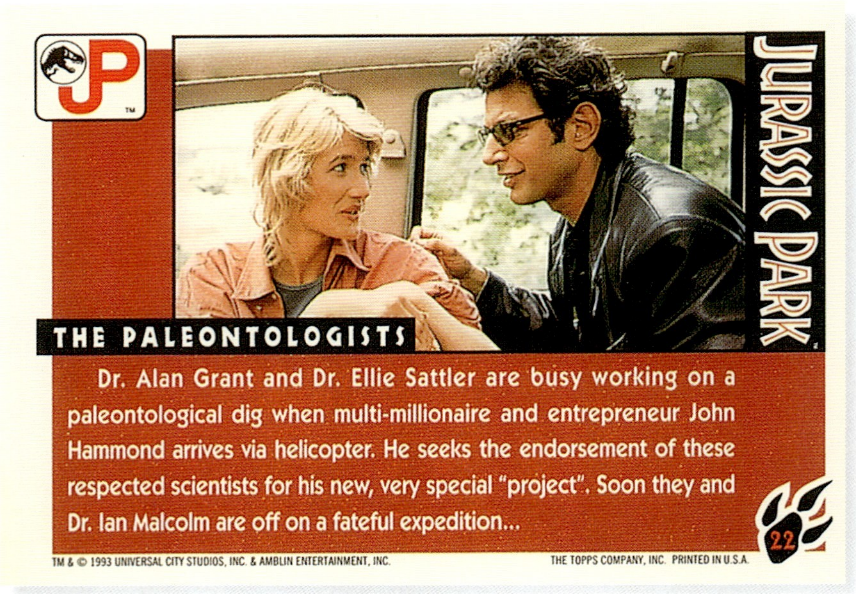
JP
JURASSIC PARK
THE PALEONTOLOGISTS
Dr. Alan Grant and Dr. Ellie Sattler are busy working on a paleontological dig when multi-millionaire and entrepreneur John Hammond arrives via helicopter. He seeks the endorsement of these respected scientists for his new, very special "project". Soon they and Dr. Ian Malcolm are off on a fateful expedition...
22
TM & © 1993 UNIVERSAL CITY STUDIOS, INC. & AMBLIN ENTERTAINMENT, INC.
THE TOPPS COMPANY, INC. PRINTED IN U.S.A.

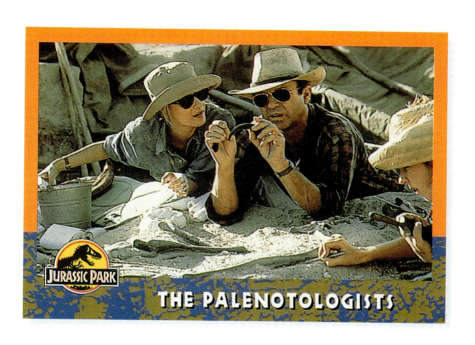

JURASSIC PARK

THE PALENOTOLOGISTS

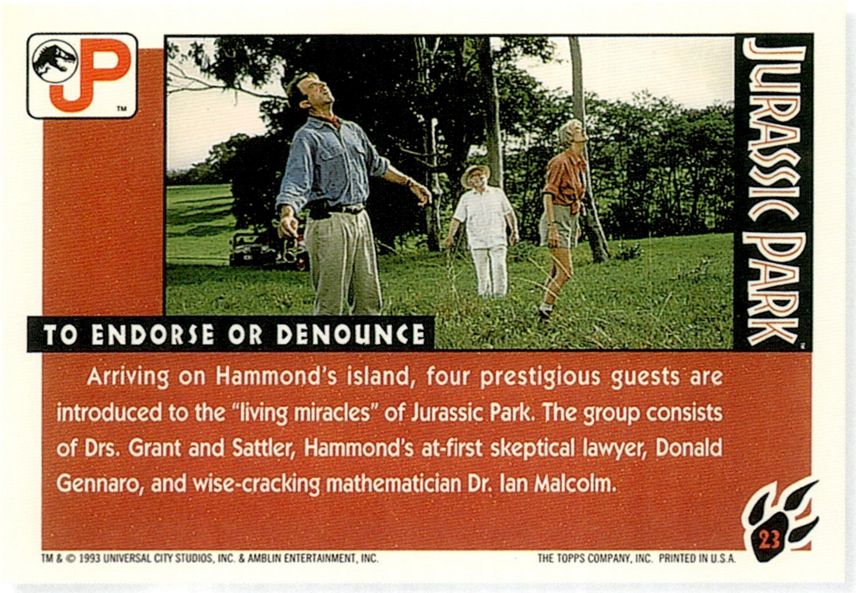
JURASSIC PARK
TO ENDORSE OR DENOUNCE
Arriving on Hammond's island, four prestigious guests are introduced to the "living miracles" of Jurassic Park. The group consists of Drs. Grant and Sattler, Hammond's at-first skeptical lawyer, Donald Gennaro, and wise-cracking mathematician Dr. Ian Malcolm.
23
TM & © 1993 UNIVERSAL CITY STUDIOS, INC. & AMBLIN ENTERTAINMENT, INC.
THE TOPPS COMPANY, INC. PRINTED IN U.S.A.

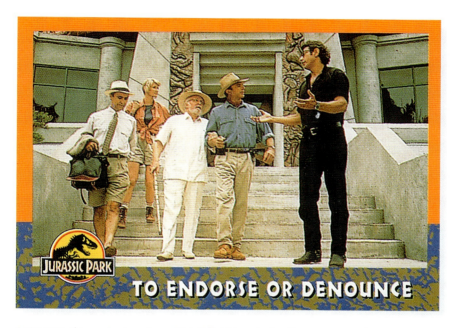

TO ENDORSE OR DENOUNCE

A nice view of our main characters, with Jeff Goldblum stealing the scene, as usual.

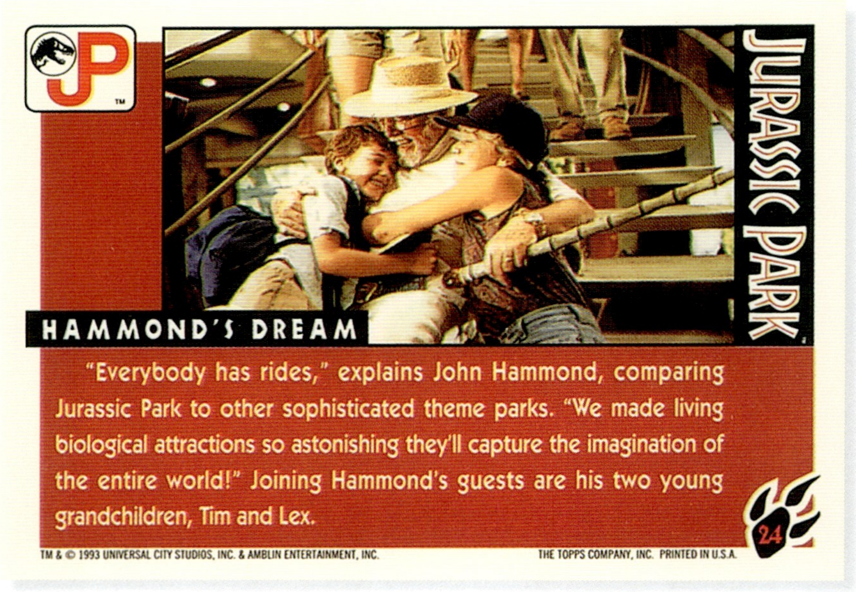
JP
JURASSIC PARK
HAMMOND'S DREAM
"Everybody has rides," explains John Hammond, comparing Jurassic Park to other sophisticated theme parks. "We made living biological attractions so astonishing they'll capture the imagination of the entire world!" Joining Hammond's guests are his two young grandchildren, Tim and Lex.
24
TM & © 1993 UNIVERSAL CITY STUDIOS, INC. & AMBLIN ENTERTAINMENT, INC.
THE TOPPS COMPANY, INC. PRINTED IN U.S.A.

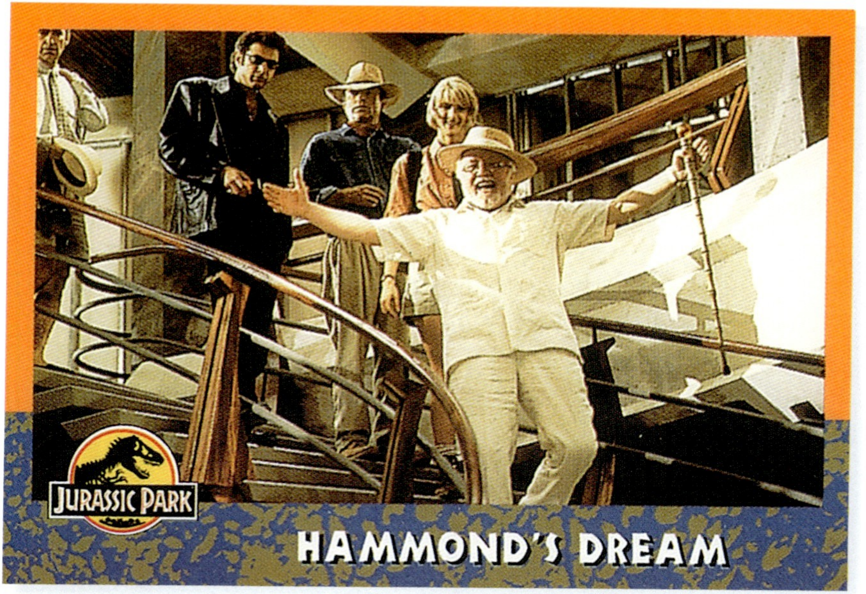
JURASSIC PARK
HAMMOND'S DREAM

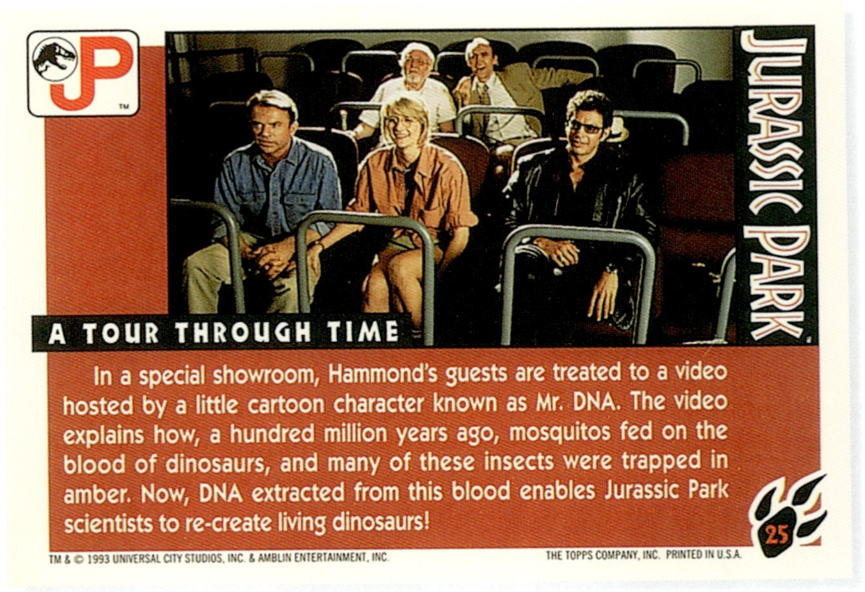
JP
JURASSIC PARK
A TOUR THROUGH TIME
In a special showroom, Hammond's guests are treated to a video hosted by a little cartoon character known as Mr. DNA. The video explains how, a hundred million years ago, mosquitos fed on the blood of dinosaurs, and many of these insects were trapped in amber. Now, DNA extracted from this blood enables Jurassic Park scientists to re-create living dinosaurs!
25
TM & © 1993 UNIVERSAL CITY STUDIOS, INC. & AMBLIN ENTERTAINMENT, INC.
THE TOPPS COMPANY, INC. PRINTED IN U.S.A.

JURASSIC PARK
A TOUR THROUGH TIME

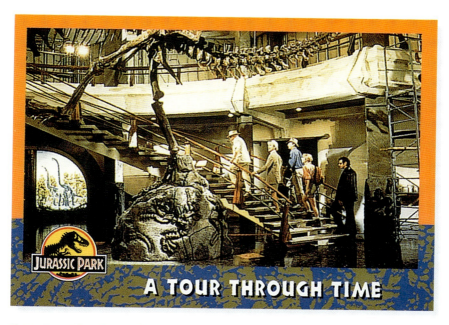

The caption "A Tour Through Time" was inspired by a line of dialogue from the 1936 science-fiction movie *The Invisible Ray*, released by Universal and starring Boris Karloff.

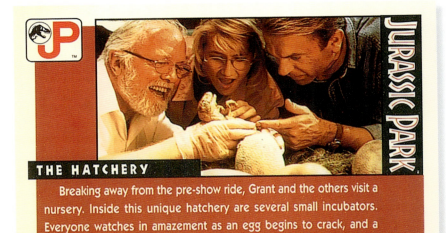

JURASSIC PARK
THE HATCHERY
Breaking away from the pre-show ride, Grant and the others visit a nursery. Inside this unique hatchery are several small incubators. Everyone watches in amazement as an egg begins to crack, and a baby dinosaur tries to waddle free of its shell.
26
TM & © 1993 UNIVERSAL CITY STUDIOS, INC. & AMBLIN ENTERTAINMENT, INC.
THE TOPPS COMPANY, INC. PRINTED IN U.S.A.

JURASSIC PARK

THE HATCHERY

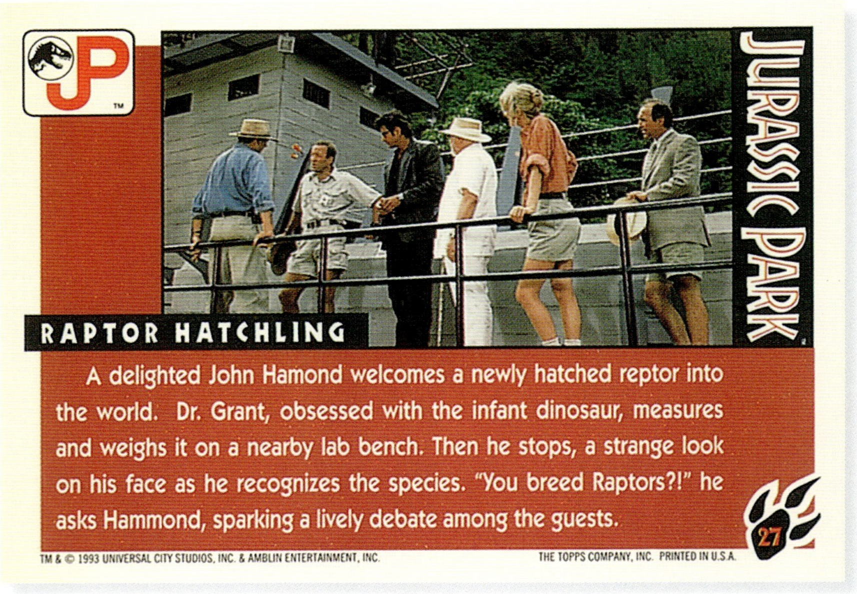
JP
JURASSIC PARK
RAPTOR HATCHLING
A delighted John Hamond welcomes a newly hatched reptor into the world. Dr. Grant, obsessed with the infant dinosaur, measures and weighs it on a nearby lab bench. Then he stops, a strange look on his face as he recognizes the species. "You breed Raptors?!" he asks Hammond, sparking a lively debate among the guests.
27
TM & © 1993 UNIVERSAL CITY STUDIOS, INC. & AMBLIN ENTERTAINMENT, INC.
THE TOPPS COMPANY, INC. PRINTED IN U.S.A.

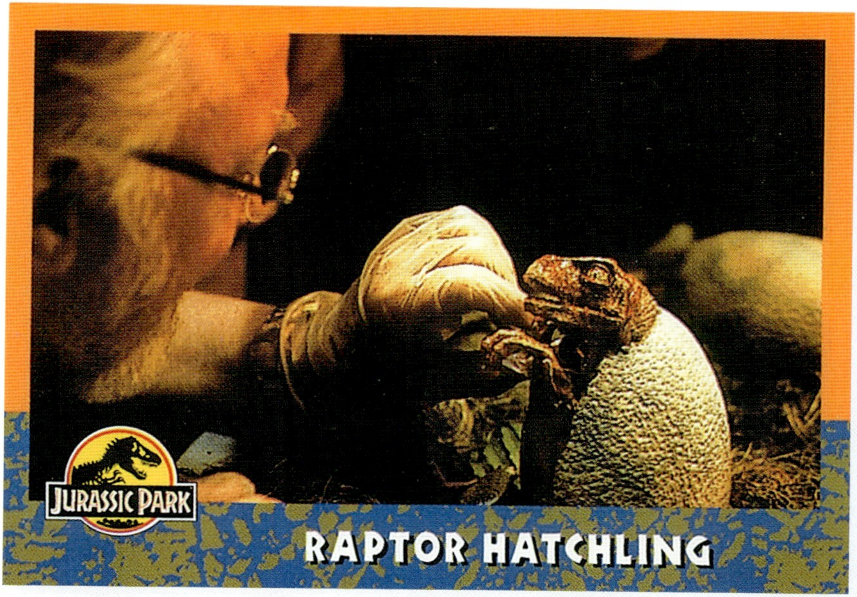
JURASSIC PARK
RAPTOR HATCHLING

Although we established the hatchery on card no. 26, the money shot of the baby raptor was saved for the front of this card. The back image of the raptor pen anticipates where the action is going, suggesting that the principal characters will soon be debating the wisdom of breeding these animals.

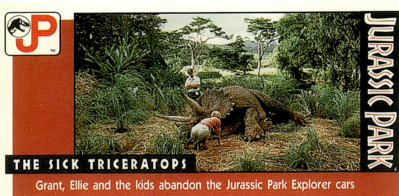

JP
JURASSIC PARK
THE SICK TRICERATOPS
Grant, Ellie and the kids abandon the Jurassic Park Explorer cars when Grant spots something curious out in the field. Soon joined by Malcolm and Gennaro, they stumble upon a large Triceratops, lying on its side, obviously ill...
28
TM & © 1993 UNIVERSAL CITY STUDIOS, INC. & AMBLIN ENTERTAINMENT, INC.
THE TOPPS COMPANY, INC. PRINTED IN U.S.A.

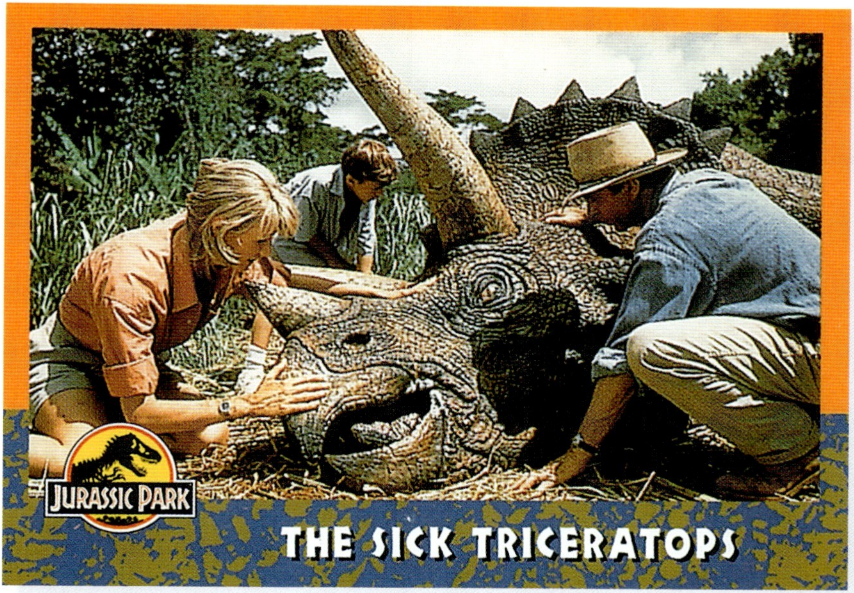
JURASSIC PARK
THE SICK TRICERATOPS

Practical special effects, meaning that they're physically on set, enabled actors to interact with extremely realistic-looking dinosaurs, which in reality were mostly sophisticated puppets.

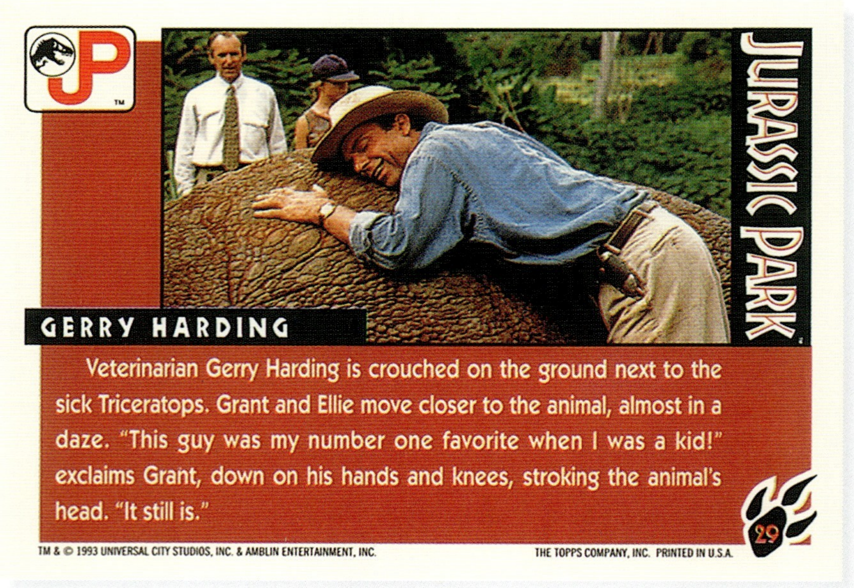
JURASSIC PARK
GERRY HARDING
Veterinarian Gerry Harding is crouched on the ground next to the sick Triceratops. Grant and Ellie move closer to the animal, almost in a daze. "This guy was my number one favorite when I was a kid!" exclaims Grant, down on his hands and knees, stroking the animal's head. "It still is."
29
TM & © 1993 UNIVERSAL CITY STUDIOS, INC. & AMBLIN ENTERTAINMENT, INC.
THE TOPPS COMPANY, INC. PRINTED IN U.S.A.

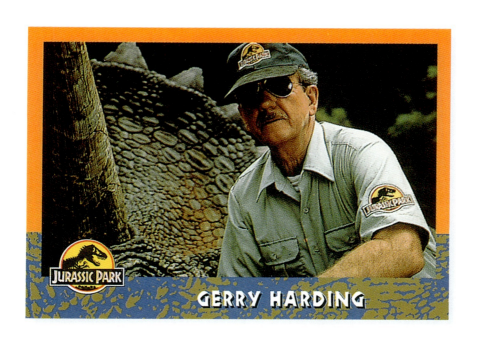

JURASSIC PARK

GERRY HARDING

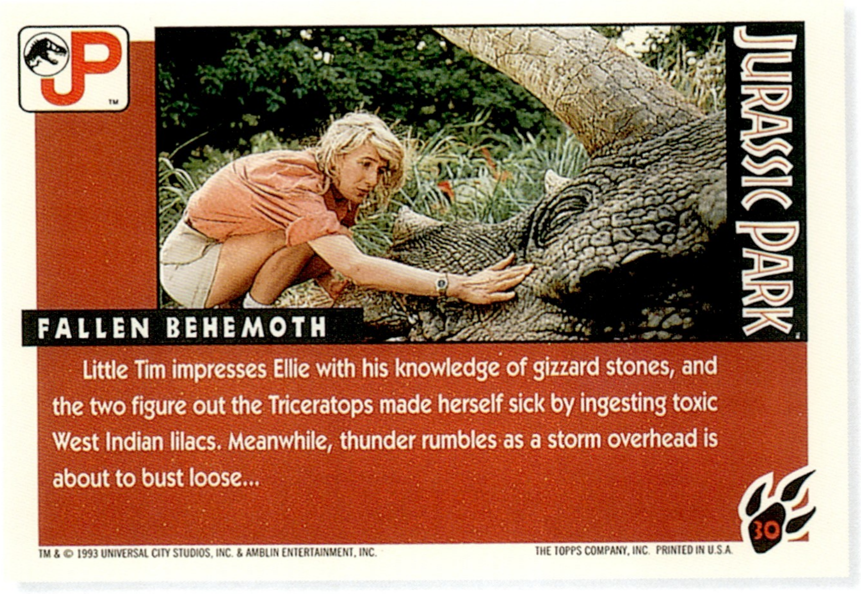
JP
JURASSIC PARK
FALLEN BEHEMOTH
Little Tim impresses Ellie with his knowledge of gizzard stones, and the two figure out the Triceratops made herself sick by ingesting toxic West Indian lilacs. Meanwhile, thunder rumbles as a storm overhead is about to bust loose...
30
TM & © 1993 UNIVERSAL CITY STUDIOS, INC. & AMBLIN ENTERTAINMENT, INC.
THE TOPPS COMPANY, INC. PRINTED IN U.S.A.

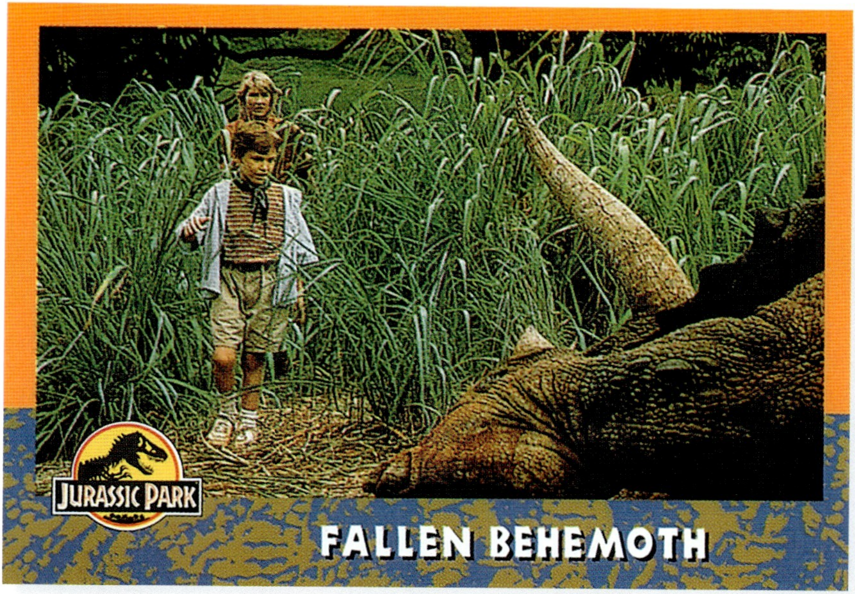
JURASSIC PARK
FALLEN BEHEMOTH

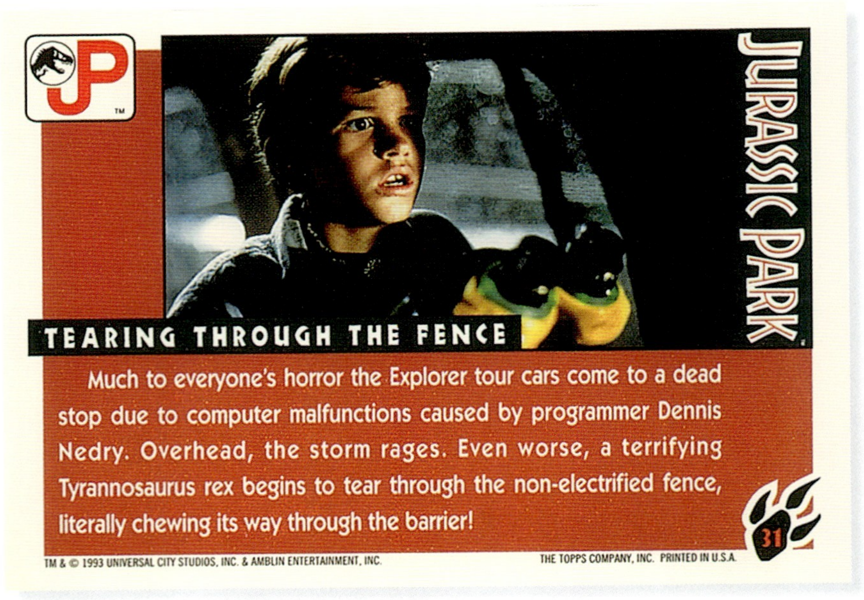
JURASSIC PARK
TEARING THROUGH THE FENCE
Much to everyone's horror the Explorer tour cars come to a dead stop due to computer malfunctions caused by programmer Dennis Nedry. Overhead, the storm rages. Even worse, a terrifying Tyrannosaurus rex begins to tear through the non-electrified fence, literally chewing its way through the barrier!
31
TM & © 1993 UNIVERSAL CITY STUDIOS, INC. & AMBLIN ENTERTAINMENT, INC.
THE TOPPS COMPANY, INC. PRINTED IN U.S.A.

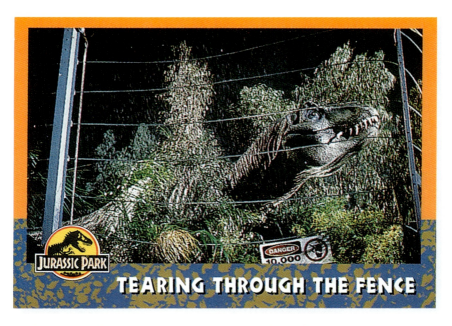

TEARING THROUGH THE FENCE

The *T. rex* makes its first appearance in the storyline cards. As was often the case with movies that employed extensive special effects, our photo selection was relatively limited. On-set practical costumes gave us a fighting chance, however.

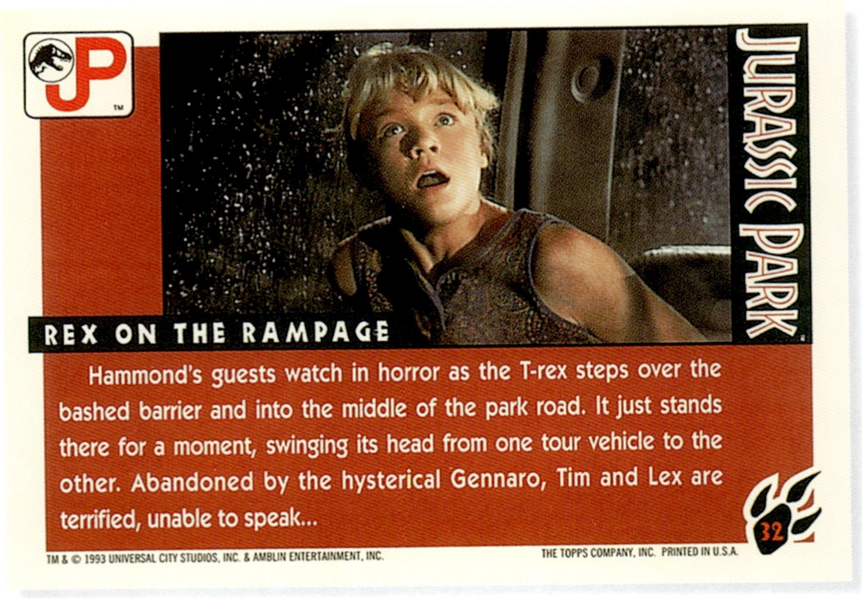
JP
JURASSIC PARK
REX ON THE RAMPAGE
Hammond's guests watch in horror as the T-rex steps over the bashed barrier and into the middle of the park road. It just stands there for a moment, swinging its head from one tour vehicle to the other. Abandoned by the hysterical Gennaro, Tim and Lex are terrified, unable to speak...
32
TM & © 1993 UNIVERSAL CITY STUDIOS, INC. & AMBLIN ENTERTAINMENT, INC.
THE TOPPS COMPANY, INC. PRINTED IN U.S.A.

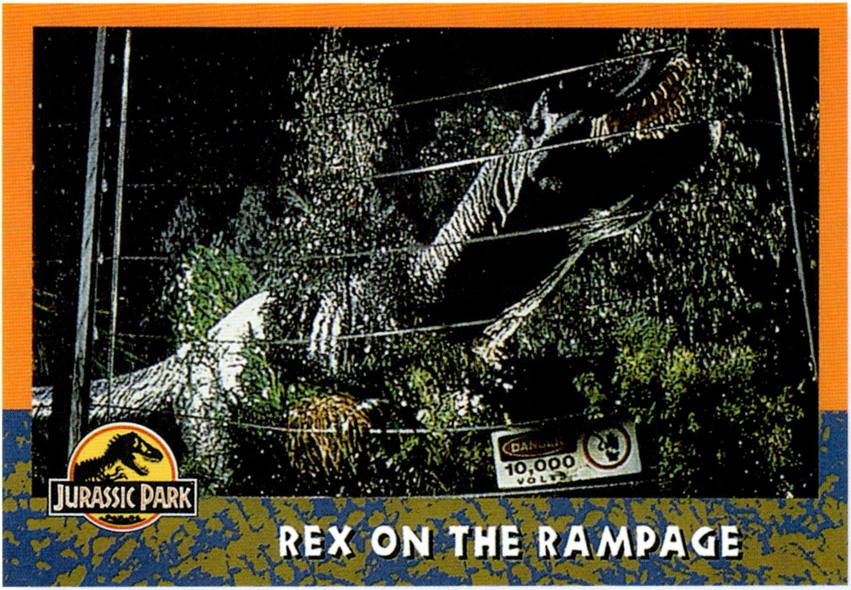
DANGER
10,000
VOLTS
JURASSIC PARK
REX ON THE RAMPAGE

This photo is pretty much the same setup as the last. But instead of the *T. rex* pushing through the fence, her massive mouth is open, and probably roaring loudly.

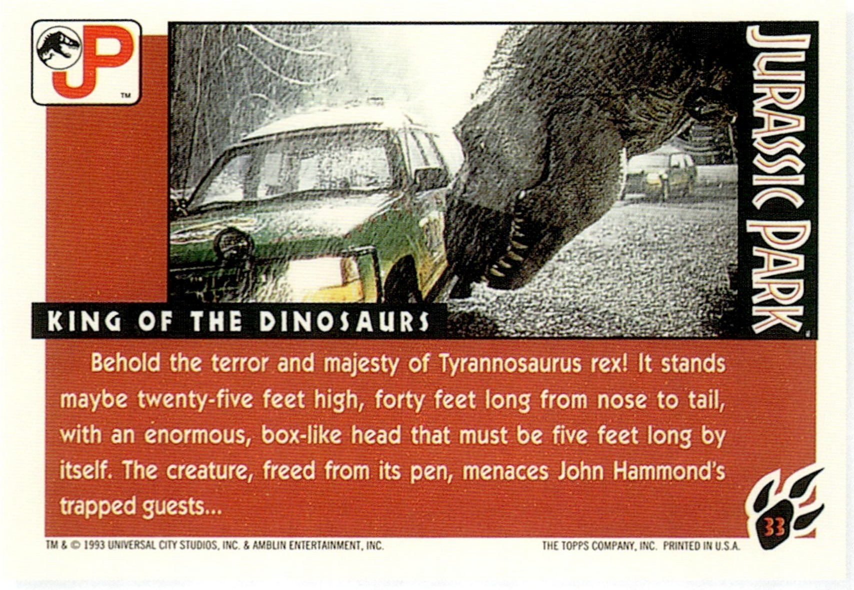
JP
JURASSIC PARK
KING OF THE DINOSAURS
Behold the terror and majesty of Tyrannosaurus rex! It stands maybe twenty-five feet high, forty feet long from nose to tail, with an enormous, box-like head that must be five feet long by itself. The creature, freed from its pen, menaces John Hammond's trapped guests...
33
TM & © 1993 UNIVERSAL CITY STUDIOS, INC. & AMBLIN ENTERTAINMENT, INC.
THE TOPPS COMPANY, INC. PRINTED IN U.S.A.

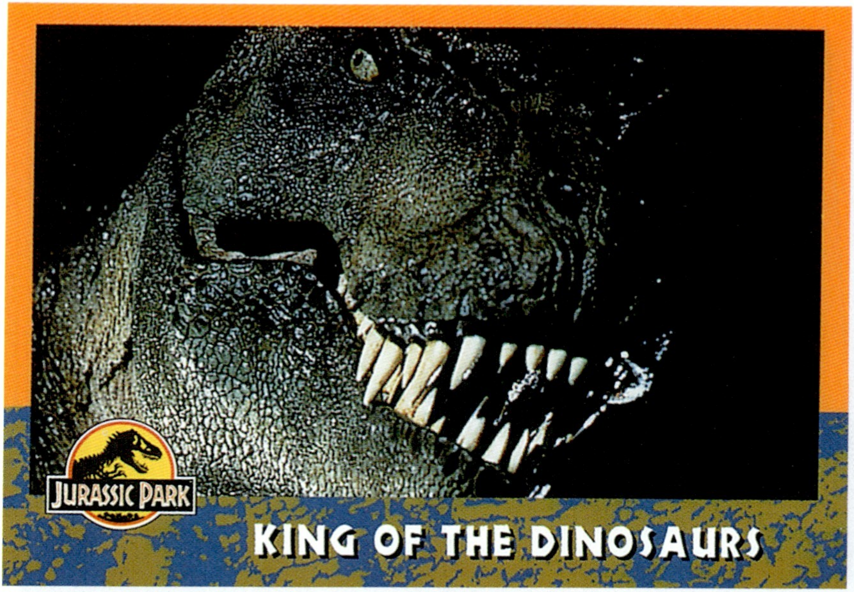
JURASSIC PARK
KING OF THE DINOSAURS

"I'm ready for my close-up!" This great headshot shows off the intricate work put into the massive full-scale puppet provided by special effects master Stan Winston and his on-set team.

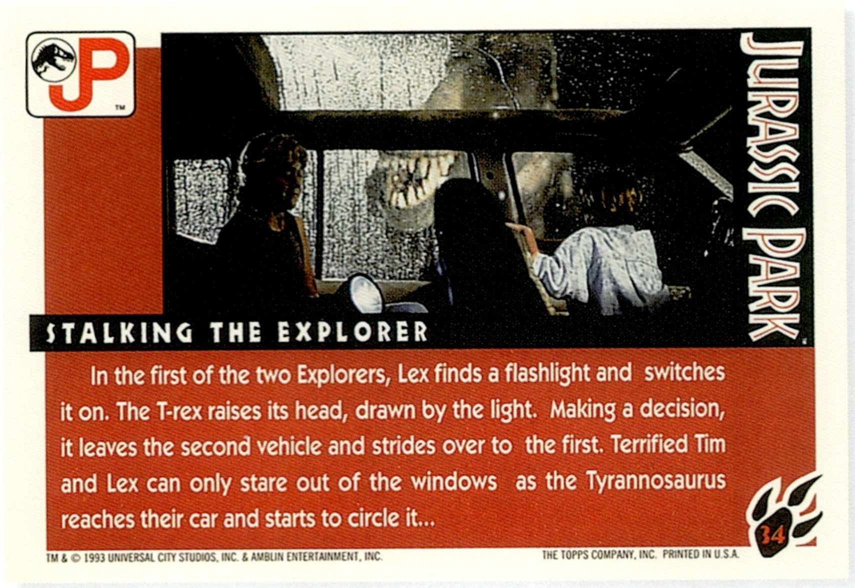
JP
JURASSIC PARK
STALKING THE EXPLORER
In the first of the two Explorers, Lex finds a flashlight and switches it on. The T-rex raises its head, drawn by the light. Making a decision, it leaves the second vehicle and strides over to the first. Terrified Tim and Lex can only stare out of the windows as the Tyrannosaurus reaches their car and starts to circle it...
34
TM & © 1993 UNIVERSAL CITY STUDIOS, INC. & AMBLIN ENTERTAINMENT, INC.
THE TOPPS COMPANY, INC. PRINTED IN U.S.A.

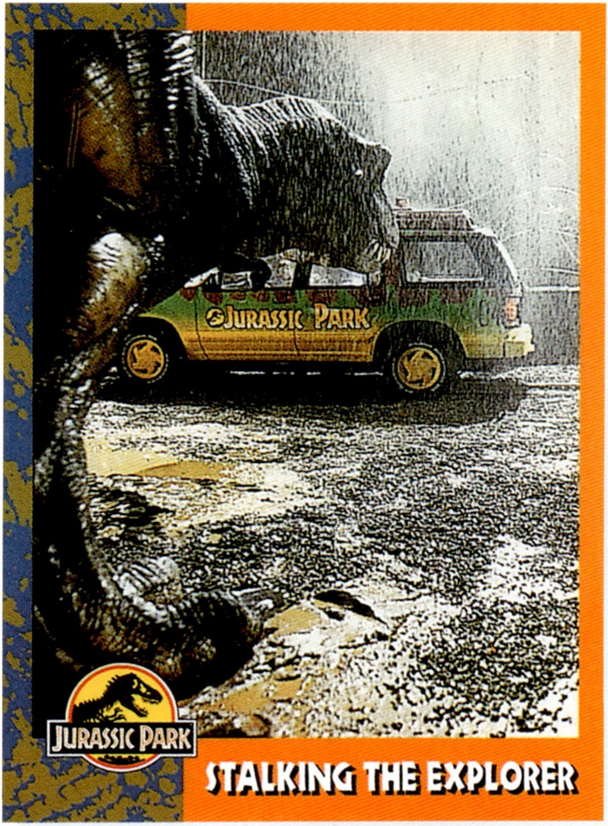
JURASSIC PARK
JURASSIC PARK
STALKING THE EXPLORER

We're looking at beautiful on-set unit photography of the initial *T. rex* attack. This image was shot with a wide-angle lens to exaggerate the dinosaur's already huge size.

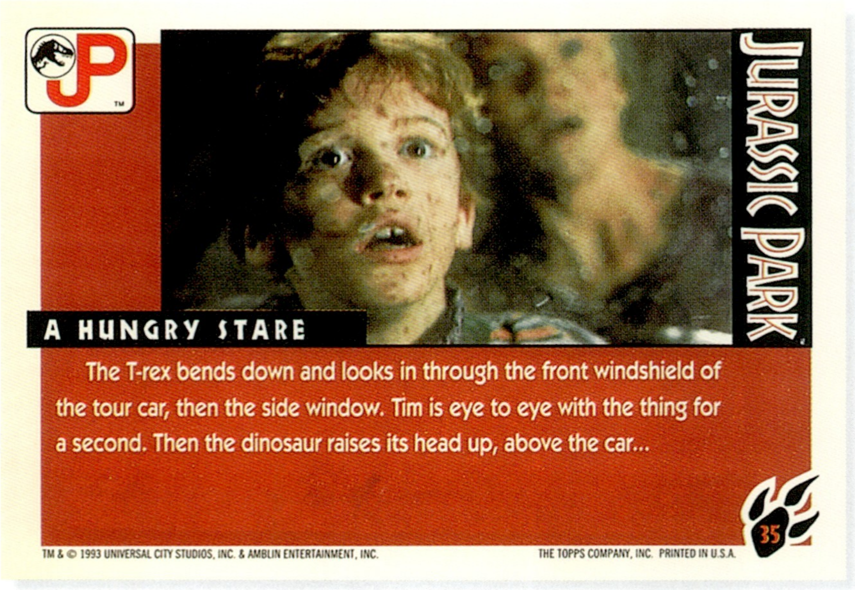
JURASSIC PARK
A HUNGRY STARE
The T-rex bends down and looks in through the front windshield of the tour car, then the side window. Tim is eye to eye with the thing for a second. Then the dinosaur raises its head up, above the car...
35
TM & © 1993 UNIVERSAL CITY STUDIOS, INC. & AMBLIN ENTERTAINMENT, INC.
THE TOPPS COMPANY, INC. PRINTED IN U.S.A.

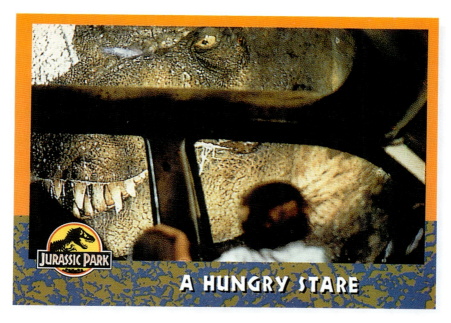

A HUNGRY STARE

John Hammond envisioned Jurassic Park as the ultimate theme-park experience, but he never bargained for thrills of this nature.

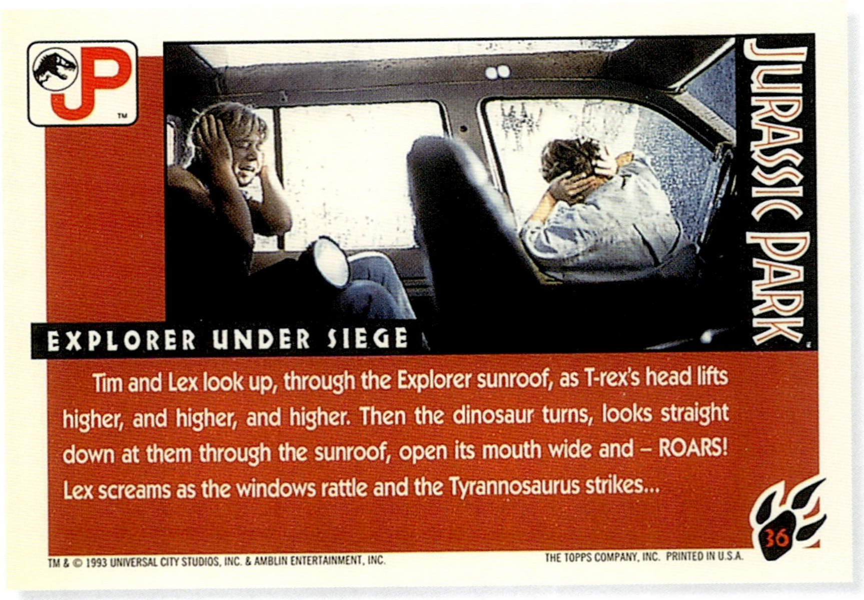
JP
JURASSIC PARK
EXPLORER UNDER SIEGE
Tim and Lex look up, through the Explorer sunroof, as T-rex's head lifts higher, and higher, and higher. Then the dinosaur turns, looks straight down at them through the sunroof, open its mouth wide and – ROARS! Lex screams as the windows rattle and the Tyrannosaurus strikes...
36
TM & © 1993 UNIVERSAL CITY STUDIOS, INC. & AMBLIN ENTERTAINMENT, INC.
THE TOPPS COMPANY, INC. PRINTED IN U.S.A.

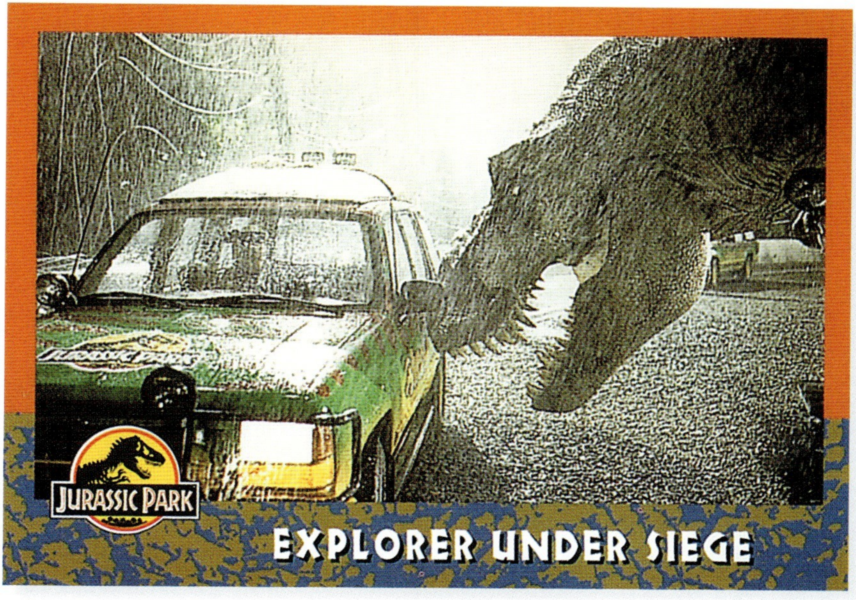
JURASSIC PARK
EXPLORER UNDER SIEGE

A nice view of the *Tyrannosaurus rex*'s profile. The rainstorm adds atmosphere and texture to the scene.

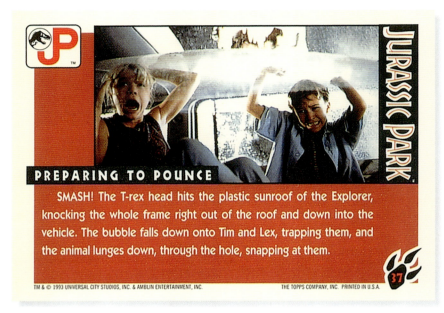

JURASSIC PARK
PREPARING TO POUNCE
SMASH! The T-rex head hits the plastic sunroof of the Explorer, knocking the whole frame right out of the roof and down into the vehicle. The bubble falls down onto Tim and Lex, trapping them, and the animal lunges down, through the hole, snapping at them.
37
TM & © 1993 UNIVERSAL CITY STUDIOS, INC. & AMBLIN ENTERTAINMENT, INC.
THE TOPPS COMPANY, INC. PRINTED IN U.S.A.

JURASSIC PARK
JURASSIC PARK
PREPARING TO POUNCE

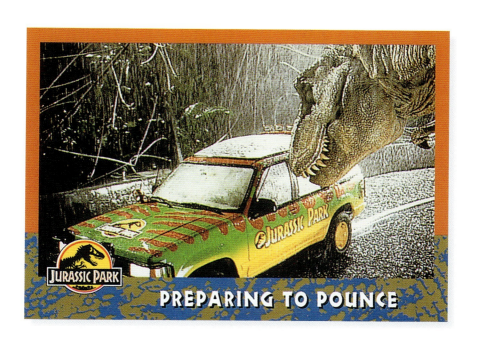

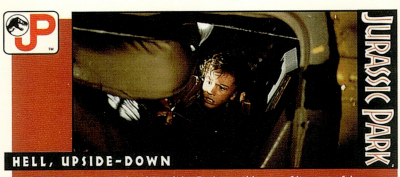

JP
JURASSIC PARK
HELL, UPSIDE-DOWN
The T-rex claws at the side of the Explorer with one of its powerful hind legs, tipping the vehicle over. The glass windows shatter, the kids are thrown to the side and the besieged tour car tilts. Relentless, the dinosaur bends down and nudges the Explorer with its head, pushing it near the edge of a sharp precipice.
38
TM & © 1993 UNIVERSAL CITY STUDIOS, INC. & AMBLIN ENTERTAINMENT, INC.
THE TOPPS COMPANY, INC. PRINTED IN U.S.A.

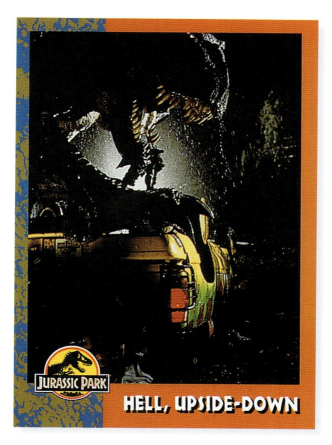

HELL, UPSIDE-DOWN

Topps often revisits great movie dialogue for its captions, but in this case I was inspired by the advertising tagline from another movie, *The Poseidon Adventure* (1972), to be exact. It really seemed to fit, and if those massive *T. rex* jaws don't seem hellish to you, then we're not looking at the same photo!

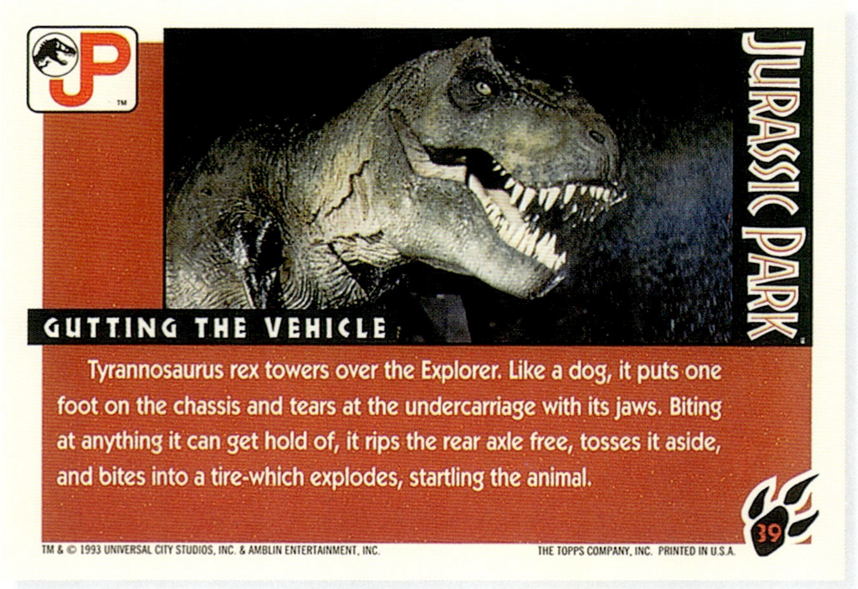
JP
JURASSIC PARK
GUTTING THE VEHICLE
Tyrannosaurus rex towers over the Explorer. Like a dog, it puts one foot on the chassis and tears at the undercarriage with its jaws. Biting at anything it can get hold of, it rips the rear axle free, tosses it aside, and bites into a tire-which explodes, startling the animal.
39
TM & © 1993 UNIVERSAL CITY STUDIOS, INC. & AMBLIN ENTERTAINMENT, INC.
THE TOPPS COMPANY, INC. PRINTED IN U.S.A.

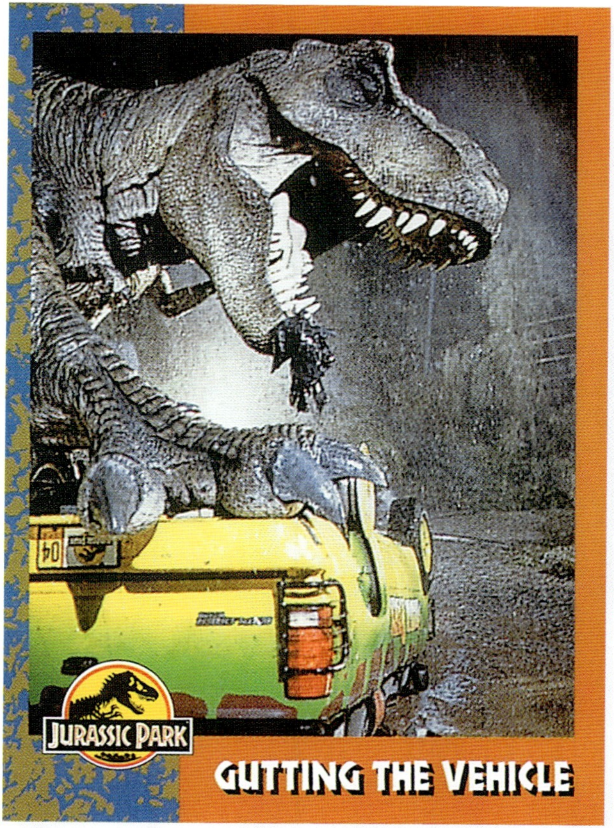
JURASSIC PARK
GUTTING THE VEHICLE

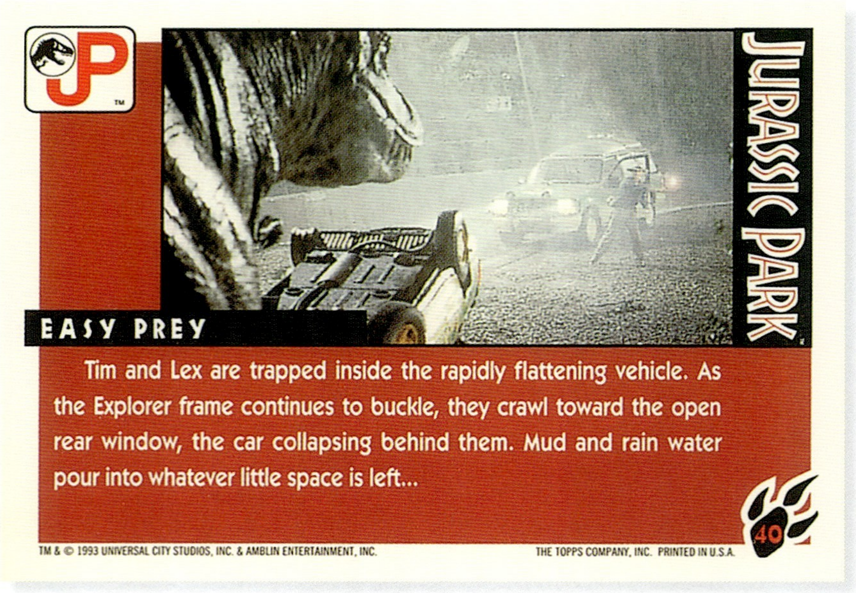
JURASSIC PARK
EASY PREY
Tim and Lex are trapped inside the rapidly flattening vehicle. As the Explorer frame continues to buckle, they crawl toward the open rear window, the car collapsing behind them. Mud and rain water pour into whatever little space is left...
40
TM & © 1993 UNIVERSAL CITY STUDIOS, INC. & AMBLIN ENTERTAINMENT, INC.
THE TOPPS COMPANY, INC. PRINTED IN U.S.A.

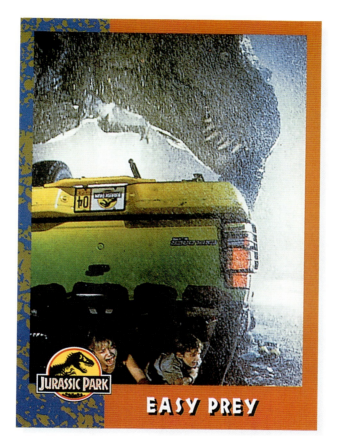

EASY PREY

Actually, these kids should be easy prey . . . but in truth, they spend most of the movie being highly elusive snacks for a variety of hungry dinosaurs.

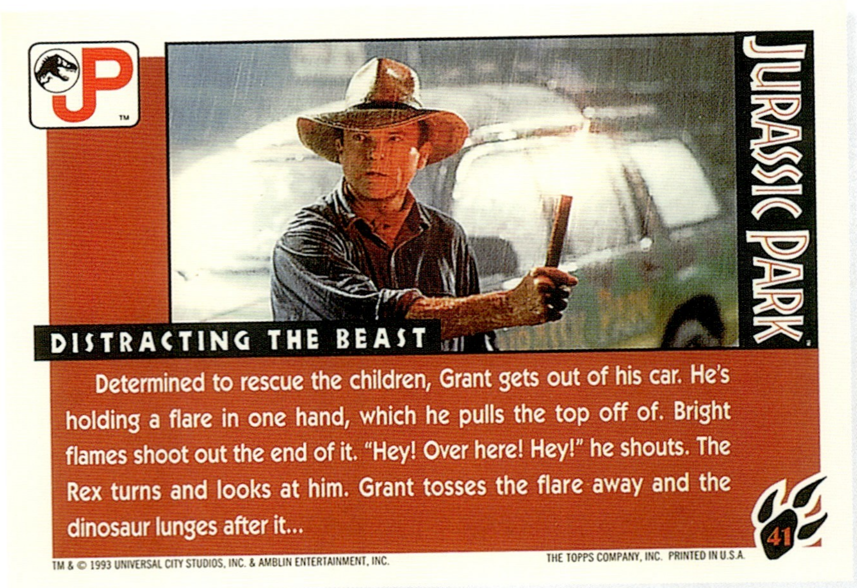
JURASSIC PARK
DISTRACTING THE BEAST
Determined to rescue the children, Grant gets out of his car. He's holding a flare in one hand, which he pulls the top off of. Bright flames shoot out the end of it. "Hey! Over here! Hey!" he shouts. The Rex turns and looks at him. Grant tosses the flare away and the dinosaur lunges after it...
41
TM & © 1993 UNIVERSAL CITY STUDIOS, INC. & AMBLIN ENTERTAINMENT, INC.
THE TOPPS COMPANY, INC. PRINTED IN U.S.A.

JURASSIC PARK

DISTRACTING THE BEAST

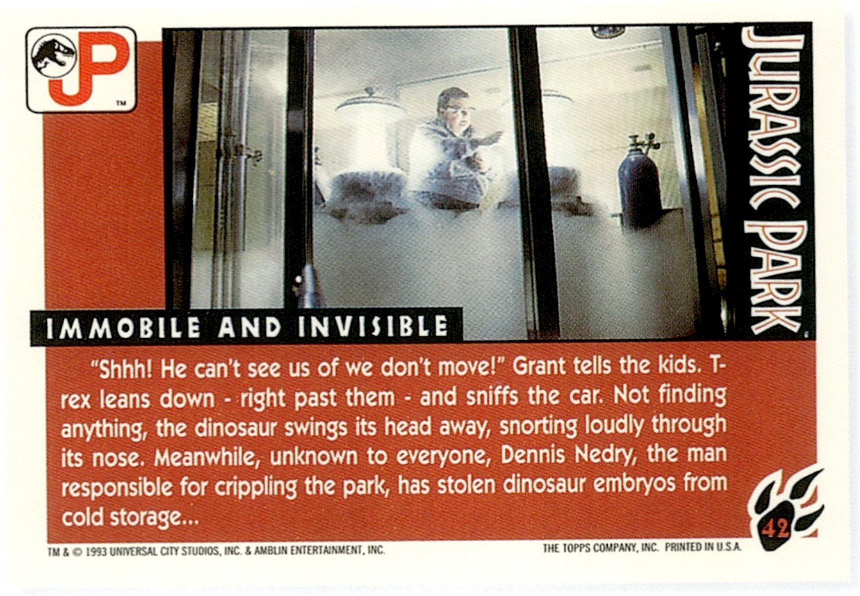
JURASSIC PARK
IMMOBILE AND INVISIBLE
"Shhh! He can't see us of we don't move!" Grant tells the kids. T-rex leans down - right past them - and sniffs the car. Not finding anything, the dinosaur swings its head away, snorting loudly through its nose. Meanwhile, unknown to everyone, Dennis Nedry, the man responsible for crippling the park, has stolen dinosaur embryos from cold storage...
42
TM & © 1993 UNIVERSAL CITY STUDIOS, INC. & AMBLIN ENTERTAINMENT, INC.
THE TOPPS COMPANY, INC. PRINTED IN U.S.A.

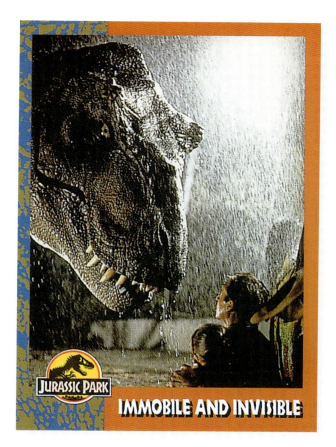

IMMOBILE AND INVISIBLE

The heart-pounding encounter between Dr. Grant and the *T. rex* makes for a standout trading card; perhaps it's no surprise "Immobile and Invisible" was chosen to represent *Jurassic Park* in the Topps 75th Anniversary trading card set released in 2013, which was comprised of a single card from 100 of the company's previous sets.

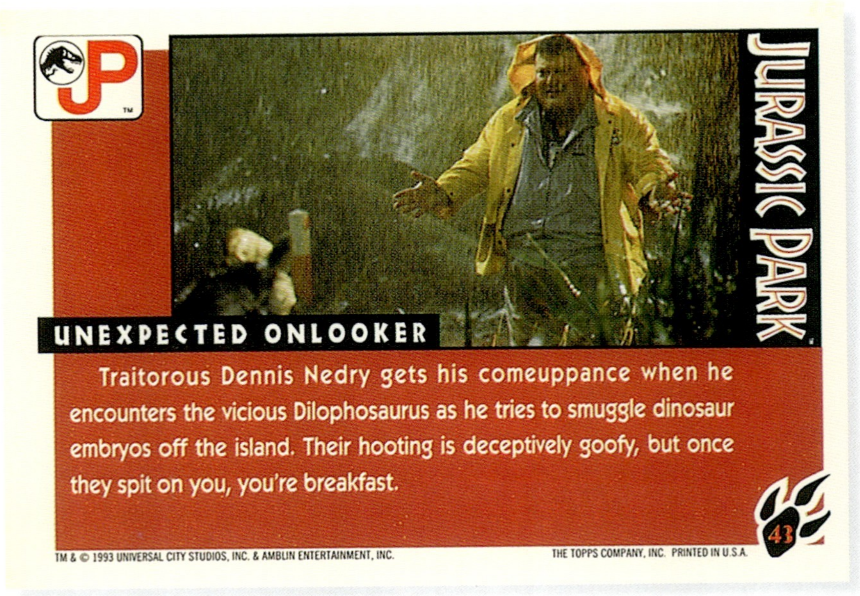
JP
JURASSIC PARK
UNEXPECTED ONLOOKER
Traitorous Dennis Nedry gets his comeuppance when he encounters the vicious Dilophosaurus as he tries to smuggle dinosaur embryos off the island. Their hooting is deceptively goofy, but once they spit on you, you're breakfast.
43
TM & © 1993 UNIVERSAL CITY STUDIOS, INC. & AMBLIN ENTERTAINMENT, INC.
THE TOPPS COMPANY, INC. PRINTED IN U.S.A.

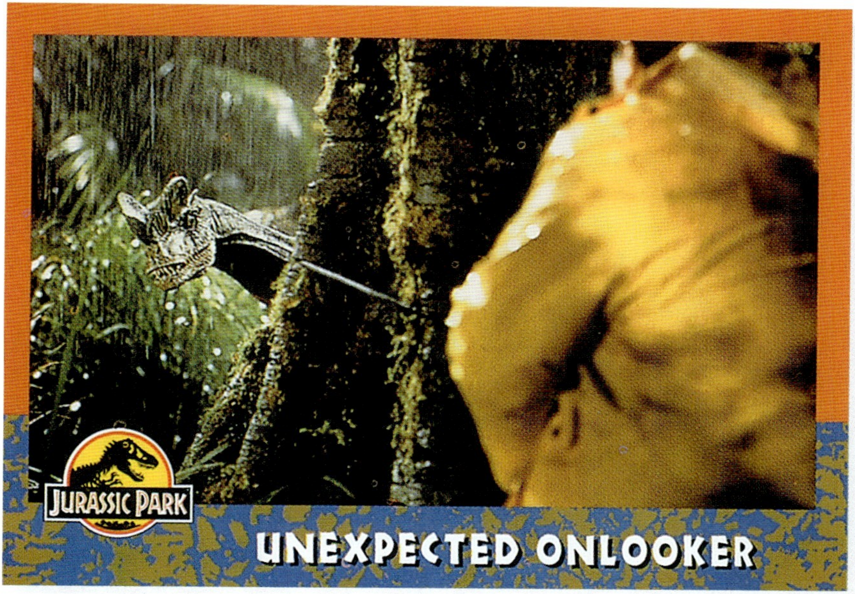
JURASSIC PARK
UNEXPECTED ONLOOKER

While raptors were prominent villains in *Jurassic Park*, the *Dilophosaurus* made an equally strong impression by providing both comic relief and, ultimately, deceitful danger. The setup for its attack was certainly humorous enough, with this colorful little creature playing hide-and-seek with a hapless human pursuer.

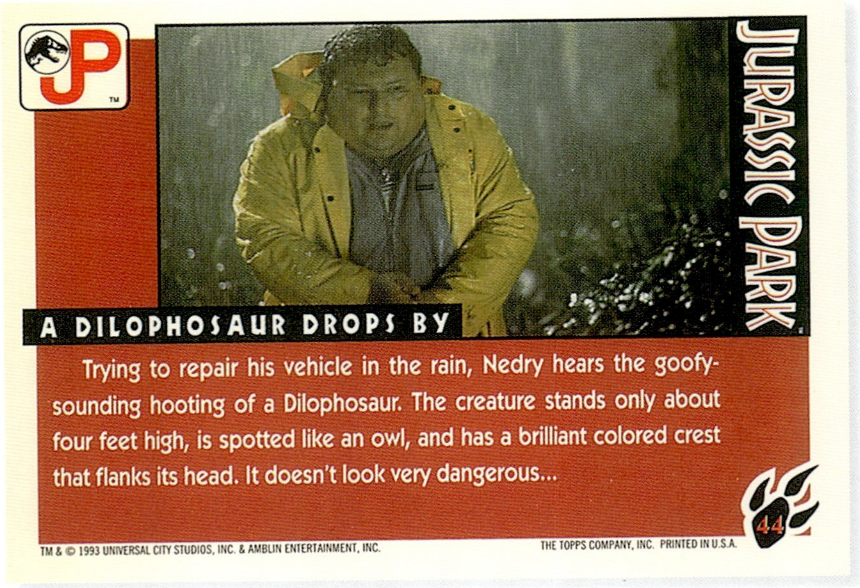
JP
JURASSIC PARK
A DILOPHOSAUR DROPS BY
Trying to repair his vehicle in the rain, Nedry hears the goofy-sounding hooting of a Dilophosaur. The creature stands only about four feet high, is spotted like an owl, and has a brilliant colored crest that flanks its head. It doesn't look very dangerous...
44
TM & © 1993 UNIVERSAL CITY STUDIOS, INC. & AMBLIN ENTERTAINMENT, INC.
THE TOPPS COMPANY, INC. PRINTED IN U.S.A.

JURASSIC PARK
A DILOPHOSAUR DROPS BY

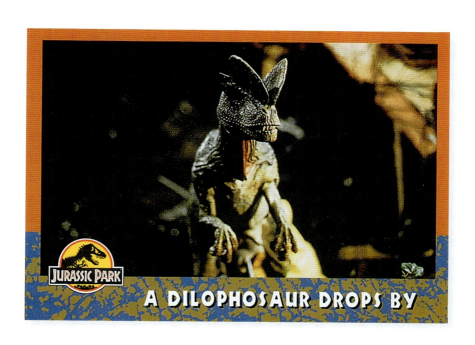

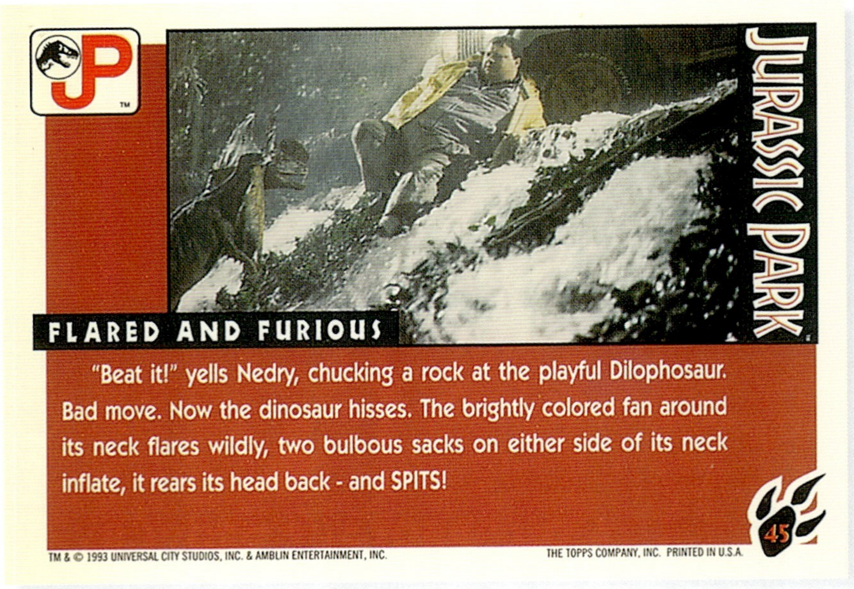
JURASSIC PARK
FLARED AND FURIOUS
"Beat it!" yells Nedry, chucking a rock at the playful Dilophosaur. Bad move. Now the dinosaur hisses. The brightly colored fan around its neck flares wildly, two bulbous sacks on either side of its neck inflate, it rears its head back - and SPITS!
45
TM & © 1993 UNIVERSAL CITY STUDIOS, INC. & AMBLIN ENTERTAINMENT, INC.
THE TOPPS COMPANY, INC. PRINTED IN U.S.A.

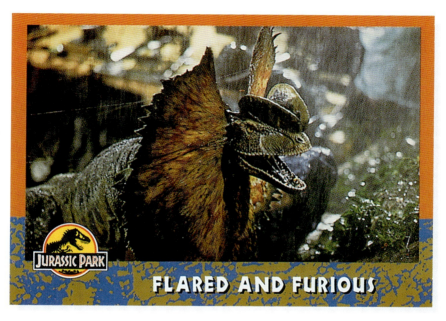

FLARED AND FURIOUS

This beauty shot of the *Dilophosaurus* made a wonderful horizontal trading card. The creature itself was an on-camera puppet created by Stan Winston and his effects team.

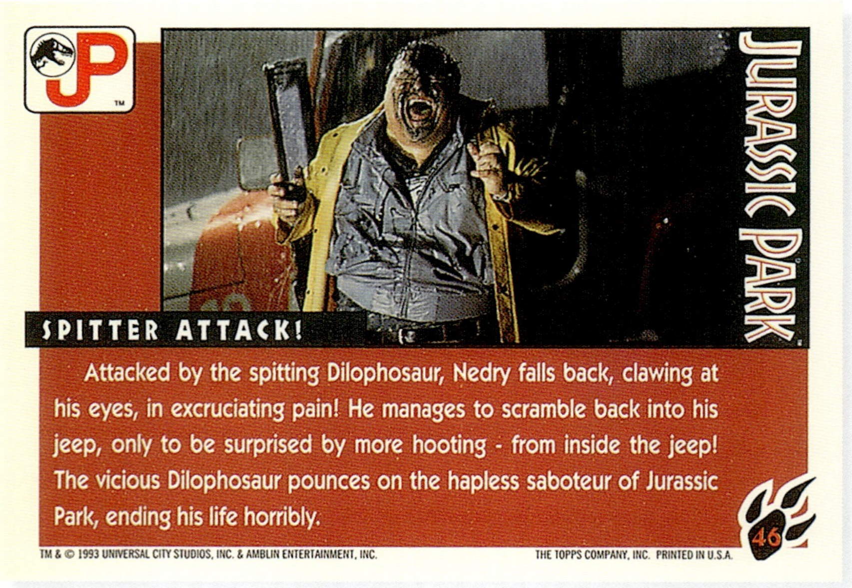
JP
JURASSIC PARK
SPITTER ATTACK!
Attacked by the spitting Dilophosaur, Nedry falls back, clawing at his eyes, in excruciating pain! He manages to scramble back into his jeep, only to be surprised by more hooting - from inside the jeep! The vicious Dilophosaur pounces on the hapless saboteur of Jurassic Park, ending his life horribly.
46
TM & © 1993 UNIVERSAL CITY STUDIOS, INC. & AMBLIN ENTERTAINMENT, INC.
THE TOPPS COMPANY, INC. PRINTED IN U.S.A.

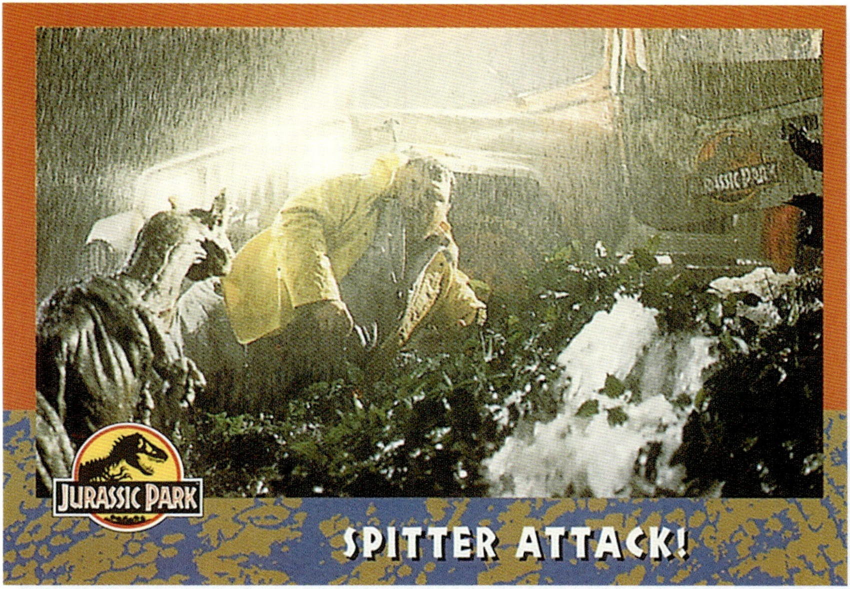
JURASSIC PARK
SPITTER ATTACK!

Although humor was built into this sequence, it was still pretty dark, especially with the *Dilophosaurus* turning quite nasty. Even so, the beautiful but deadly "Spitter" became one of the movie's most memorable dinosaurs.

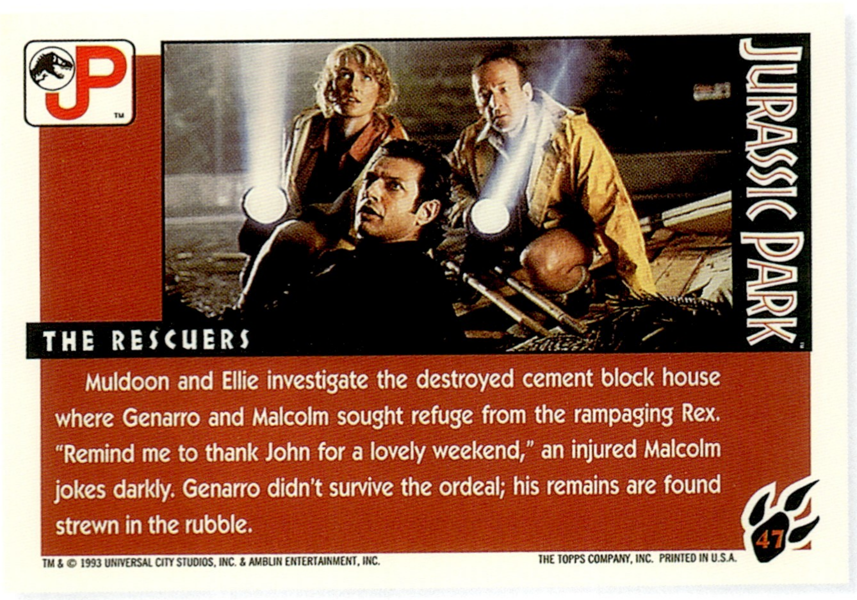
JURASSIC PARK
THE RESCUERS
Muldoon and Ellie investigate the destroyed cement block house where Genarro and Malcolm sought refuge from the rampaging Rex. "Remind me to thank John for a lovely weekend," an injured Malcolm jokes darkly. Genarro didn't survive the ordeal; his remains are found strewn in the rubble.
47
TM & © 1993 UNIVERSAL CITY STUDIOS, INC. & AMBLIN ENTERTAINMENT, INC.
THE TOPPS COMPANY, INC. PRINTED IN U.S.A.

JURASSIC PARK

THE RESCUERS

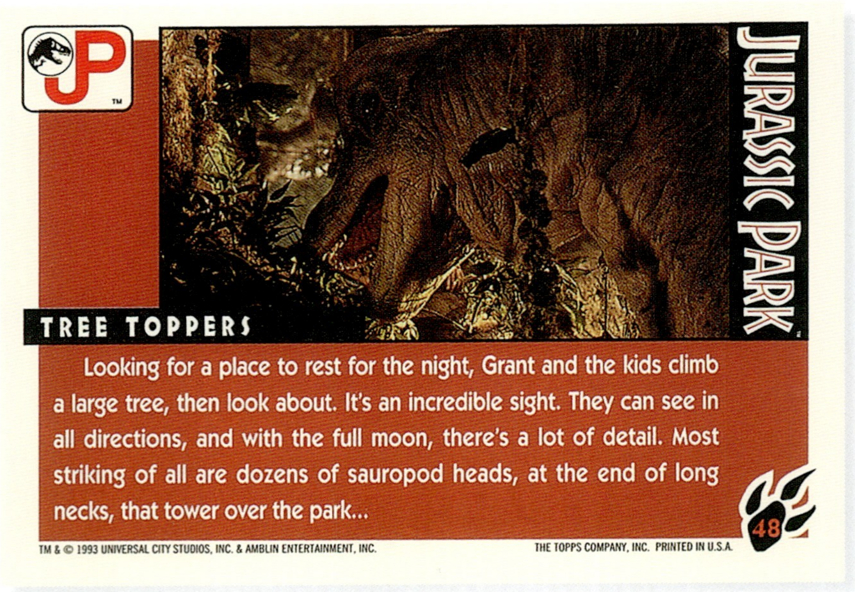
JP
JURASSIC PARK
TREE TOPPERS
Looking for a place to rest for the night, Grant and the kids climb a large tree, then look about. It's an incredible sight. They can see in all directions, and with the full moon, there's a lot of detail. Most striking of all are dozens of sauropod heads, at the end of long necks, that tower over the park...
48
TM & © 1993 UNIVERSAL CITY STUDIOS, INC. & AMBLIN ENTERTAINMENT, INC.
THE TOPPS COMPANY, INC. PRINTED IN U.S.A.

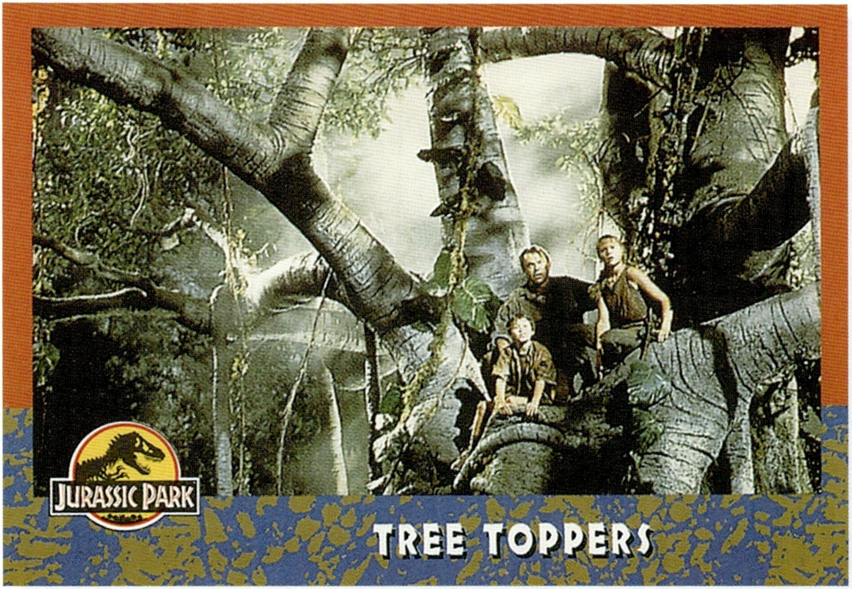
JURASSIC PARK
TREE TOPPERS

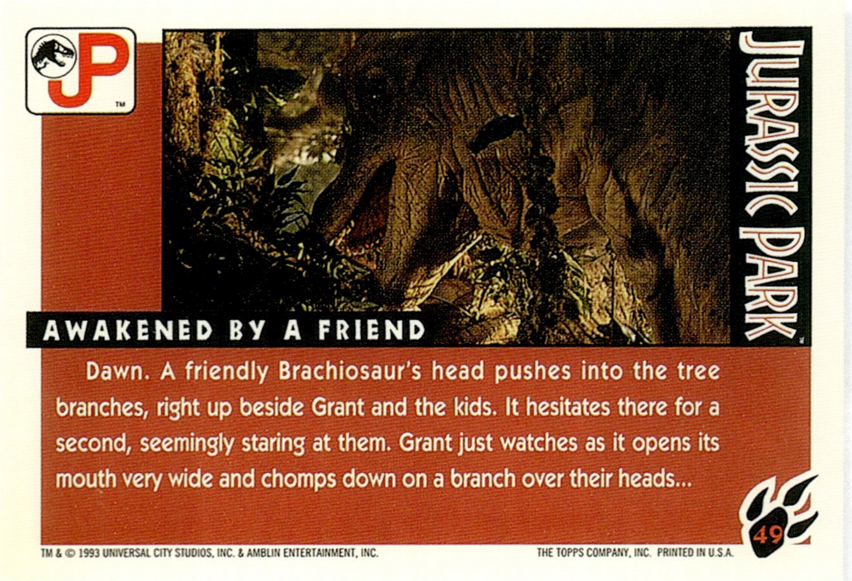
JP
JURASSIC PARK
AWAKENED BY A FRIEND
Dawn. A friendly Brachiosaur's head pushes into the tree branches, right up beside Grant and the kids. It hesitates there for a second, seemingly staring at them. Grant just watches as it opens its mouth very wide and chomps down on a branch over their heads...
49
TM & © 1993 UNIVERSAL CITY STUDIOS, INC. & AMBLIN ENTERTAINMENT, INC.
THE TOPPS COMPANY, INC. PRINTED IN U.S.A.

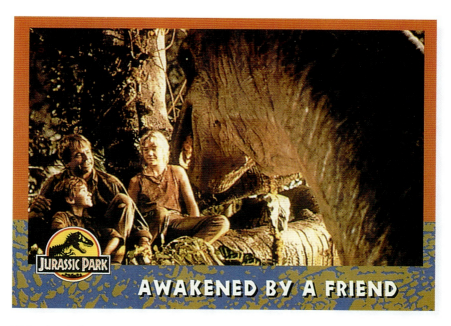

AWAKENED BY A FRIEND

While a lot of what we thought we knew about dinosaurs has been proven incorrect over the years, the giant Bronto-like sauropods of the Jurassic age continue to be characterized as creatures with essentially gentle dispositions, according to most paleontologists.

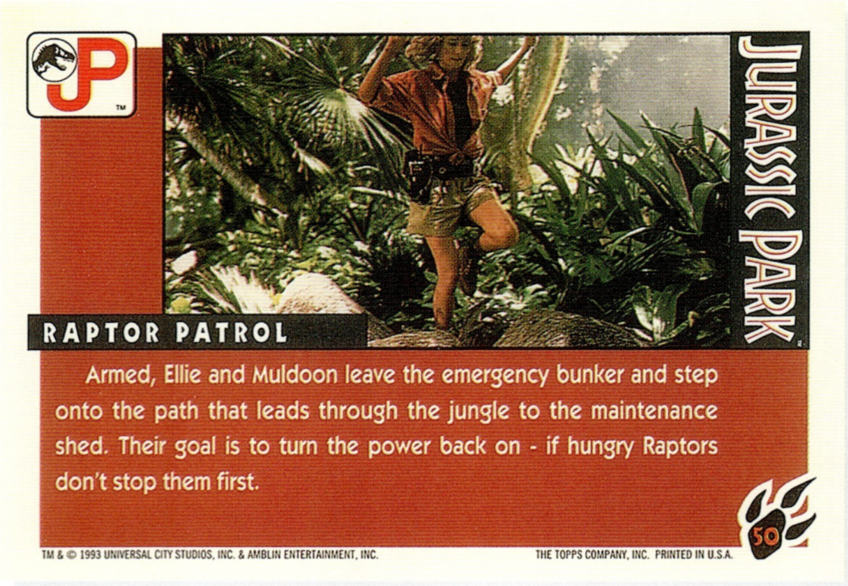
JURASSIC PARK
RAPTOR PATROL
Armed, Ellie and Muldoon leave the emergency bunker and step onto the path that leads through the jungle to the maintenance shed. Their goal is to turn the power back on - if hungry Raptors don't stop them first.
50
TM & © 1993 UNIVERSAL CITY STUDIOS, INC. & AMBLIN ENTERTAINMENT, INC.
THE TOPPS COMPANY, INC. PRINTED IN U.S.A.

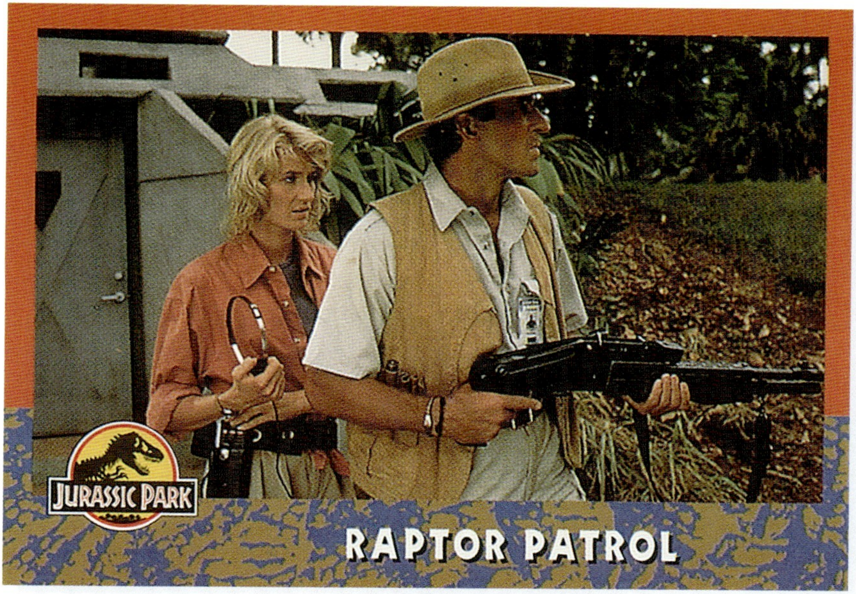
JURASSIC PARK
RAPTOR PATROL

Muldoon, as played by Bob Peck, pits his hunter's instincts against the greatest predators of natural history. It's a battle to the death that he's fated to lose.

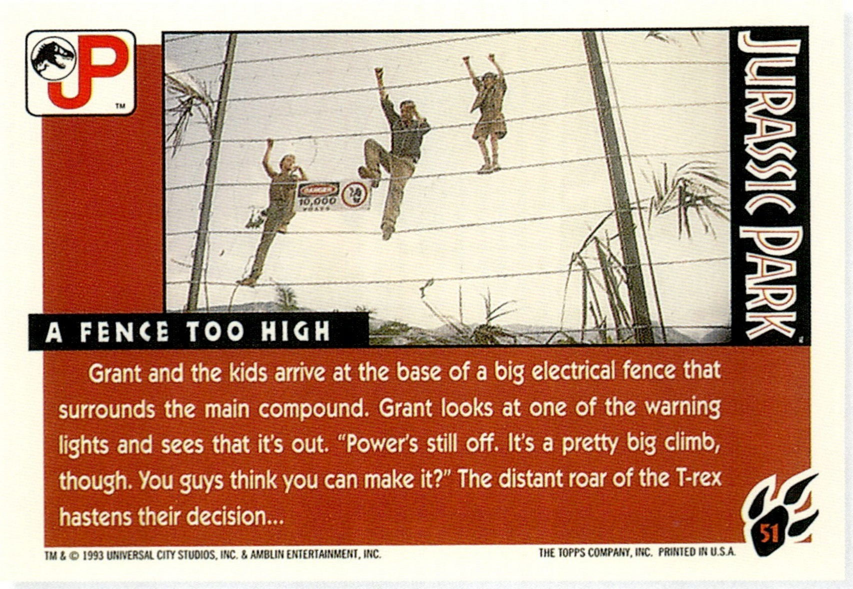
JURASSIC PARK
JP
A FENCE TOO HIGH
Grant and the kids arrive at the base of a big electrical fence that surrounds the main compound. Grant looks at one of the warning lights and sees that it's out. "Power's still off. It's a pretty big climb, though. You guys think you can make it?" The distant roar of the T-rex hastens their decision...
51
TM & © 1993 UNIVERSAL CITY STUDIOS, INC. & AMBLIN ENTERTAINMENT, INC.
THE TOPPS COMPANY, INC. PRINTED IN U.S.A.

DANGER
10,000 VOLTS

JURASSIC PARK

A FENCE TOO HIGH

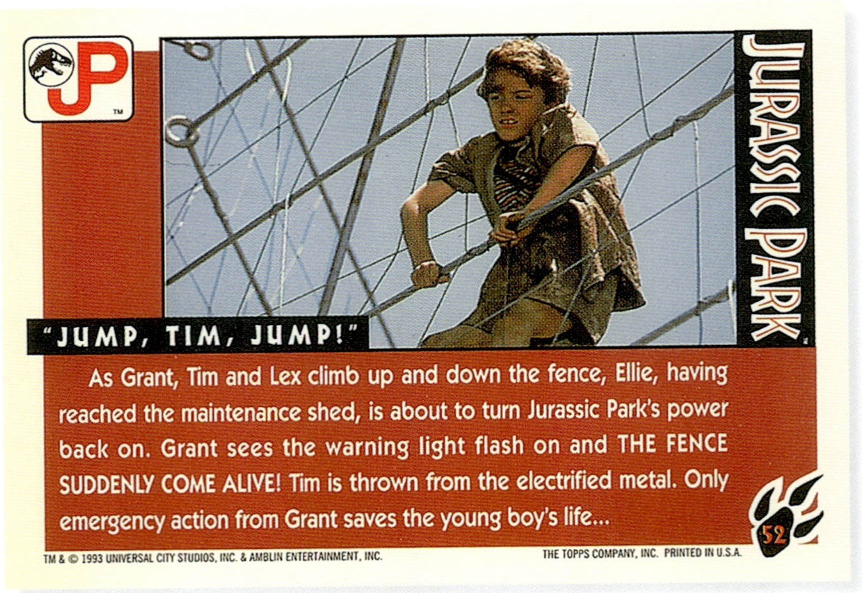
JP
JURASSIC PARK
"JUMP, TIM, JUMP!"
As Grant, Tim and Lex climb up and down the fence, Ellie, having reached the maintenance shed, is about to turn Jurassic Park's power back on. Grant sees the warning light flash on and THE FENCE SUDDENLY COME ALIVE! Tim is thrown from the electrified metal. Only emergency action from Grant saves the young boy's life...
52
TM & © 1993 UNIVERSAL CITY STUDIOS, INC. & AMBLIN ENTERTAINMENT, INC.
THE TOPPS COMPANY, INC. PRINTED IN U.S.A.

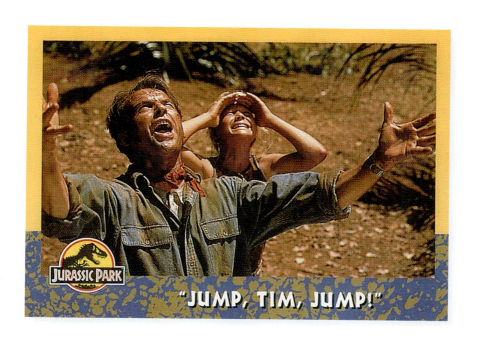

JURASSIC PARK

"JUMP, TIM, JUMP!"

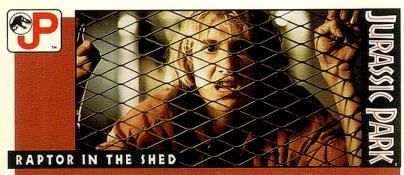

JP
JURASSIC PARK
RAPTOR IN THE SHED
After restoring power from the maintenance shed, Ellie comes face- to-face with a hungry Raptor. It takes a lunging sweep at the scientist, but gets stuck, its feet and legs tangled in debris. Ellie slams a wire mesh door closed behind her. The Raptor untangles itself and gives chase, slashing easily through the mesh with one of its talons.
53
TM & © 1993 UNIVERSAL CITY STUDIOS, INC. & AMBLIN ENTERTAINMENT, INC.
THE TOPPS COMPANY, INC. PRINTED IN U.S.A.

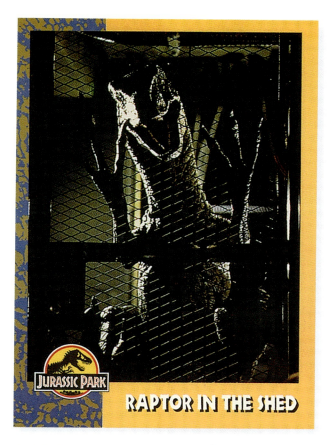

RAPTOR IN THE SHED

Here's an epic image of a raptor trying to claw its way to imperiled Dr. Ellie Sattler (Laura Dern). In the back photo, a trapped and desperate Sattler is trying to claw her own way out.

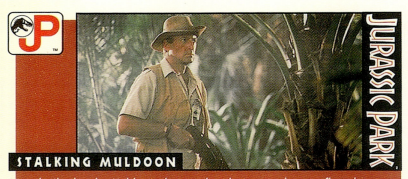

JURASSIC PARK
STALKING MULDOON
In the jungle, Muldoon draws a bead on a semi-camouflaged Raptor. Suddenly, a terrible thought hits him. His eyes flick to the side - which is where the attack comes from. With a roar, a second Raptor comes flashing out of nowhere and pounces on Muldoon, slashing through the hunter's midsection.
54
TM & © 1993 UNIVERSAL CITY STUDIOS, INC. & AMBLIN ENTERTAINMENT, INC.
THE TOPPS COMPANY, INC. PRINTED IN U.S.A.

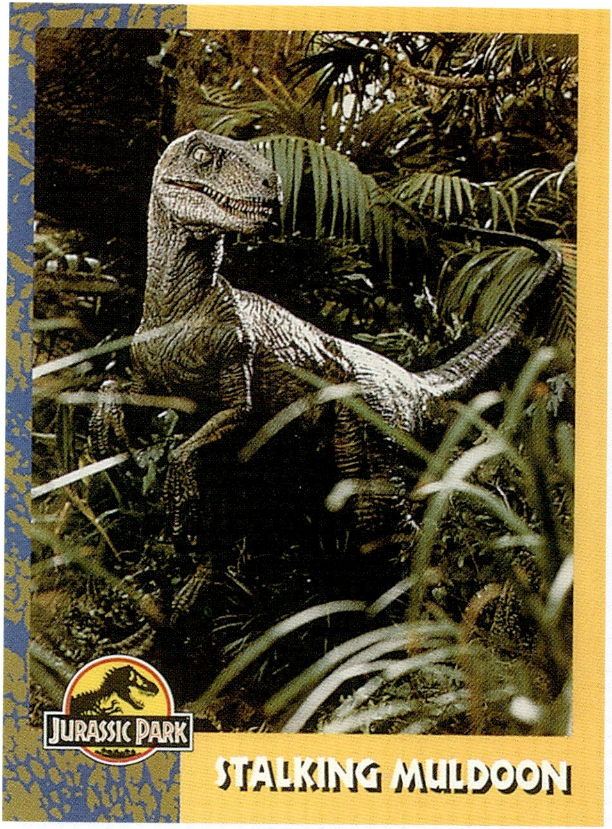
JURASSIC PARK
STALKING MULDOON

Muldoon's grisly demise was tastefully (sorry about that!) handled off-camera. Our front image is a wonderful photo of a raptor in the wild, used extensively in the movie's advertising campaign. On the back, hunter Muldoon becomes the hunted.

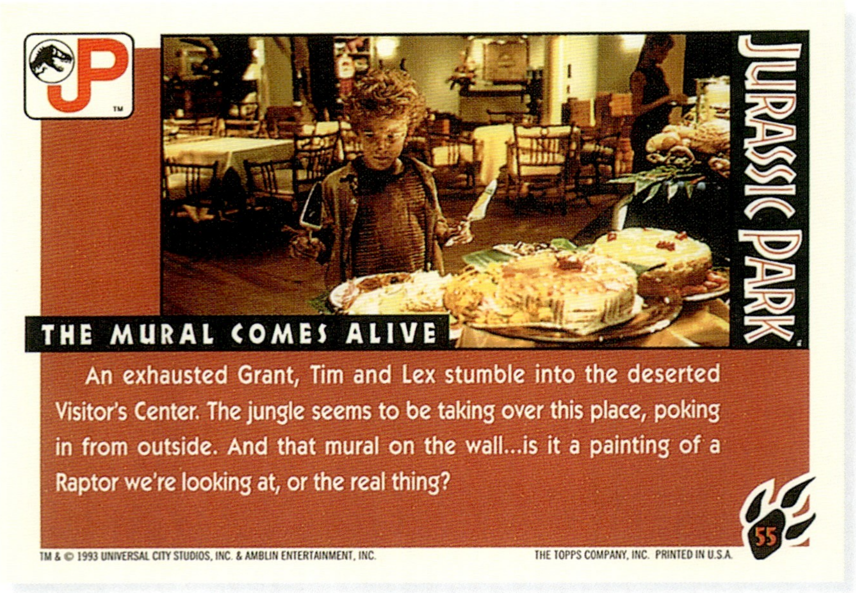
JP
JURASSIC PARK
THE MURAL COMES ALIVE
An exhausted Grant, Tim and Lex stumble into the deserted Visitor's Center. The jungle seems to be taking over this place, poking in from outside. And that mural on the wall...is it a painting of a Raptor we're looking at, or the real thing?
55
TM & © 1993 UNIVERSAL CITY STUDIOS, INC. & AMBLIN ENTERTAINMENT, INC.
THE TOPPS COMPANY, INC. PRINTED IN U.S.A.

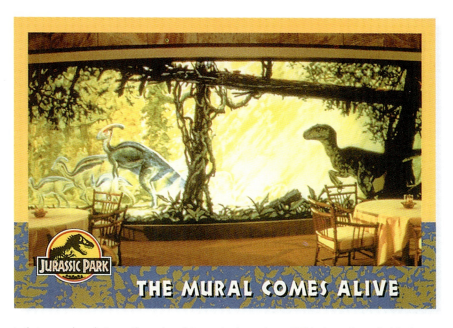

THE MURAL COMES ALIVE

Is that a mural rendering or the real predatory animal creeping up? This clever cinematic bit-of-business was nicely captured in trading card form. Heads up, Tim!

IT HUNGERS
Unaware that there are Raptors in the Visitor's Center, Grant separates from the kids. After spotting one of the hungry dinosaurs, Lex quickly loops an arm under her brother's, hauls him to his feet, and races into the nearby kitchen with him...
JP
EXIT
JURASSIC PARK
56
TM & © 1993 UNIVERSAL CITY STUDIOS, INC. & AMBLIN ENTERTAINMENT, INC.
THE TOPPS COMPANY, INC. PRINTED IN U.S.A.

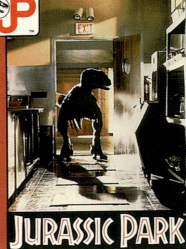

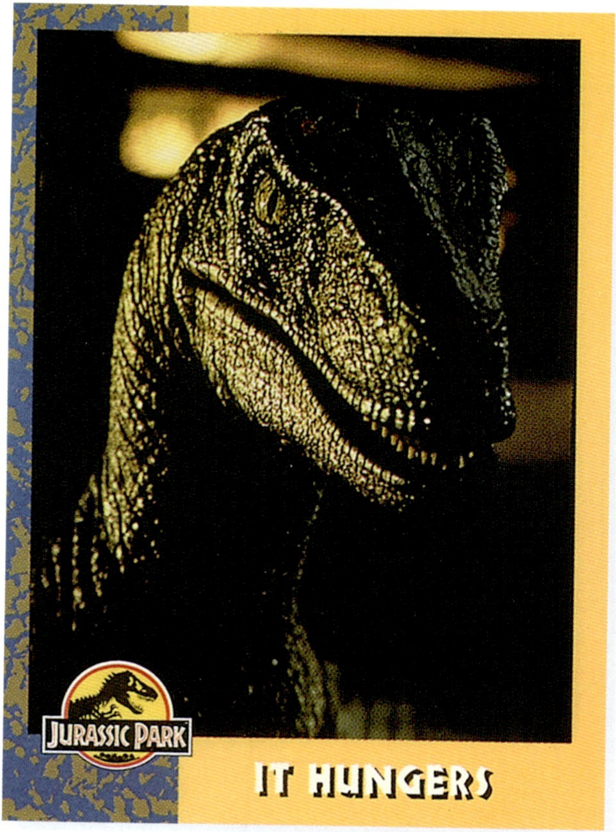
JURASSIC PARK
IT HUNGERS

Great close-up of the raptor. This elaborate costume and others like it were worn by the same special effects experts who inhabited the various *Alien* and *Pumpkinhead* suits over the years.

HIDING IN THE KITCHEN
Lex helps Tim down an aisle in the kitchen and they hide at the end, behind a counter, breathing hard. Suddenly, the kitchen door opens and a Raptor strides forward, snarling. A second of its kind joins it in the doorway and they both move into the room, looking for the kids...
JP
JURASSIC PARK
57
TM & © 1993 UNIVERSAL CITY STUDIOS, INC. & AMBLIN ENTERTAINMENT, INC.
THE TOPPS COMPANY, INC. PRINTED IN U.S.A.

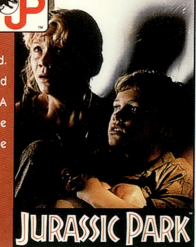

JURASSIC PARK
HIDING IN THE KITCHEN

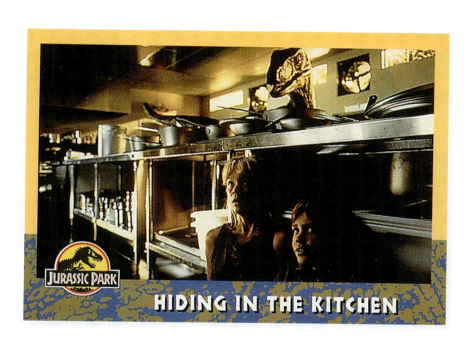

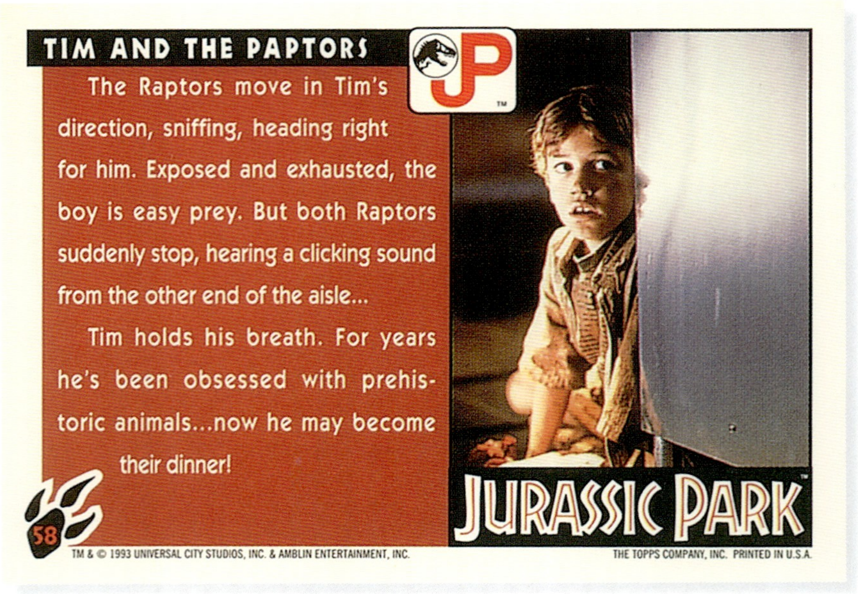
TIM AND THE RAPTORS
The Raptors move in Tim's direction, sniffing, heading right for him. Exposed and exhausted, the boy is easy prey. But both Raptors suddenly stop, hearing a clicking sound from the other end of the aisle...
Tim holds his breath. For years he's been obsessed with prehistoric animals...now he may become their dinner!
58
JP
JURASSIC PARK
TM & © 1993 UNIVERSAL CITY STUDIOS, INC. & AMBLIN ENTERTAINMENT, INC.
THE TOPPS COMPANY, INC. PRINTED IN U.S.A.

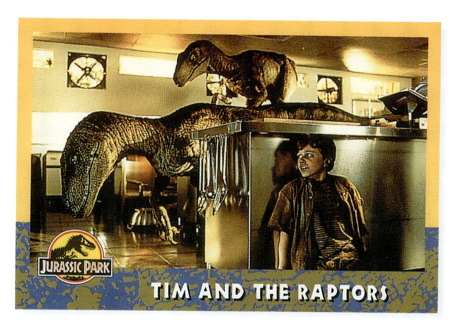

TIM AND THE RAPTORS

This extremely suspenseful moment in *Jurassic Park* was later revisited in 2005 by director Steven Spielberg in his *War of the Worlds* movie, with a terrified child once again trying to hide from prowling, deadly creatures.

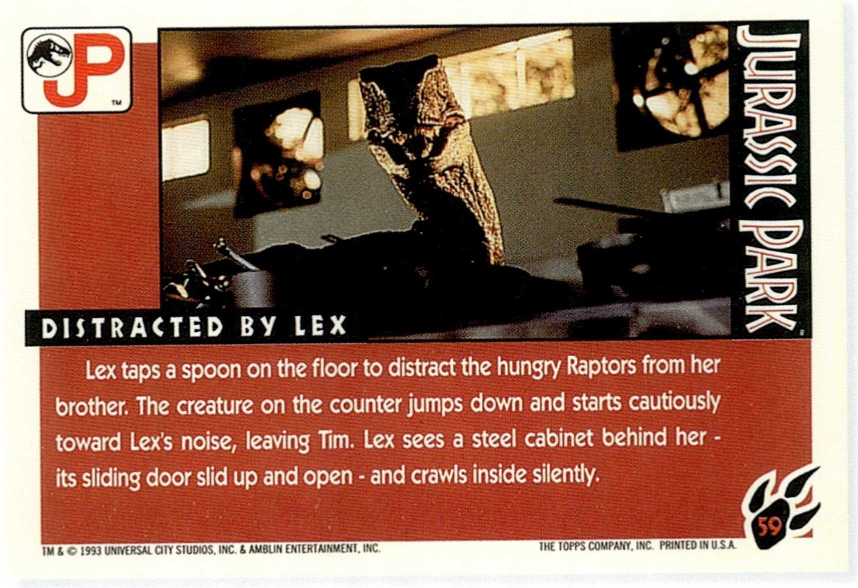
JURASSIC PARK
DISTRACTED BY LEX
Lex taps a spoon on the floor to distract the hungry Raptors from her brother. The creature on the counter jumps down and starts cautiously toward Lex's noise, leaving Tim. Lex sees a steel cabinet behind her - its sliding door slid up and open - and crawls inside silently.
59
TM & © 1993 UNIVERSAL CITY STUDIOS, INC. & AMBLIN ENTERTAINMENT, INC.
THE TOPPS COMPANY, INC. PRINTED IN U.S.A.

JURASSIC PARK

DISTRACTED BY LEX

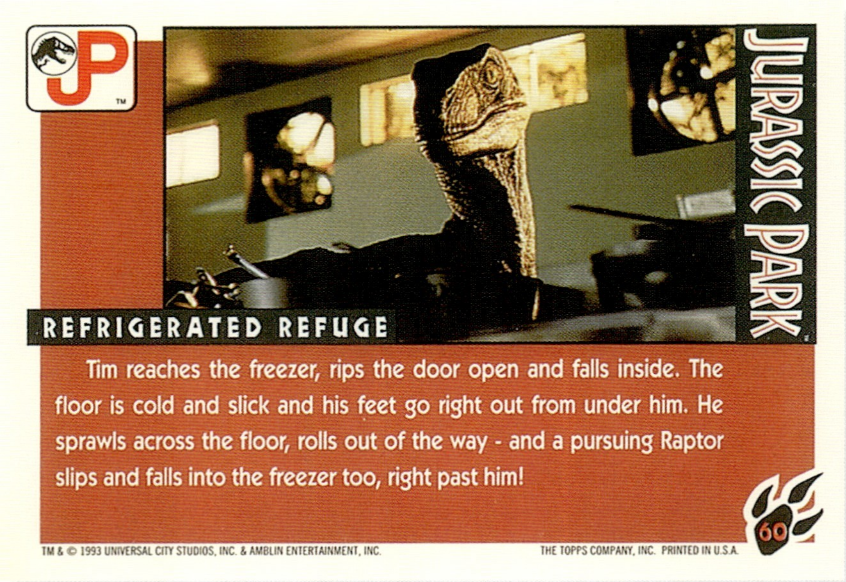
JP™
JURASSIC PARK
REFRIGERATED REFUGE
Tim reaches the freezer, rips the door open and falls inside. The floor is cold and slick and his feet go right out from under him. He sprawls across the floor, rolls out of the way - and a pursuing Raptor slips and falls into the freezer too, right past him!
60
TM & © 1993 UNIVERSAL CITY STUDIOS, INC. & AMBLIN ENTERTAINMENT, INC.
THE TOPPS COMPANY, INC. PRINTED IN U.S.A.

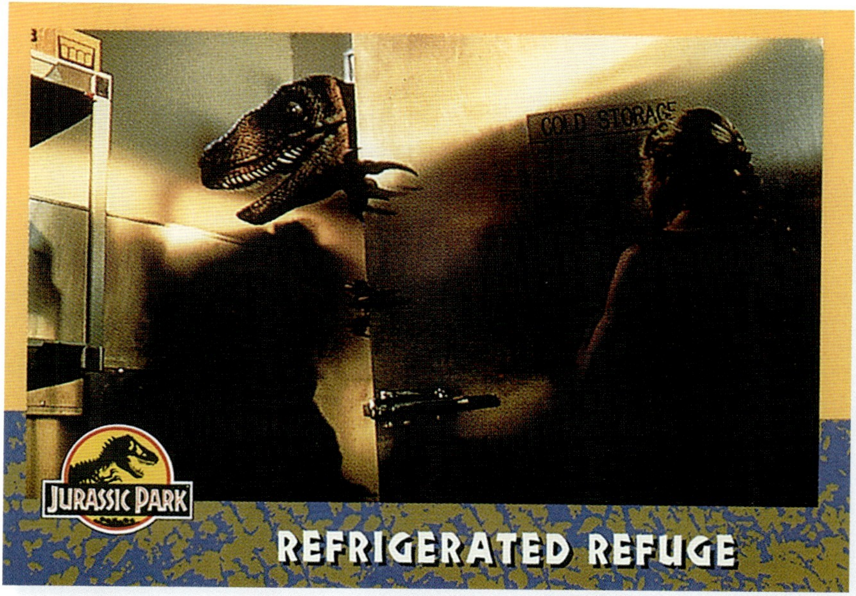
COLD STORAGE
JURASSIC PARK
REFRIGERATED REFUGE

Raptors raid the fridge, with cringing Lex Murphy (Ariana Richards) fearing she might be a potential snack. These predators' smarts, with their ability to open doors and enter rooms, gave them a disturbing edge over their more lumbering counterparts.

INVADING THE CONTROL ROOM
Escaping from the reptors, Tim and Lex run into Grant and Ellie and they all rush to the Control Room. Unable to lock the door, Grant hurls his back against it as a Raptor snarls and snaps, ramming with all its might, trying to force its way into the Control Room.
61
JURASSIC PARK
TM & © 1993 UNIVERSAL CITY STUDIOS, INC. & AMBLIN ENTERTAINMENT, INC.
THE TOPPS COMPANY, INC. PRINTED IN U.S.A.

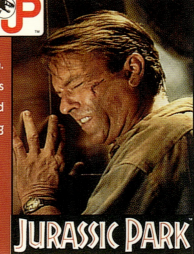

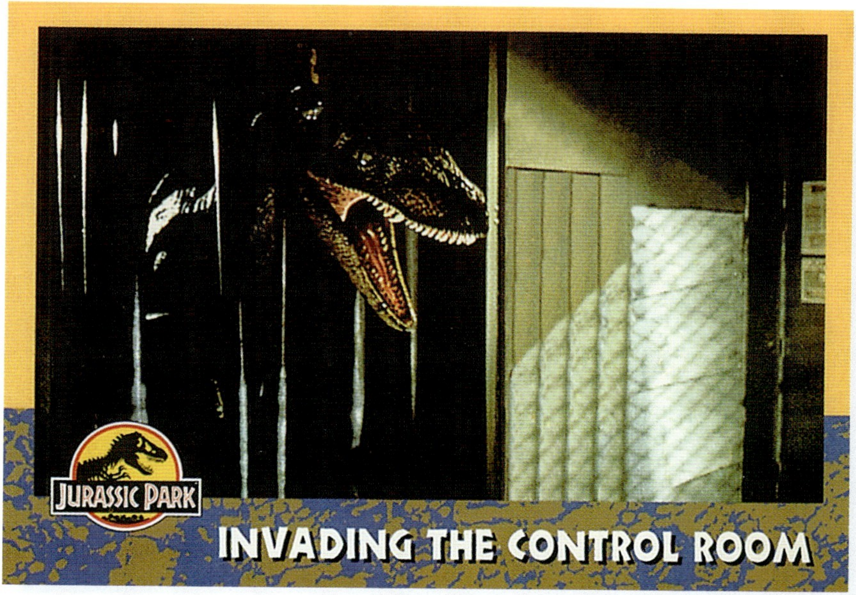
JURASSIC PARK
INVADING THE CONTROL ROOM

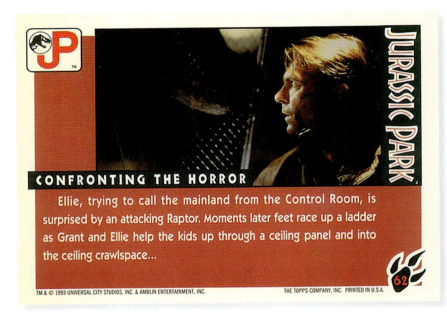

CONFRONTING THE HORROR

Ellie, trying to call the mainland from the Control Room, is surprised by an attacking Raptor. Moments later feet race up a ladder as Grant and Ellie help the kids up through a ceiling panel and into the ceiling crawlspace...

62

TM & © 1993 UNIVERSAL CITY STUDIOS, INC. & AMBLIN ENTERTAINMENT, INC.   THE TOPPS COMPANY, INC. PRINTED IN U.S.A.

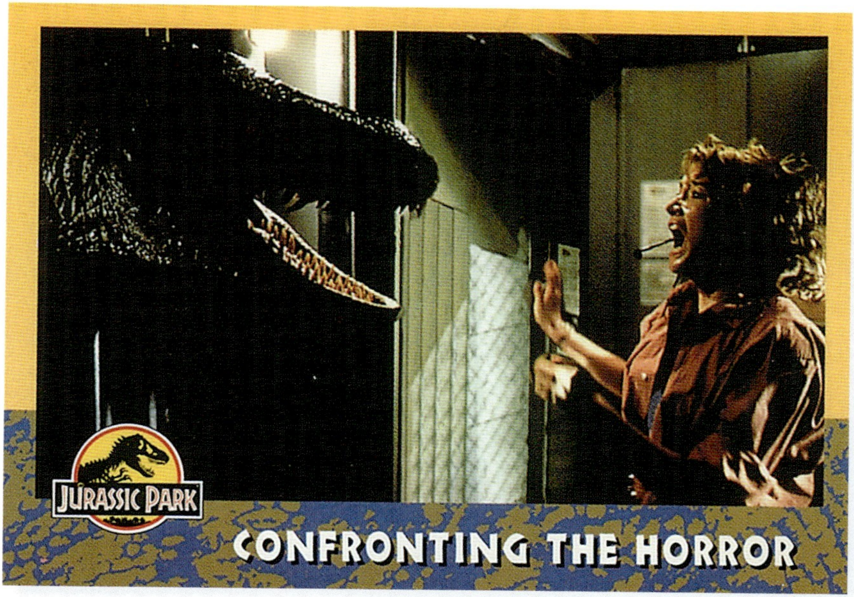
JURASSIC PARK
CONFRONTING THE HORROR

. . . and quite a horror it is! Dinosaurs have been imperiling humans since the earliest days of the silent cinema, and here, on-the-run heroine Ellie Sattler has her own raptor run-in.

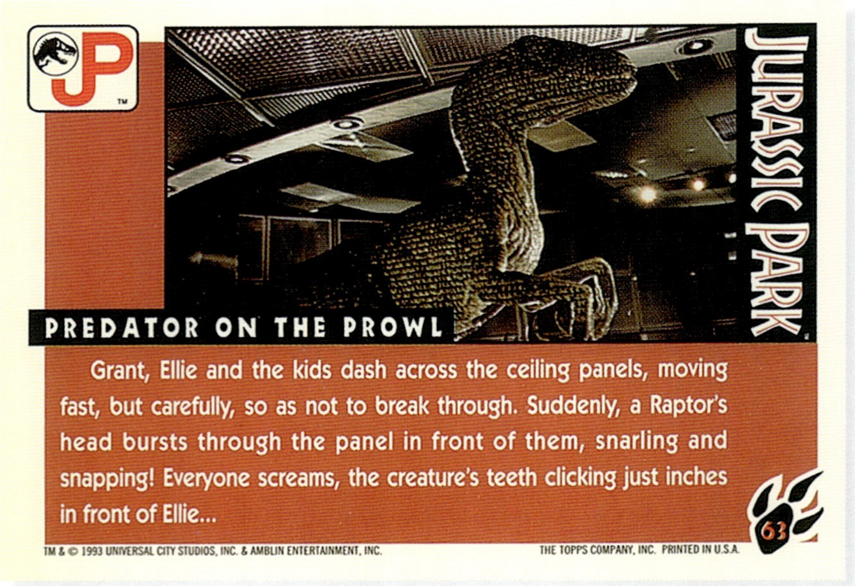
JURASSIC PARK
PREDATOR ON THE PROWL
Grant, Ellie and the kids dash across the ceiling panels, moving fast, but carefully, so as not to break through. Suddenly, a Raptor's head bursts through the panel in front of them, snarling and snapping! Everyone screams, the creature's teeth clicking just inches in front of Ellie...
63
TM & © 1993 UNIVERSAL CITY STUDIOS, INC. & AMBLIN ENTERTAINMENT, INC.
THE TOPPS COMPANY, INC. PRINTED IN U.S.A.

PREDATOR ON THE PROWL

JURASSIC PARK

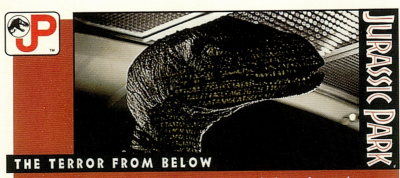

JURASSIC PARK
THE TERROR FROM BELOW
Grant looks around frantically and spots an air duct a few yards away. They move for it, but the Raptor's head crashes through the ceiling again, this time right underneath Lex! Grant smashes his boot into the dinosaur's reptilian face, and, summoning his strength, jerks Lex to safety...
64
TM & © 1993 UNIVERSAL CITY STUDIOS, INC. & AMBLIN ENTERTAINMENT, INC.
THE TOPPS COMPANY, INC. PRINTED IN U.S.A.

JURASSIC PARK

THE TERROR FROM BELOW

I always thought there was an interesting, jack-in-the-box flavor to this photo. The expression "heads up" takes on startling new meaning!

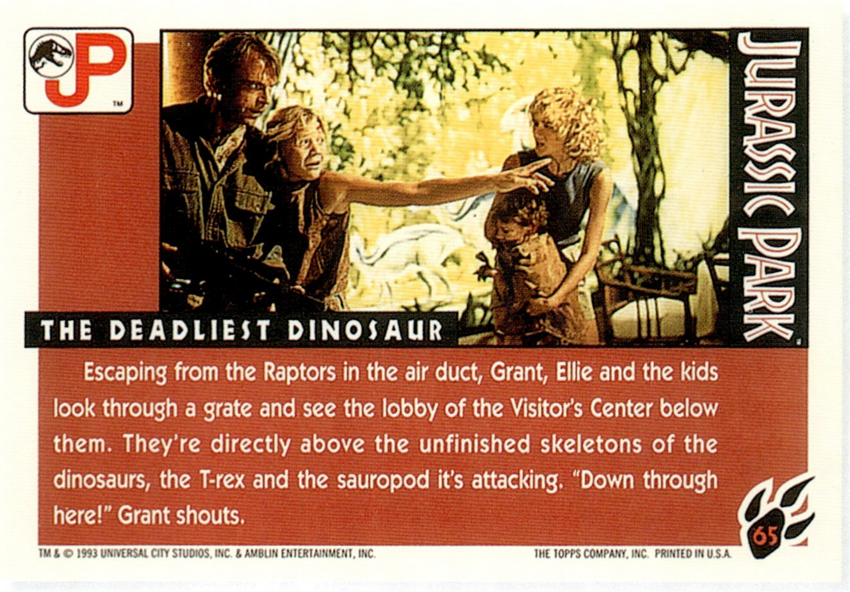
JP
JURASSIC PARK
THE DEADLIEST DINOSAUR
Escaping from the Raptors in the air duct, Grant, Ellie and the kids look through a grate and see the lobby of the Visitor's Center below them. They're directly above the unfinished skeletons of the dinosaurs, the T-rex and the sauropod it's attacking. "Down through here!" Grant shouts.
65
TM & © 1993 UNIVERSAL CITY STUDIOS, INC. & AMBLIN ENTERTAINMENT, INC.
THE TOPPS COMPANY, INC. PRINTED IN U.S.A.

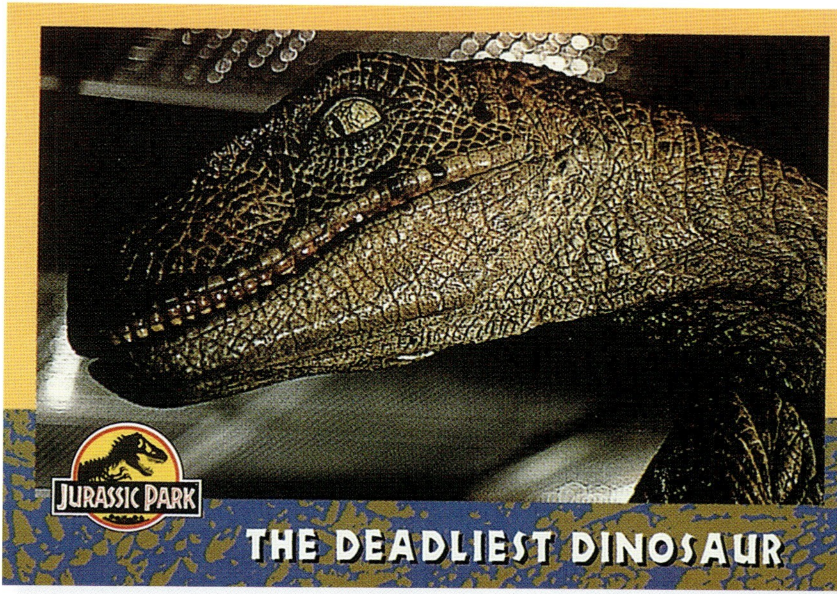
JURASSIC PARK
THE DEADLIEST DINOSAUR

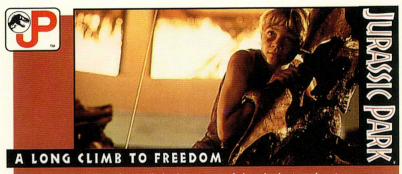

JP
JURASSIC PARK
A LONG CLIMB TO FREEDOM
Grant and the others climb down out of the air duct and onto a platform of the scaffolding that stands along side of the dinosaur skeletons. It's much too far to jump to the lobby floor, so Grant climbs gingerly onto the nearest skeleton, the towering Alamosaur. Ellie and the kids follow...
66
TM & © 1993 UNIVERSAL CITY STUDIOS, INC. & AMBLIN ENTERTAINMENT, INC.
THE TOPPS COMPANY, INC. PRINTED IN U.S.A.

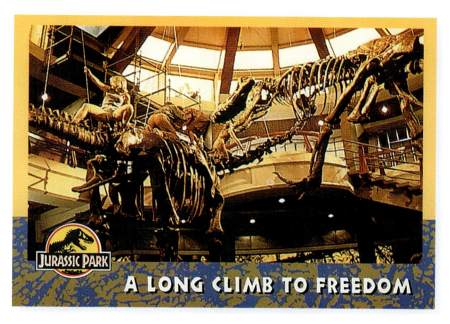

A LONG CLIMB TO FREEDOM

It was a stroke of genius to set *Jurassic Park*'s final confrontation scene among displays of actual dinosaur skeletons. Without a word being spoken, the past and present fully collide, driving home the moral difference between what nature created ages ago, proper in its time and place, and what mankind, misusing modern science, has recklessly wrought today.

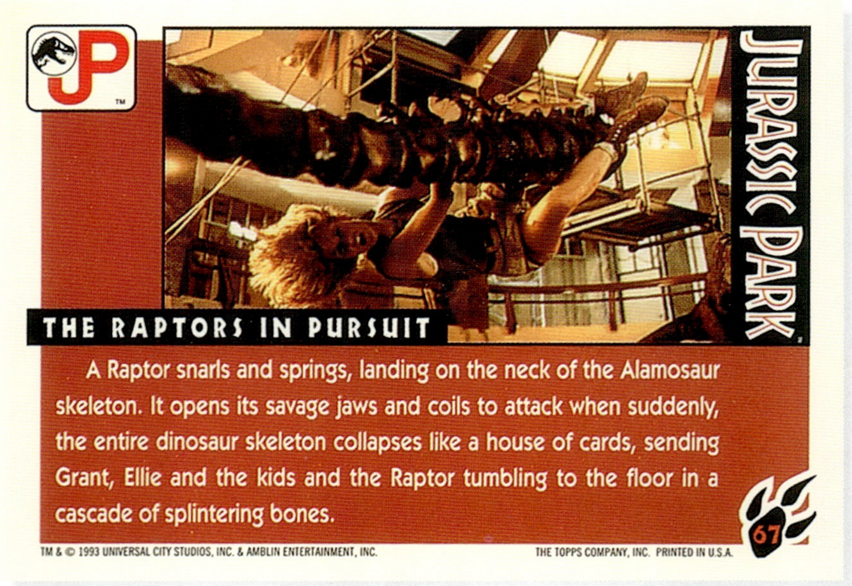
JP
TM
JURASSIC PARK
THE RAPTORS IN PURSUIT
A Raptor snarls and springs, landing on the neck of the Alamosaur skeleton. It opens its savage jaws and coils to attack when suddenly, the entire dinosaur skeleton collapses like a house of cards, sending Grant, Ellie and the kids and the Raptor tumbling to the floor in a cascade of splintering bones.
67
TM & © 1993 UNIVERSAL CITY STUDIOS, INC. & AMBLIN ENTERTAINMENT, INC.
THE TOPPS COMPANY, INC. PRINTED IN U.S.A.

JURASSIC PARK
THE RAPTORS IN PURSUIT

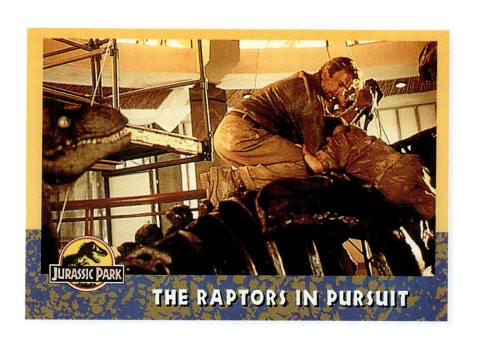

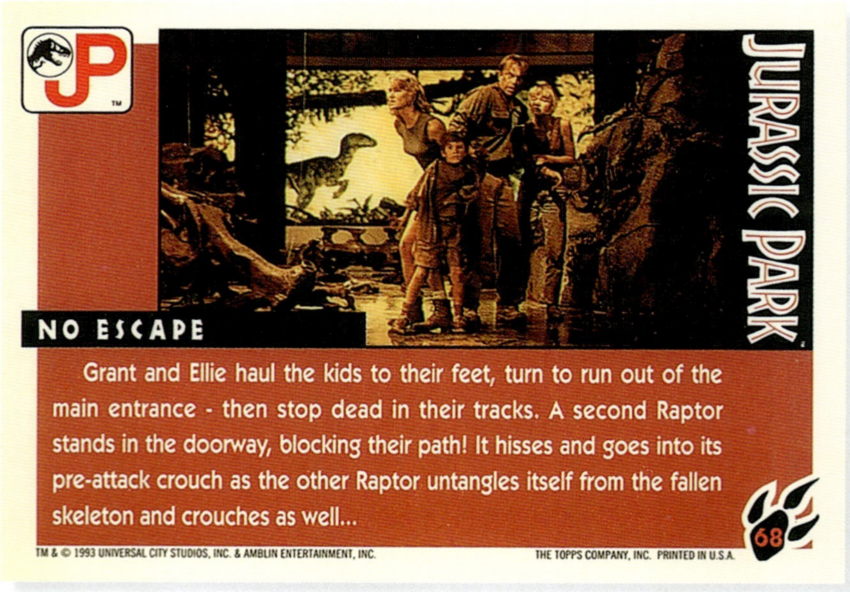
JP
JURASSIC PARK
NO ESCAPE
Grant and Ellie haul the kids to their feet, turn to run out of the main entrance - then stop dead in their tracks. A second Raptor stands in the doorway, blocking their path! It hisses and goes into its pre-attack crouch as the other Raptor untangles itself from the fallen skeleton and crouches as well...
68
TM & © 1993 UNIVERSAL CITY STUDIOS, INC. & AMBLIN ENTERTAINMENT, INC.
THE TOPPS COMPANY, INC. PRINTED IN U.S.A.

JURASSIC PARK
NO ESCAPE

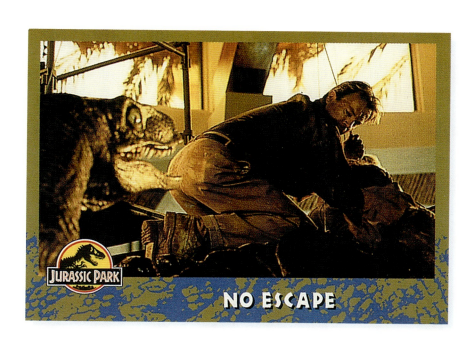

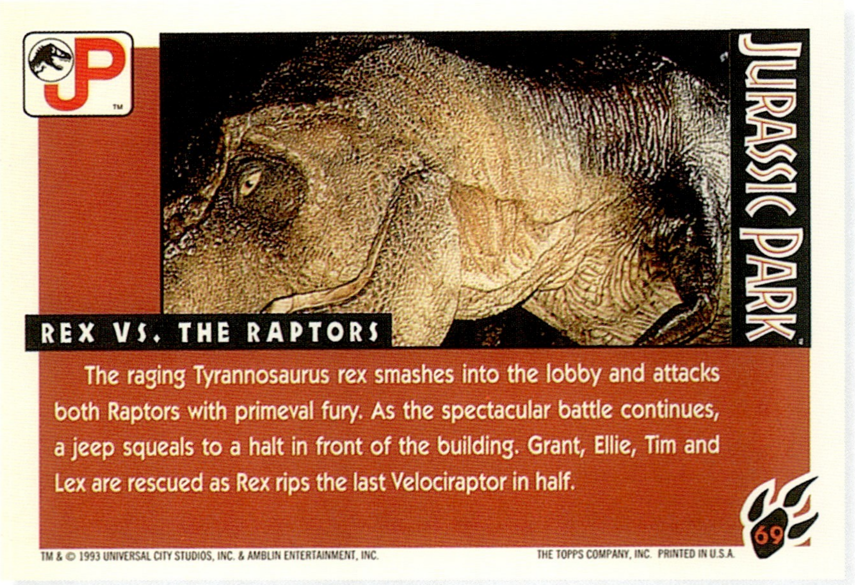
JP
JURASSIC PARK
REX VS. THE RAPTORS
The raging Tyrannosaurus rex smashes into the lobby and attacks both Raptors with primeval fury. As the spectacular battle continues, a jeep squeals to a halt in front of the building. Grant, Ellie, Tim and Lex are rescued as Rex rips the last Velociraptor in half.
69
TM & © 1993 UNIVERSAL CITY STUDIOS, INC. & AMBLIN ENTERTAINMENT, INC.
THE TOPPS COMPANY, INC. PRINTED IN U.S.A.

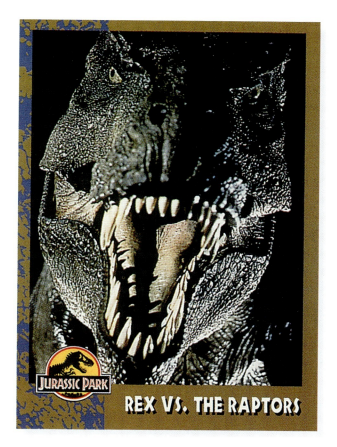

REX VS. THE RAPTORS

For all the freshness and novelty of the raptors, it was the good old *Tyrannosaurus rex* who saves the day at the end of *Jurassic Park*. The *T. rex* dramatically rescues our human characters and gives those nasty raptors some well-earned grief.

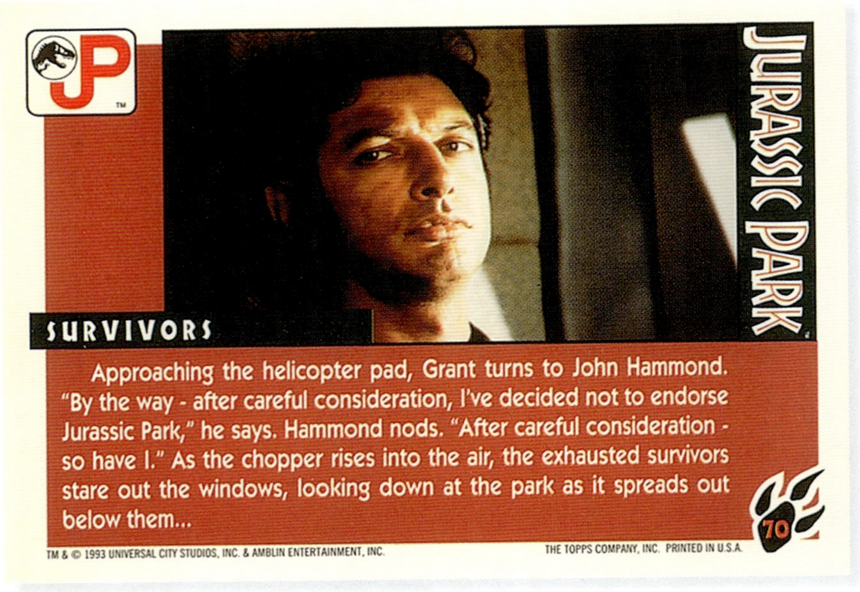
JURASSIC PARK
JP
SURVIVORS
Approaching the helicopter pad, Grant turns to John Hammond. "By the way - after careful consideration, I've decided not to endorse Jurassic Park," he says. Hammond nods. "After careful consideration - so have I." As the chopper rises into the air, the exhausted survivors stare out the windows, looking down at the park as it spreads out below them...
70
TM & © 1993 UNIVERSAL CITY STUDIOS, INC. & AMBLIN ENTERTAINMENT, INC.
THE TOPPS COMPANY, INC. PRINTED IN U.S.A.

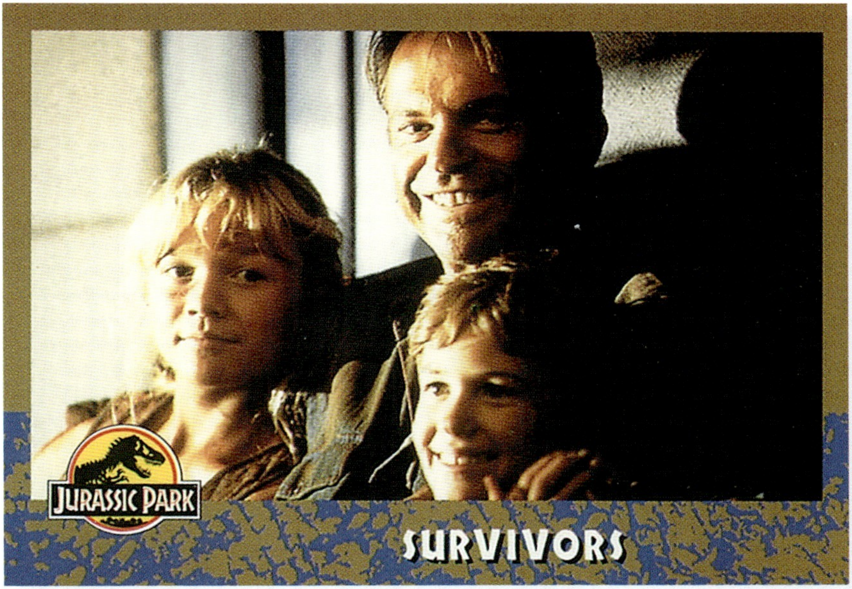
JURASSIC PARK
SURVIVORS

Dr. Grant has finally learned how to be comfortable around children, after having risked his own life to save young Lex and Tim during their harrowing trek through Jurassic Park. This subtheme was nicely captured in our final storyline photo (front).

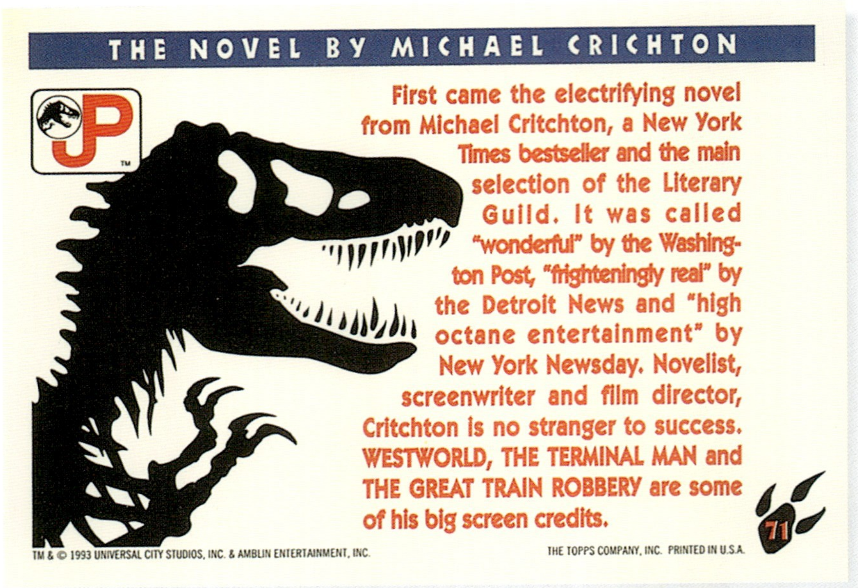
THE NOVEL BY MICHAEL CRICHTON
JP
First came the electrifying novel from Michael Critchton, a New York Times bestseller and the main selection of the Literary Guild. It was called "wonderful" by the Washington Post, "frighteningly real" by the Detroit News and "high octane entertainment" by New York Newsday. Novelist, screenwriter and film director, Critchton is no stranger to success. WESTWORLD, THE TERMINAL MAN and THE GREAT TRAIN ROBBERY are some of his big screen credits.
71
TM & © 1993 UNIVERSAL CITY STUDIOS, INC. & AMBLIN ENTERTAINMENT, INC.
THE TOPPS COMPANY, INC. PRINTED IN U.S.A.

#1 BESTSELLER
MICHAEL CRICHTON
AUTHOR OF THE
#1 BESTSELLER
RISING SUN
JURASSIC
PARK
JP
TM

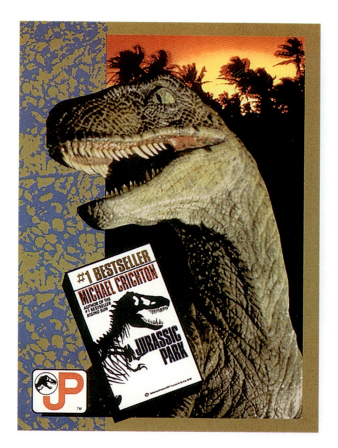

We included two different behind-the-scenes subsets for *Jurassic Park*, making prudent use of imagery that showcased dinosaurs. It made sense to start off with an overview of Michael Crichton's bestselling book, which inspired the mega-movie and franchise that followed.

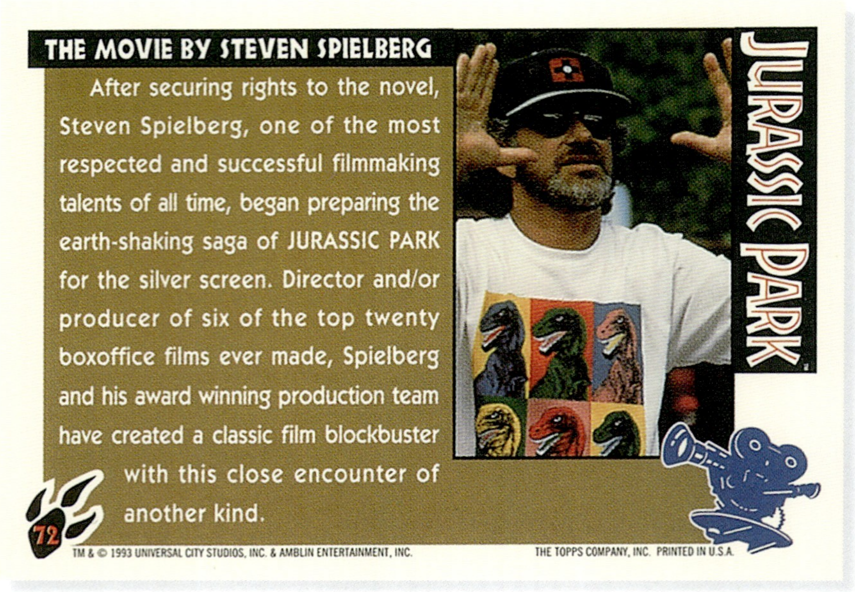

THE MOVIE BY STEVEN SPIELBERG
After securing rights to the novel, Steven Spielberg, one of the most respected and successful filmmaking talents of all time, began preparing the earth-shaking saga of JURASSIC PARK for the silver screen. Director and/or producer of six of the top twenty boxoffice films ever made, Spielberg and his award winning production team have created a classic film blockbuster with this close encounter of another kind.
JURASSIC PARK
72
TM & © 1993 UNIVERSAL CITY STUDIOS, INC. & AMBLIN ENTERTAINMENT, INC.
THE TOPPS COMPANY, INC. PRINTED IN U.S.A.

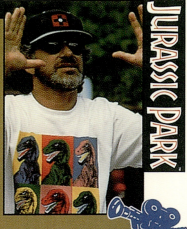

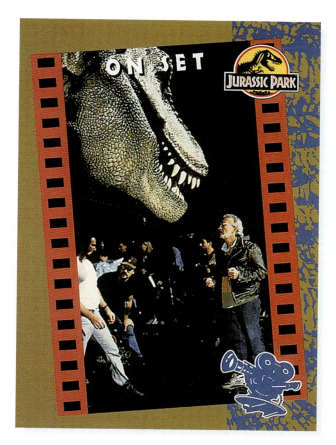

We're on set with the life-size *T. rex* "puppet," an enormous and terrifying creation. That's director Steven Spielberg crouching on the left and special effects master Stan Winston (with the white beard) on the right.

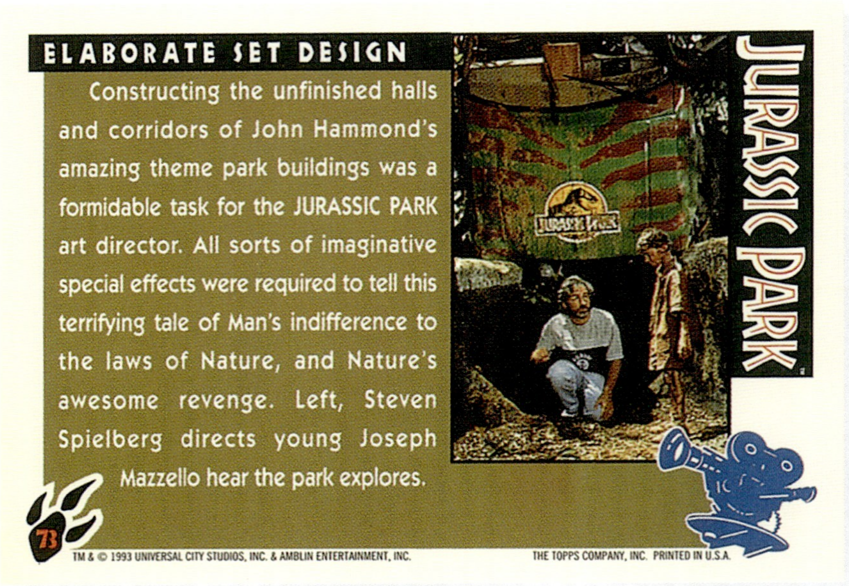

ELABORATE SET DESIGN
Constructing the unfinished halls and corridors of John Hammond's amazing theme park buildings was a formidable task for the JURASSIC PARK art director. All sorts of imaginative special effects were required to tell this terrifying tale of Man's indifference to the laws of Nature, and Nature's awesome revenge. Left, Steven Spielberg directs young Joseph Mazzello hear the park explores.
JURASSIC PARK
73
TM & © 1993 UNIVERSAL CITY STUDIOS, INC. & AMBLIN ENTERTAINMENT, INC.
THE TOPPS COMPANY, INC. PRINTED IN U.S.A.

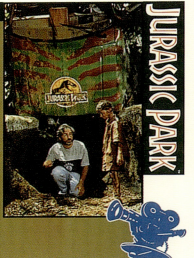

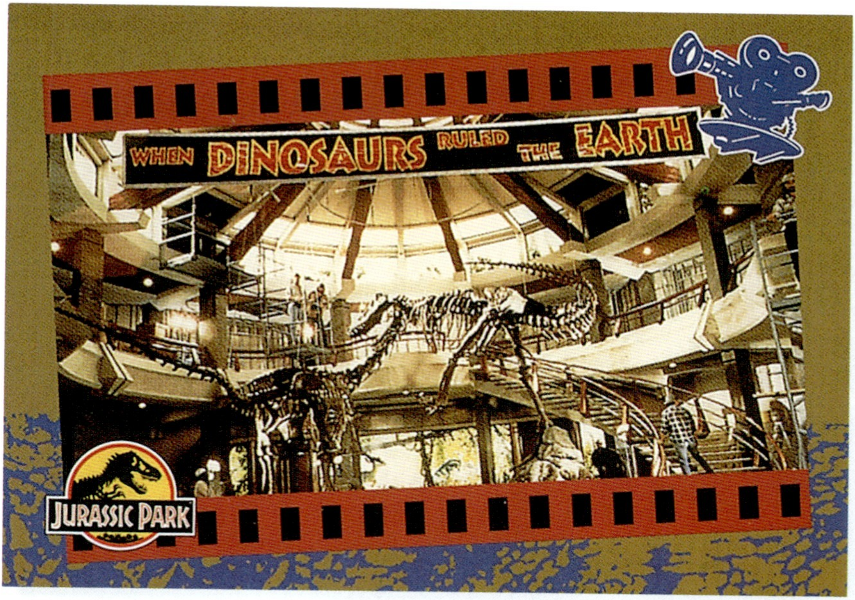
WHEN DINOSAURS RULED THE EARTH
JURASSIC PARK

NEW HEIGHTS IN SUSPENSE
An actor's life isn't easy! Here, JURASSIC PARK cast members are put through their strenuous paces in the tense and exciting "electrified fence" sequence. Earlier in the film, director Steven Spielberg had some pertinent comments for participants in the "sick triceratops" scene.
JURASSIC PARK
74
TM & © 1993 UNIVERSAL CITY STUDIOS, INC. & AMBLIN ENTERTAINMENT, INC.
THE TOPPS COMPANY, INC. PRINTED IN U.S.A.

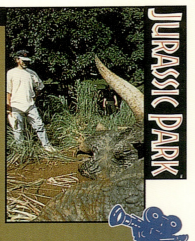

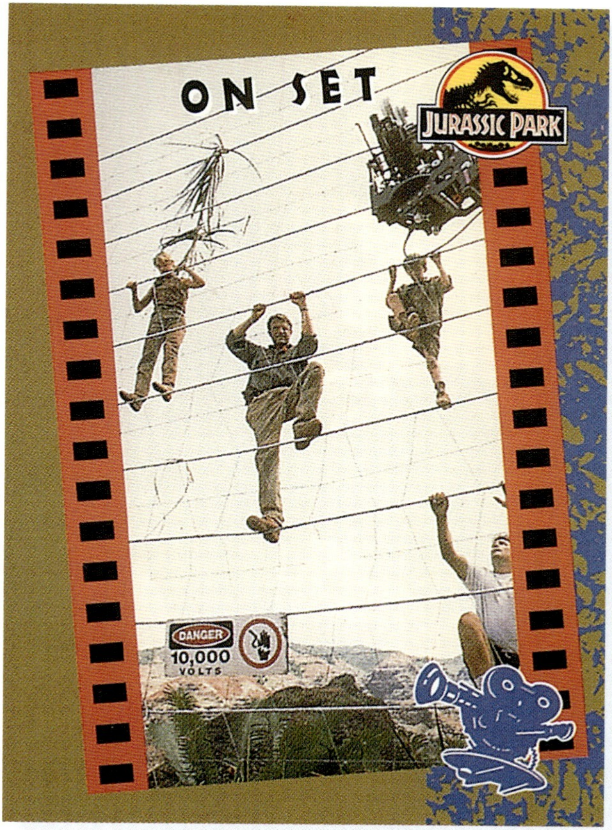
ON SET
JURASSIC PARK
DANGER
10,000
VOLTS

THE COLLOSAL T-REX PROP
The dinosaurs of JURASSIC PARK were brought to life by a number of sophisticated special effects methods. Some of the creatures were computer-generated, while others were full scale props (such as the giant Tyrannosaurus head). Producer Kathleen Kennedy recalls, "It was a dream come true to land (special effects leaders) Stan Winston, Phil Tippett, Dennis Muren, and Micheal Lantieri all on one movie."
JURASSIC PARK
75
TM & © 1993 UNIVERSAL CITY STUDIOS, INC. & AMBLIN ENTERTAINMENT, INC.
THE TOPPS COMPANY, INC. PRINTED IN U.S.A.

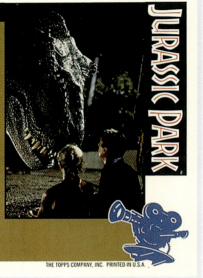

ON SET
JURASSIC PARK

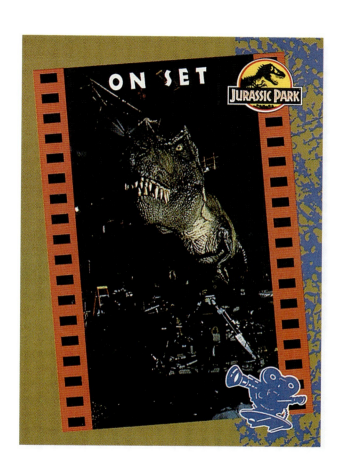

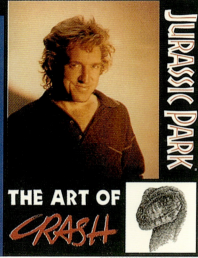

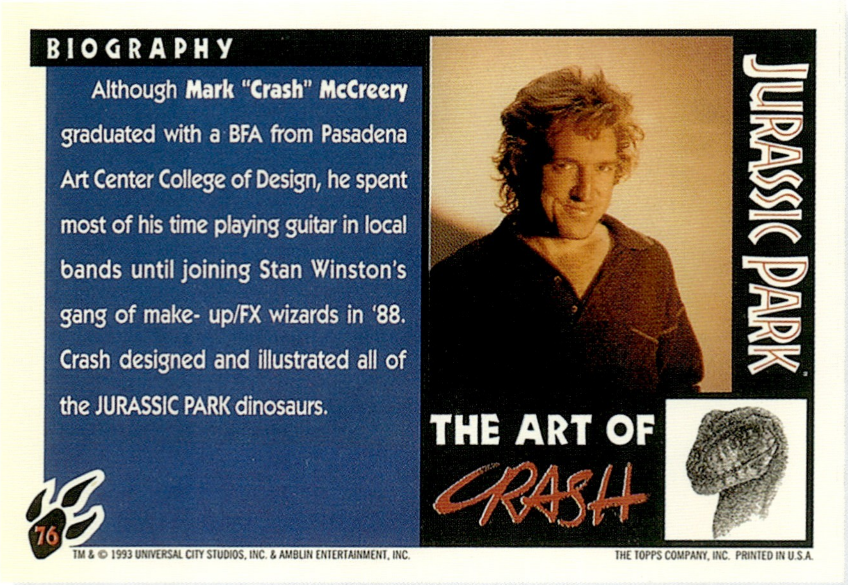

BIOGRAPHY
Although Mark "Crash" McCreery graduated with a BFA from Pasadena Art Center College of Design, he spent most of his time playing guitar in local bands until joining Stan Winston's gang of make- up/FX wizards in '88. Crash designed and illustrated all of the JURASSIC PARK dinosaurs.
JURASSIC PARK
THE ART OF
CRASH
76
TM & © 1993 UNIVERSAL CITY STUDIOS, INC. & AMBLIN ENTERTAINMENT, INC.
THE TOPPS COMPANY, INC. PRINTED IN U.S.A.

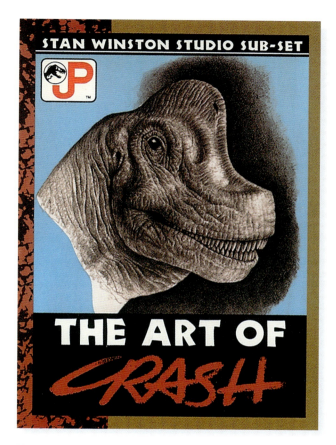

STAN WINSTON STUDIO SUB-SET

JP

THE ART OF
CRASH

This next special behind-the-scenes subset is dedicated to the artwork of Mark "Crash" McCreery, the visionary behind *Jurassic Park*'s dinosaur concepts and renderings. Interestingly, the front design of this card functioned as a mini-cover. It employed a canny variation of the distinctive Title Card design we had put into play for all Topps trading card products back in the late 1970s.

TYRANNOSAURUS REX
"This was the very first conceptual drawing I did for the project. We wanted the animal to portray agility, speed and ferocity which relates to recent popular concepts of the Rex.
"This rendering is the closest to the T-rex's final design. We made the legs a little heavier to support the weight but kept the ferocity of the mouth and eyes."
77
JURASSIC PARK
THE ART OF
CRASH
TM & © 1993 UNIVERSAL CITY STUDIOS, INC. & AMBLIN ENTERTAINMENT, INC.
THE TOPPS COMPANY, INC. PRINTED IN U.S.A.

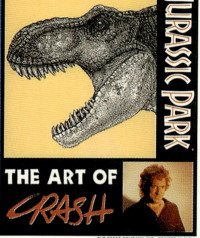

T. rex, by Crash. Uncluttered by a card caption, we can fully appreciate this wonderful combination of a *Tyrannosaurus rex* head study and the full-figure dinosaur.

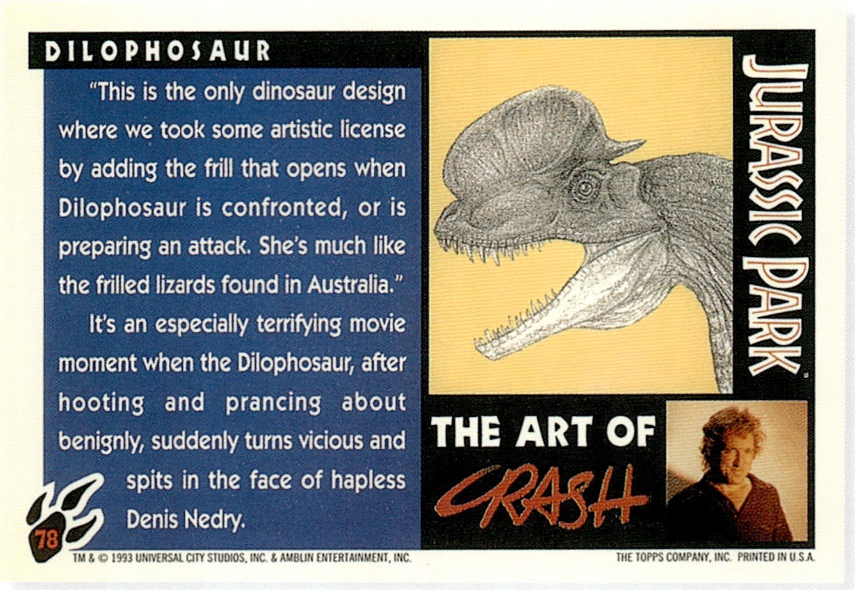

DILOPHOSAUR
"This is the only dinosaur design where we took some artistic license by adding the frill that opens when Dilophosaur is confronted, or is preparing an attack. She's much like the frilled lizards found in Australia."
It's an especially terrifying movie moment when the Dilophosaur, after hooting and prancing about benignly, suddenly turns vicious and spits in the face of hapless Denis Nedry.
78
JURASSIC PARK
THE ART OF
CRASH
TM & © 1993 UNIVERSAL CITY STUDIOS, INC. & AMBLIN ENTERTAINMENT, INC.
THE TOPPS COMPANY, INC. PRINTED IN U.S.A.

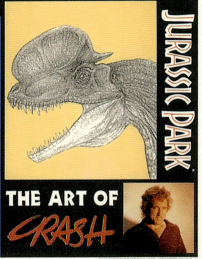

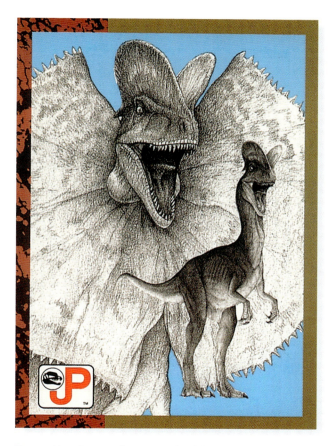

The sneakiest dinosaur of *Jurassic Park* is fully realized in Crash's detailed rendering. Sure, the *Dilophosaurus* can be amusing and somewhat cute-looking . . . until she unleashes her most devastating weapon. They don't call this dinosaur "Spitter" for nothing!

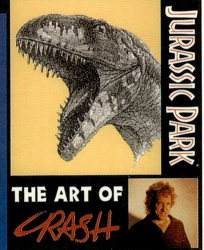

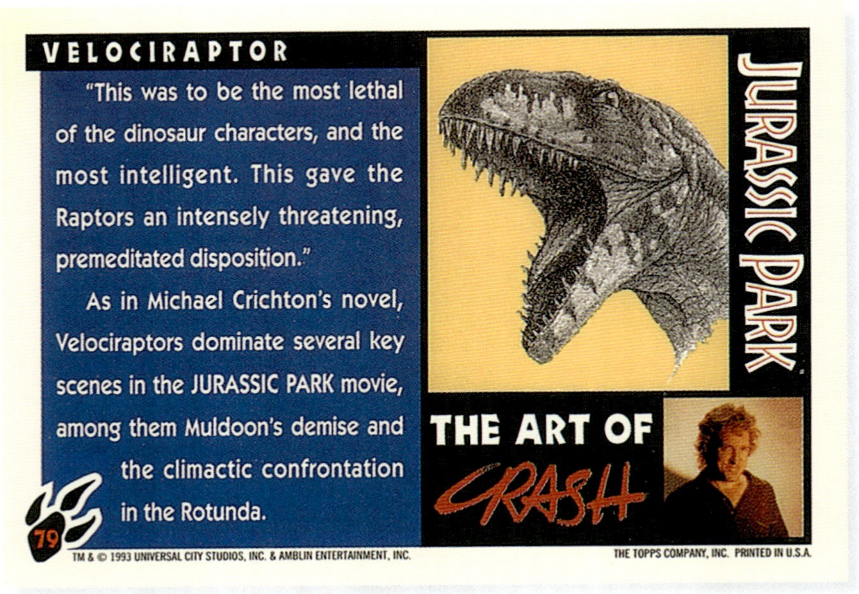

VELOCIRAPTOR
"This was to be the most lethal of the dinosaur characters, and the most intelligent. This gave the Raptors an intensely threatening, premeditated disposition."
As in Michael Crichton's novel, Velociraptors dominate several key scenes in the JURASSIC PARK movie, among them Muldoon's demise and the climactic confrontation in the Rotunda.
79
JURASSIC PARK
THE ART OF
CRASH
TM & © 1993 UNIVERSAL CITY STUDIOS, INC. & AMBLIN ENTERTAINMENT, INC.
THE TOPPS COMPANY, INC. PRINTED IN U.S.A.

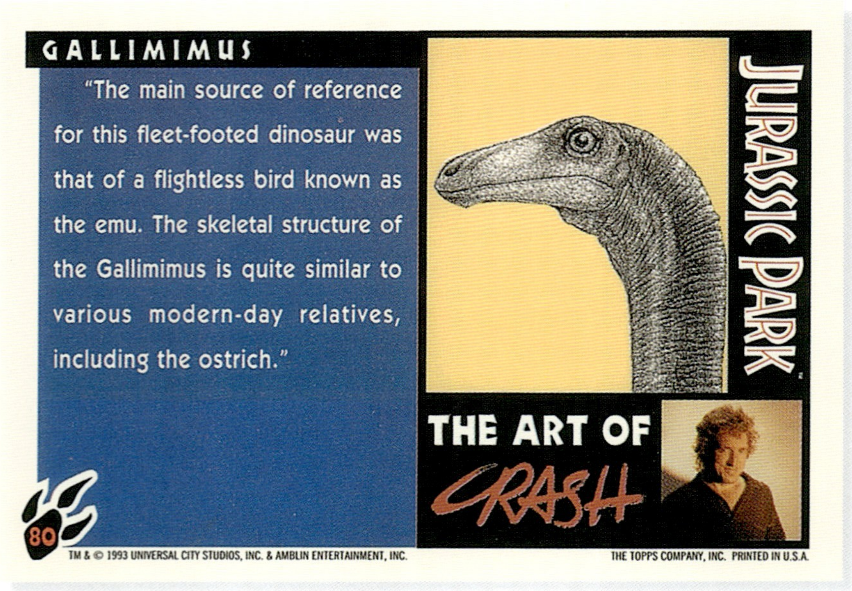

GALLIMIMUS
"The main source of reference for this fleet-footed dinosaur was that of a flightless bird known as the emu. The skeletal structure of the Gallimimus is quite similar to various modern-day relatives, including the ostrich."
JURASSIC PARK
THE ART OF
CRASH
80
TM & © 1993 UNIVERSAL CITY STUDIOS, INC. & AMBLIN ENTERTAINMENT, INC.
THE TOPPS COMPANY, INC. PRINTED IN U.S.A.

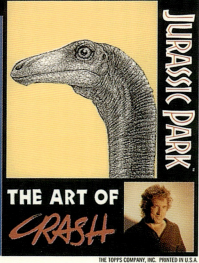

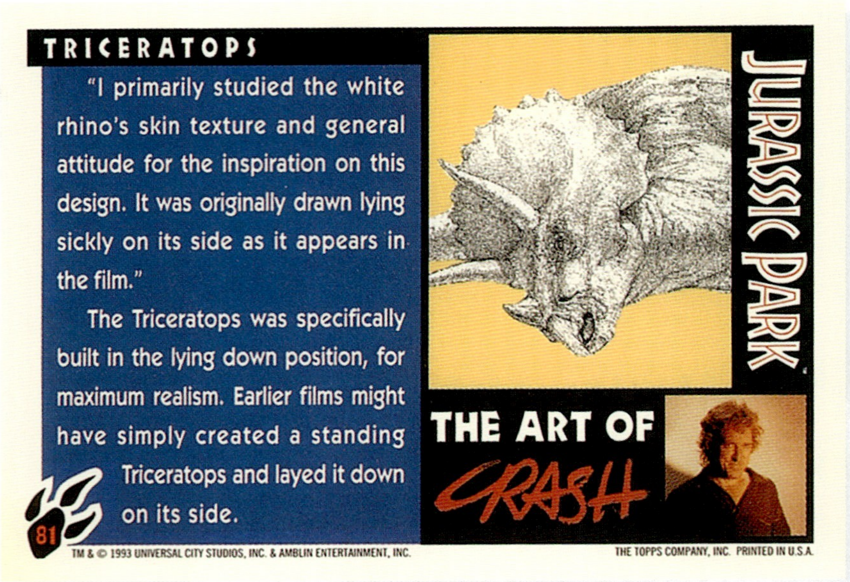

TRICERATOPS
"I primarily studied the white rhino's skin texture and general attitude for the inspiration on this design. It was originally drawn lying sickly on its side as it appears in the film."
The Triceratops was specifically built in the lying down position, for maximum realism. Earlier films might have simply created a standing Triceratops and layed it down on its side.
81
JURASSIC PARK
THE ART OF
CRASH
TM & © 1993 UNIVERSAL CITY STUDIOS, INC. & AMBLIN ENTERTAINMENT, INC.
THE TOPPS COMPANY, INC. PRINTED IN U.S.A.

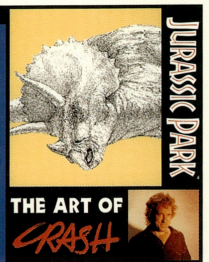

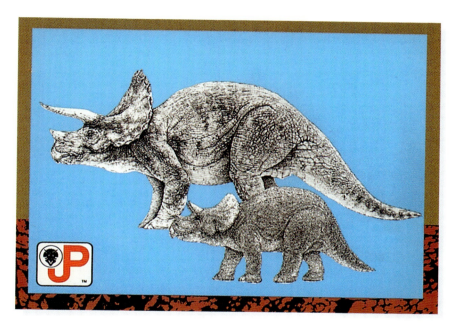

The *Triceratops* only appears briefly in *Jurassic Park*, and even then, she's in pretty sad shape, lying on the ground and sick to her stomach. Still, a dinosaur of this iconic stature couldn't be ignored in the ultimate dinosaur movie, so Spielberg and company found a place for *Triceratop*s in the story.

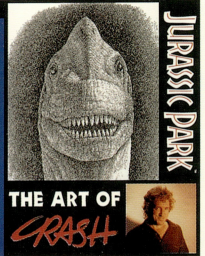

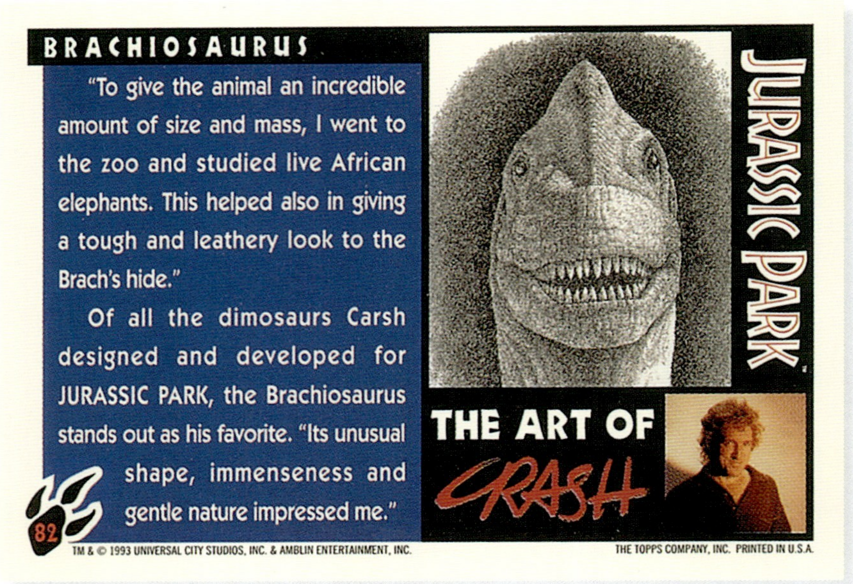

BRACHIOSAURUS
"To give the animal an incredible amount of size and mass, I went to the zoo and studied live African elephants. This helped also in giving a tough and leathery look to the Brach's hide."
Of all the dimosaurs Carsh designed and developed for JURASSIC PARK, the Brachiosaurus stands out as his favorite. "Its unusual shape, immenseness and gentle nature impressed me."
82
JURASSIC PARK
THE ART OF
CRASH
TM & © 1993 UNIVERSAL CITY STUDIOS, INC. & AMBLIN ENTERTAINMENT, INC.
THE TOPPS COMPANY, INC. PRINTED IN U.S.A.

PARASAUROLOPHUS
"Being a duck-billed dinosaur, the obvious reference for the shape of the mouth was that of a duck. I also incorporated the innocent face and eyes of a deer to make the dinosaur seem quiet and docile."
for some reason, the Parasaurolophus didn't make it into the finished film. Crash's rendering suggests how impressive and unusual the "real" creature might've been.
83
TM & © 1993 UNIVERSAL CITY STUDIOS, INC. & AMBLIN ENTERTAINMENT, INC.
JURASSIC PARK
THE ART OF
CRASH
THE TOPPS COMPANY, INC. PRINTED IN U.S.A.

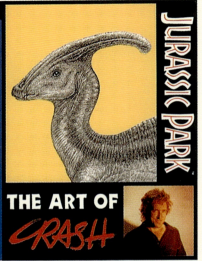

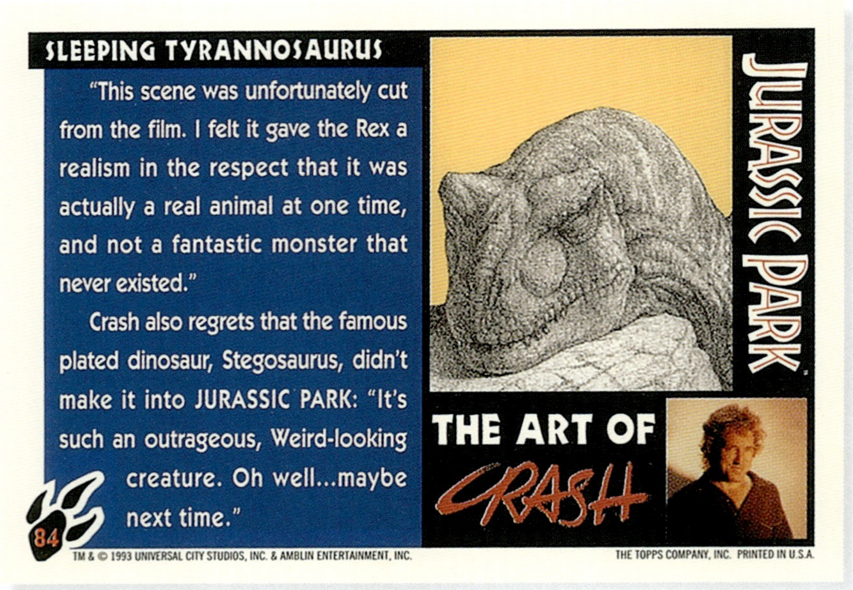

SLEEPING TYRANNOSAURUS
"This scene was unfortunately cut from the film. I felt it gave the Rex a realism in the respect that it was actually a real animal at one time, and not a fantastic monster that never existed."
Crash also regrets that the famous plated dinosaur, Stegosaurus, didn't make it into JURASSIC PARK: "It's such an outrageous, Weird-looking creature. Oh well...maybe next time."
84
JURASSIC PARK
THE ART OF
CRASH
TM & © 1993 UNIVERSAL CITY STUDIOS, INC. & AMBLIN ENTERTAINMENT, INC.
THE TOPPS COMPANY, INC. PRINTED IN U.S.A.

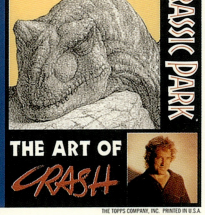

This remarkable moment was actually going to be in the movie, according to Crash McCreery. At least the artist's illustration survives. It's interesting how it gives *T. rex* a somewhat different, less terrifying, almost *approachable* persona.

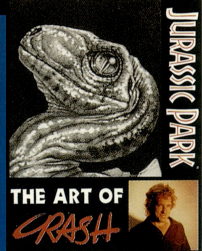

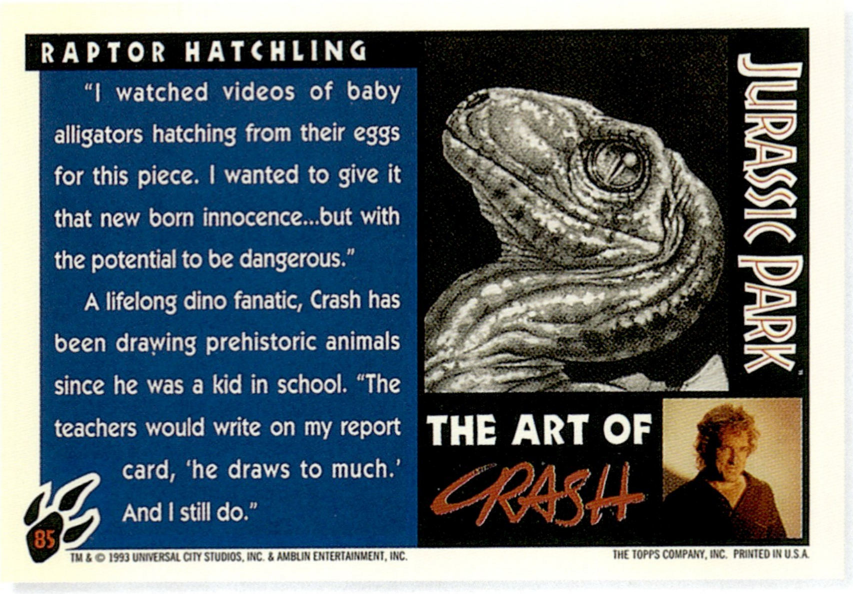

RAPTOR HATCHLING
"I watched videos of baby alligators hatching from their eggs for this piece. I wanted to give it that new born innocence...but with the potential to be dangerous."
A lifelong dino fanatic, Crash has been drawing prehistoric animals since he was a kid in school. "The teachers would write on my report card, 'he draws to much.' And I still do."
85
JURASSIC PARK
THE ART OF
CRASH
TM & © 1993 UNIVERSAL CITY STUDIOS, INC. & AMBLIN ENTERTAINMENT, INC.
THE TOPPS COMPANY, INC. PRINTED IN U.S.A.

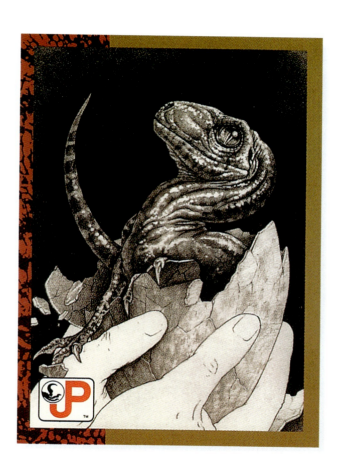

RAPTOR BABIES
"Once again I wanted to portray the young Raptors as playful, young and inexperienced. Yet - as the one in the foreground suggests - there is something very menacing and preditorial going on behind that eye!"
JURASSIC PARK
THE ART OF
CRASH
86
TM & © 1993 UNIVERSAL CITY STUDIOS, INC. & AMBLIN ENTERTAINMENT, INC.
THE TOPPS COMPANY, INC. PRINTED IN U.S.A.

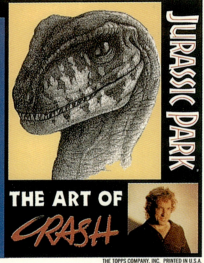

Babies of any kind are cute, even baby raptors. But, as Crash points out, these are deadly, dangerous animals, and, even in their infant state, there's a suggestion of potential menace.

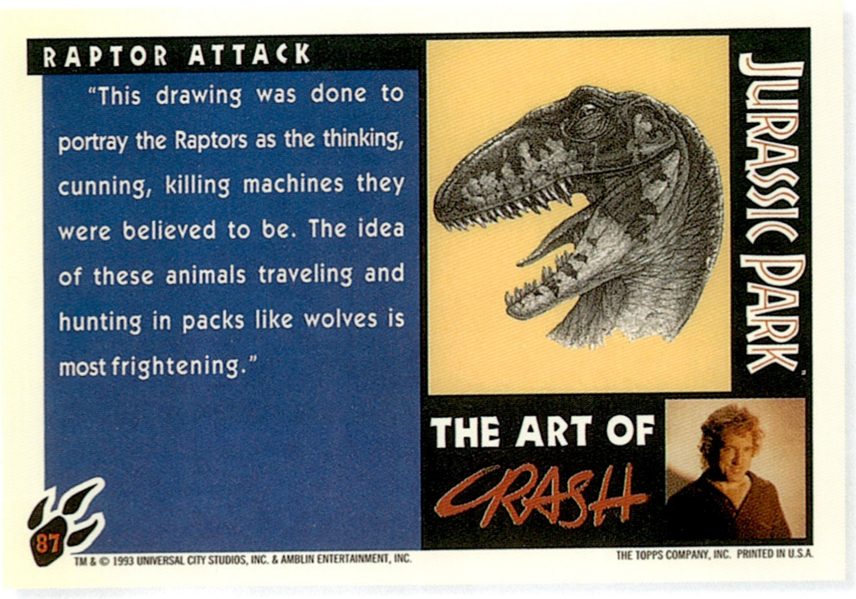

RAPTOR ATTACK
"This drawing was done to portray the Raptors as the thinking, cunning, killing machines they were believed to be. The idea of these animals traveling and hunting in packs like wolves is most frightening."
JURASSIC PARK
THE ART OF
CRASH
87
TM & © 1993 UNIVERSAL CITY STUDIOS, INC. & AMBLIN ENTERTAINMENT, INC.
THE TOPPS COMPANY, INC. PRINTED IN U.S.A.

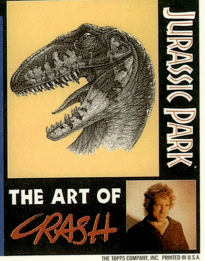

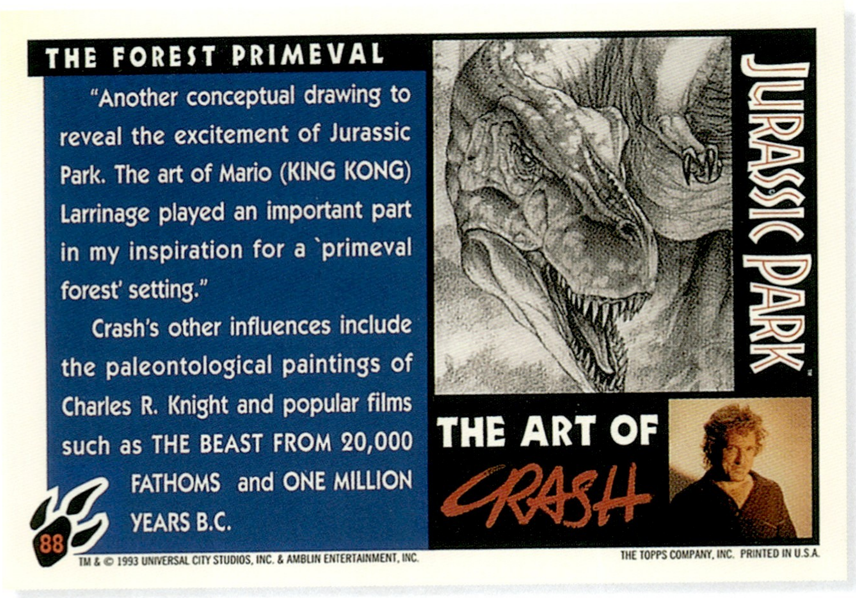

THE FOREST PRIMEVAL
"Another conceptual drawing to reveal the excitement of Jurassic Park. The art of Mario (KING KONG) Larrinage played an important part in my inspiration for a `primeval forest' setting."
Crash's other influences include the paleontological paintings of Charles R. Knight and popular films such as THE BEAST FROM 20,000 FATHOMS and ONE MILLION YEARS B.C.
88
TM & © 1993 UNIVERSAL CITY STUDIOS, INC. & AMBLIN ENTERTAINMENT, INC.
JURASSIC PARK
THE ART OF
CRASH
THE TOPPS COMPANY, INC. PRINTED IN U.S.A.

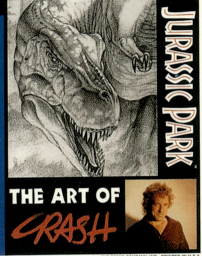

One of Crash McCreery's *Jurassic Park* masterpieces: a *Tyrannosaurus rex* on the prowl, seeking prey within the jungle environment of Hammond's island. As the artist mentions on the back of the card, his primary inspiration was the eerie black-and-white world featured in the 1933 classic *King Kong*.

STICKER CARDS

CAUTION
BIOLOGICAL HAZARD
AUTHORIZED PERSONNEL ONLY
1
PEEL
JURASSIC PARK
TYRANNOSAURUS REX

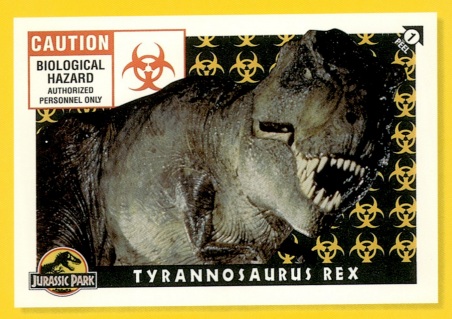

The *Tyrannosaurus rex* gets a royal horizontal treatment in this first of eleven stickers. Notice how distinctive *Jurassic Park* symbols are worked into the image.

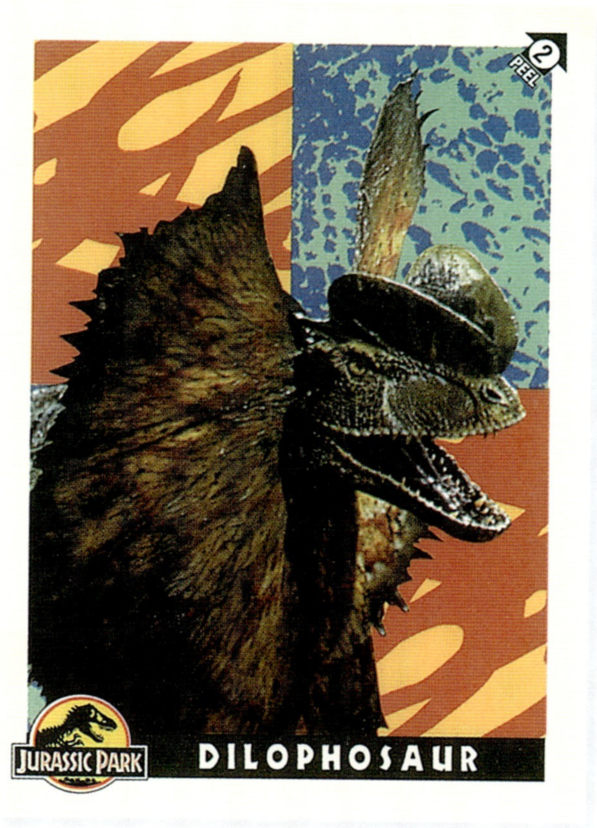
2
PEEL
JURASSIC PARK
DILOPHOSAUR

3
PEEL
JURASSIC PARK
VELOCIRAPTOR

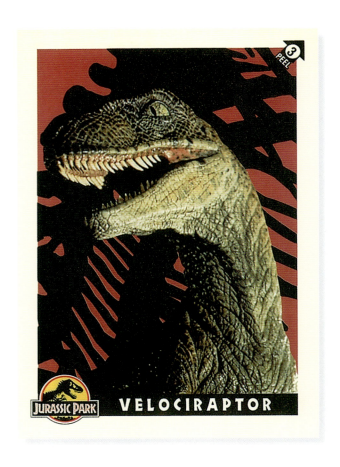

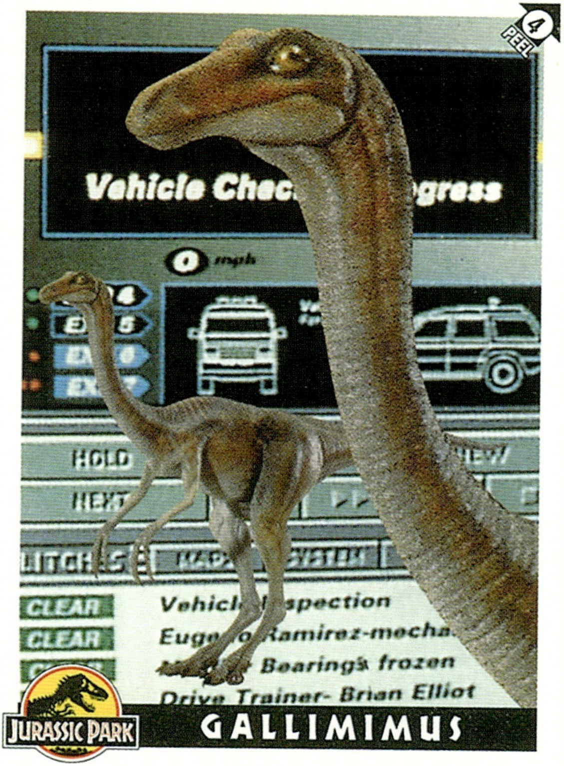
4
PEEL
HOLD
CLEAR
CLEAR
Bearings frozen
Drive Trainer- Brian Elliot
JURASSIC PARK
GALLIMIMUS

An odd idea that worked: we superimposed the *Gallimimus* over computers and high-tech scientific equipment from the studio style guide.

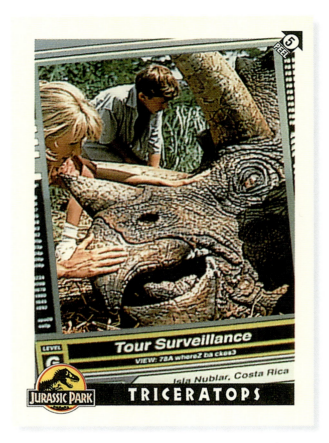

Tour Surveillance

VIEW: 78A where2 ba ckes3

Isla Nublar, Costa Rica

TRICERATOPS

JURASSIC PARK

This view of the sick *Triceratops* is just as satisfying as some of the movie scenes with her that were featured in our card set.

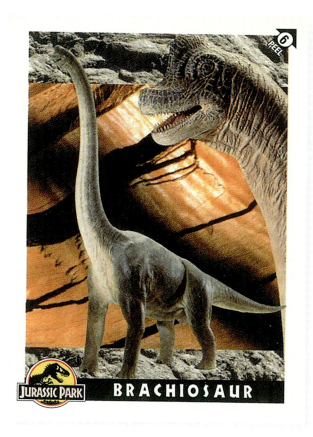

PEEL **6**

JURASSIC PARK

BRACHIOSAUR

7
PEEL
JURASSIC PARK
TYRANNOSAURUS REX

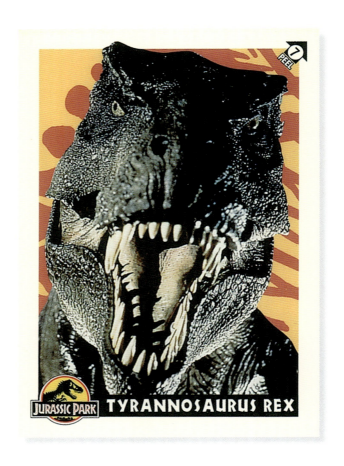

8
PEEL
JURASSIC PARK
VELOCIRAPTOR

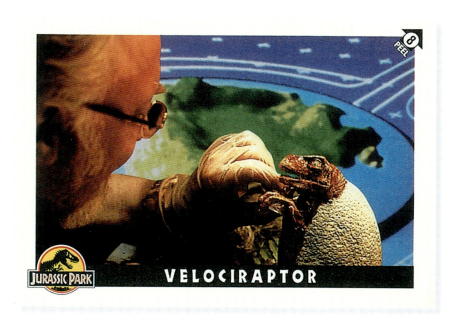

PEEL
9
DANGER
VOLTS
GER
JURASSIC PARK
TYRANNOSAURUS REX

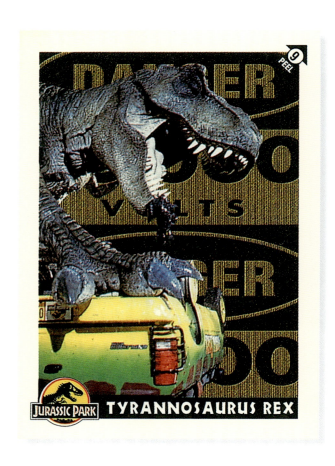

10
PEEL
JURASSIC PARK
VELOCIRAPTOR

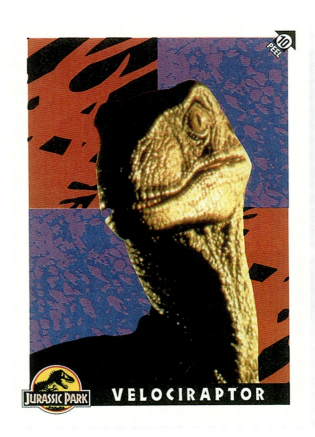

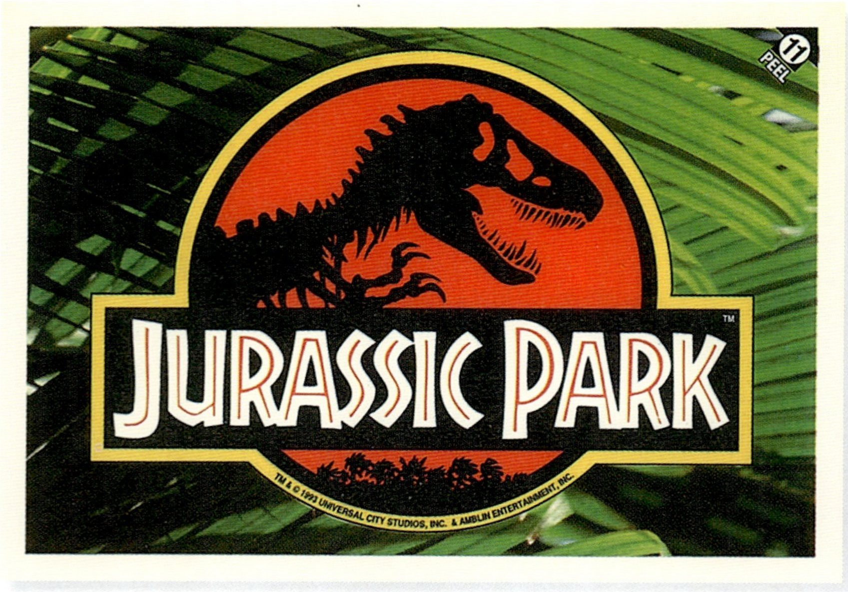
11
PEEL
JURASSIC PARK
TM
TM & © 1993 UNIVERSAL CITY STUDIOS, INC. & AMBLIN ENTERTAINMENT, INC.

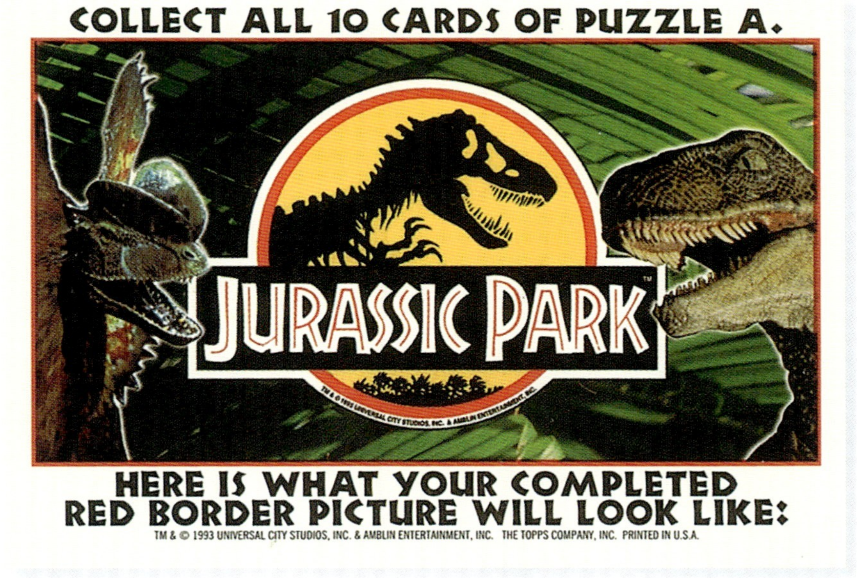
COLLECT ALL 10 CARDS OF PUZZLE A.
JURASSIC PARK
HERE IS WHAT YOUR COMPLETED
RED BORDER PICTURE WILL LOOK LIKE:
TM & © 1993 UNIVERSAL CITY STUDIOS, INC. & AMBLIN ENTERTAINMENT, INC. THE TOPPS COMPANY, INC. PRINTED IN U.S.A.

Our stickers for this movie hardly broke new creative ground, but they were still rich in entertainment value. Our theme? Dinosaurs, of course. Pulling from the studio style guide enabled us to make clever use of a variety of background visuals. We then superimposed the dinosaur in question over these graphics. Meanwhile, the backs of each sticker card acted like pieces of a puzzle, with ten cards coming together to form the image revealed on the eleventh card.

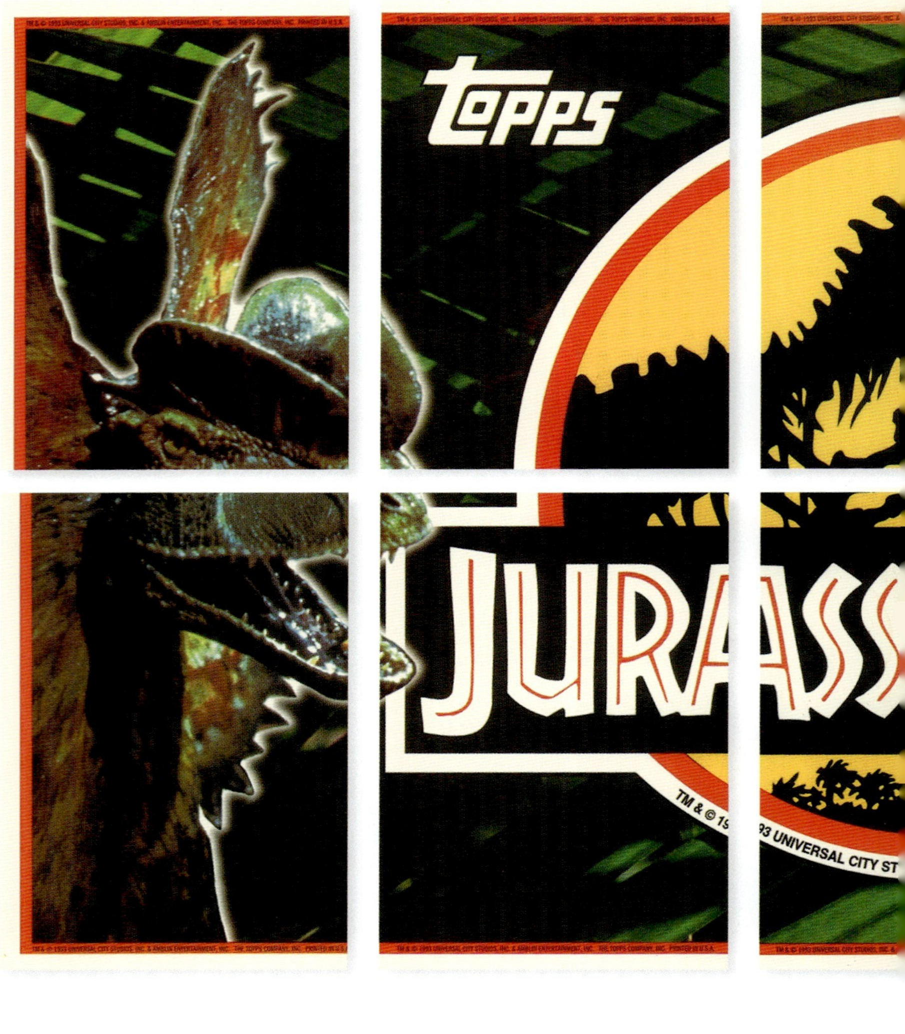
topps
JURASS
TM & © 19
93 UNIVERSAL CITY ST

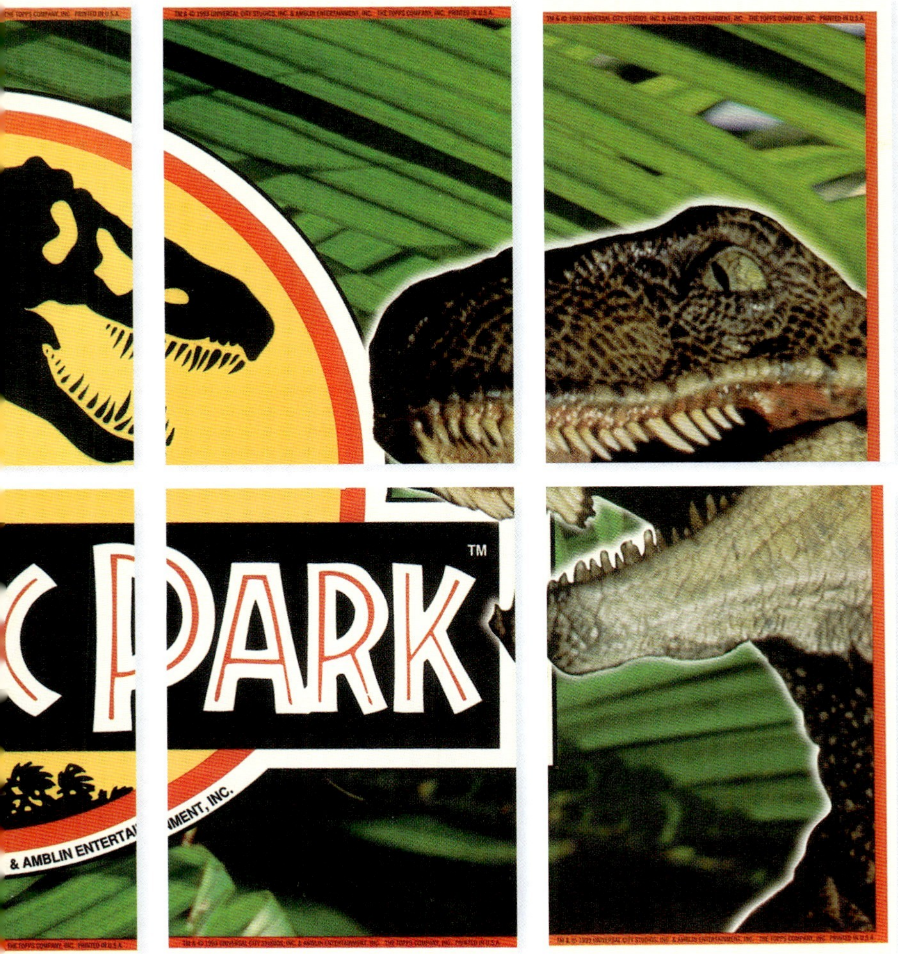
C PARK
TM
& AMBLIN ENTERTA
NMENT, INC.

HOLOGRAM CARDS

JURASSIC PARK
PEEL
TM & © 1992 U.C.S. & AMBLIN
topps

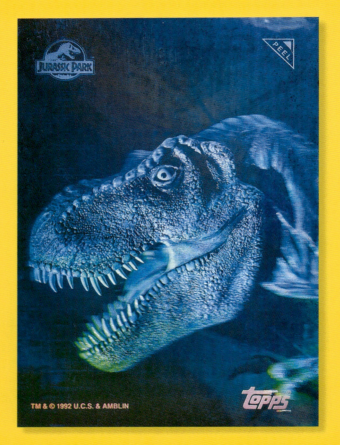

Both Series 1 and 2 featured the same four hologram cards, each showcasing a different dinosaur. The images on the following pages capture the captivating before-and-after effect, showing both possible views achieved when tilting each trading card.

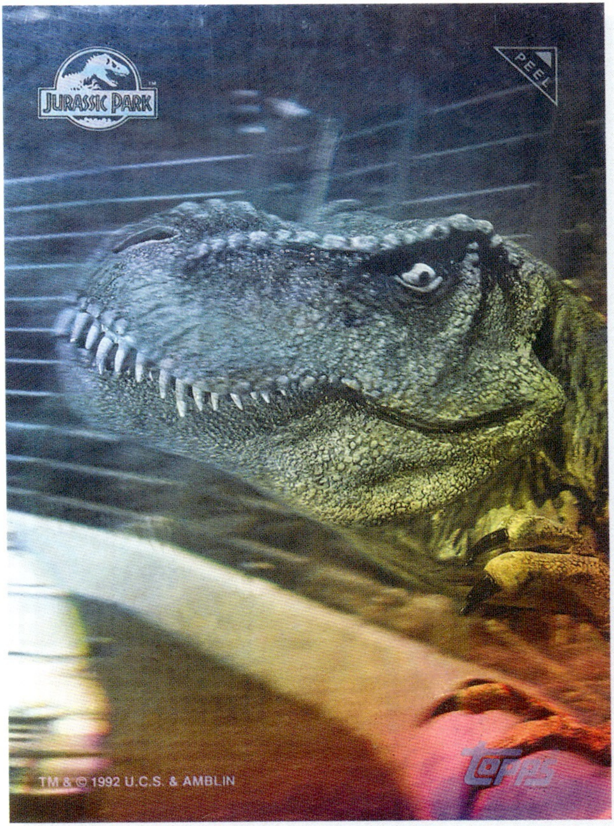
JURASSIC PARK
PEEL
TM & © 1992 U.C.S. & AMBLIN
topps

It seemed logical to showcase a powerful *T. rex* head for our first hologram sticker.

JURASSIC PARK
PEEL
TM & © 1992 U.C.S. & AMBLIN
topps

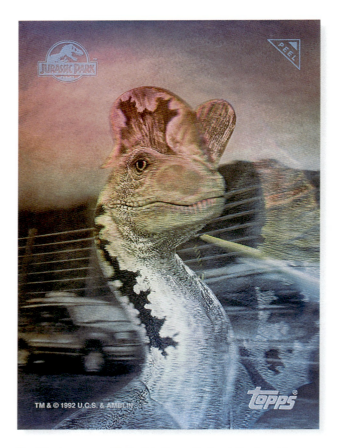

The *Dilophosaurus* or "Spitter" (with mouth closed, thank you) became our second hologram subject. Adding a Jurassic Park animal pen and other elements behind the creature enhanced the dimensional effect.

JURASSIC PARK
PEEL
TM & © 1992 U.C.S. & AMBLIN
topps

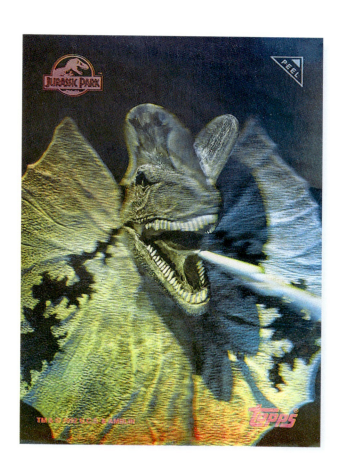

JURASSIC PARK
PEEL
TM & © 1992 U.C.S. & AMBLIN
topps

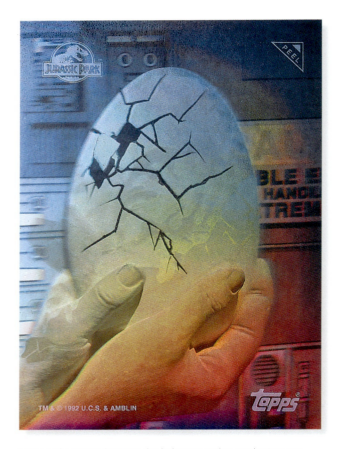

Instead of a grown dinosaur, this hologram sticker emphasizes one of the eggs, dramatically hatching before our captivated eyes. This instantly conveys John Hammond's well-intentioned dream of bringing new dinosaurs into the world, creating a species that hasn't been around for millions of years.

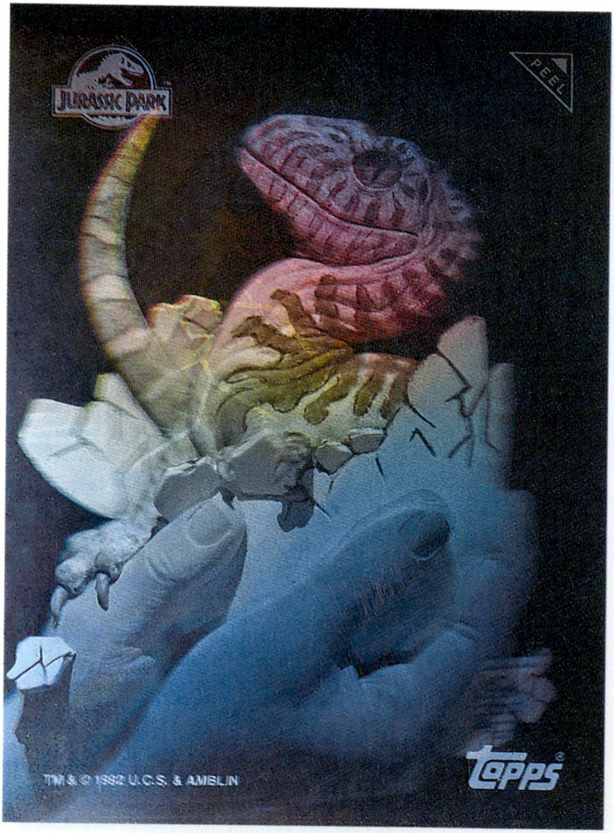
JURASSIC PARK
PEEL
TM & © 1992 U.C.S. & AMBLIN
topps

JURASSIC PARK
PEEL
TM & © 1992 U.C.S. & AMBLIN
topps

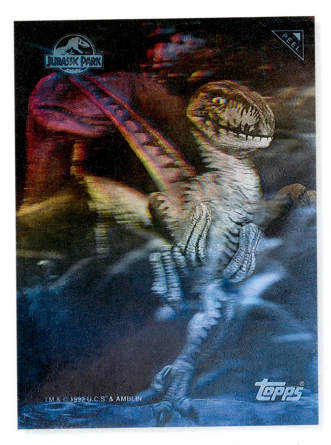

Two images of the super-fast raptor adorn this final hologram card. The one in the foreground makes excellent use of the hologram's dimensional qualities.

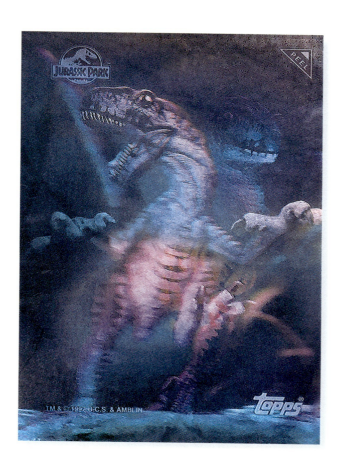

PEEL

JURASSIC PARK

TM & © 1992 U.C.S. & AMBLIN

topps ®

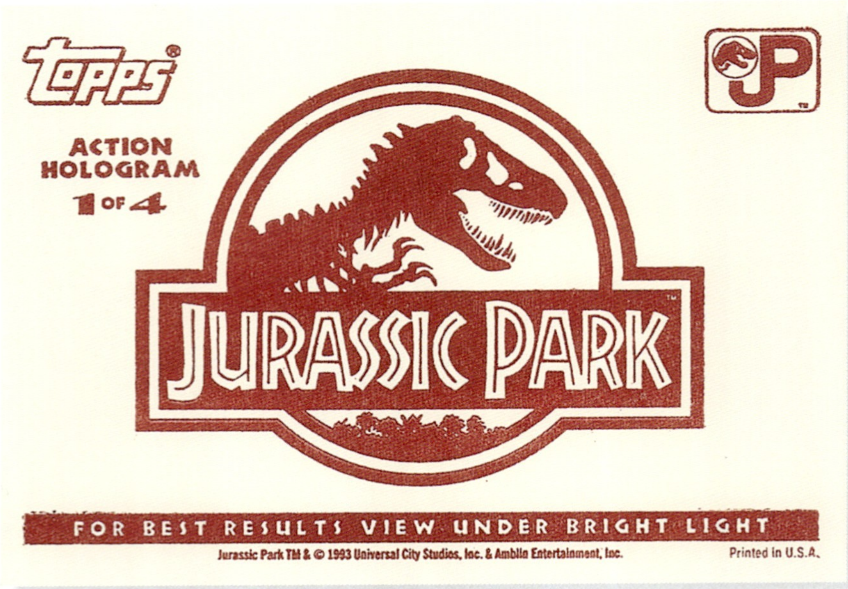
topps®
ACTION HOLOGRAM
1 OF 4
JP
JURASSIC PARK
FOR BEST RESULTS VIEW UNDER BRIGHT LIGHT
Jurassic Park TM & © 1993 Universal City Studios, Inc. & Amblin Entertainment, Inc.
Printed in U.S.A.

PROMO CARDS

TOP SECRET
NOT TO BE REVEALED
UNTIL SUMMER 1993
JURASSIC PARK

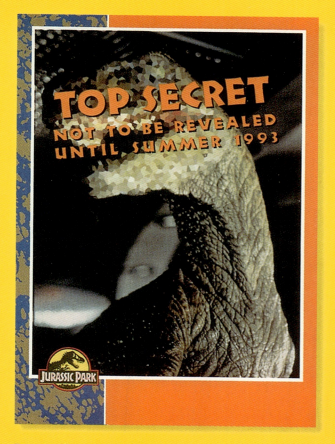

Topps would issue highly collectible promo cards for its upcoming sets, and *Jurassic Park* was certainly a striking and colorful new release to feature. In the first of these four advance cards, a hungry raptor prowls the shut-down facility, searching for prey.

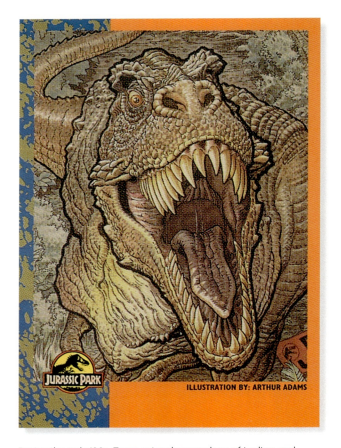

ILLUSTRATION BY: ARTHUR ADAMS

During the early '90s, Topps entered a new phase of trading-card publishing by commissioning all-new renderings from popular artists based on licensed film and TV properties. **Arthur Adams**, who had already dazzled fans with his work for Topps's *Star Wars Galaxy*, was clearly the right man to bring *Jurassic Park*'s rampaging *rex* to line-art life for this exciting promo card.

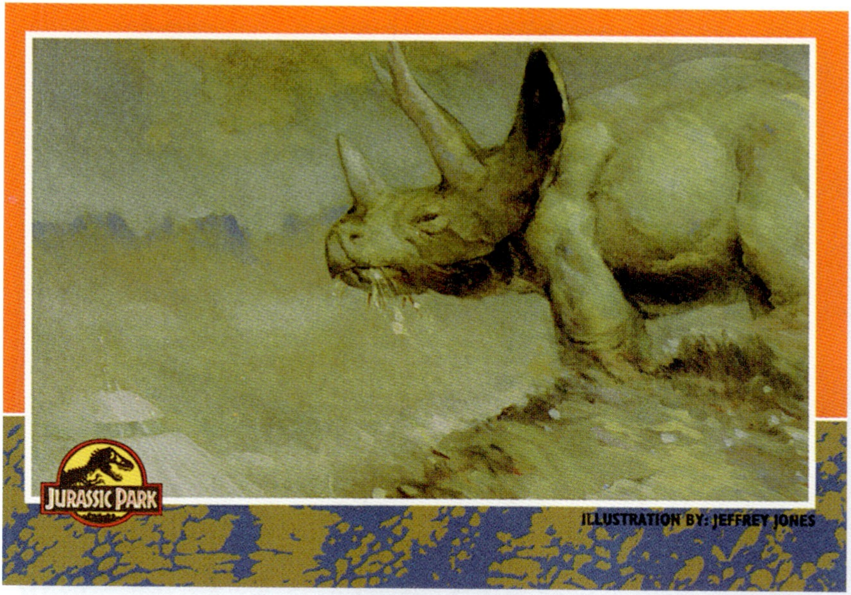
JURASSIC PARK
ILLUSTRATION BY: JEFFREY JONES

Not directly related to a specific scene from *Jurassic Park*, this lovely promo card image of a *Triceratops* munching on some flowers was rendered by illustrator **Jeffrey Jones**.

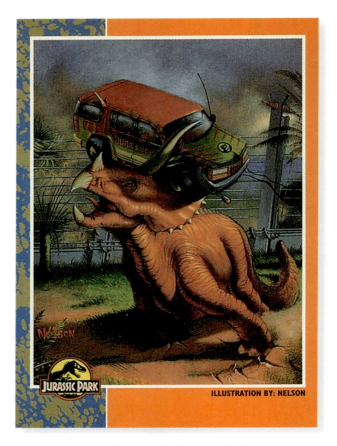

ILLUSTRATION BY: NELSON

Wow! The *Triceratops* featured in **Nelson**'s breathtaking promo card art is far more agitated than her equivalent in the movie (who was sick and out of the action). The illustrator's painted style is somewhat reminiscent of Topps's self-created prehistoric trading card epic, *Dinosaurs Attack!*

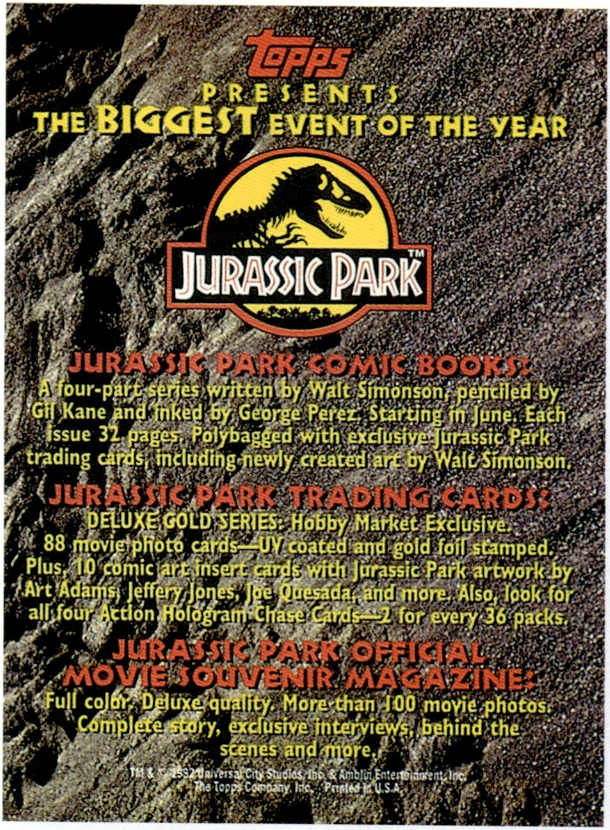

topps
PRESENTS
THE BIGGEST EVENT OF THE YEAR
JURASSIC PARK™
JURASSIC PARK COMIC BOOKS:
A four-part series written by Walt Simonson, penciled by Gil Kane and inked by George Perez. Starting in June. Each issue 32 pages. Polybagged with exclusive Jurassic Park trading cards, including newly created art by Walt Simonson.
JURASSIC PARK TRADING CARDS:
DELUXE GOLD SERIES: Hobby Market Exclusive.
88 movie photo cards—UV coated and gold foil stamped. Plus, 10 comic art insert cards with Jurassic Park artwork by Art Adams, Jeffery Jones, Joe Quesada, and more. Also, look for all four Action Hologram Chase Cards—2 for every 36 packs.
JURASSIC PARK OFFICIAL MOVIE SOUVENIR MAGAZINE:
Full color. Deluxe quality. More than 100 movie photos. Complete story, exclusive interviews, behind the scenes and more.
The Topps Company, Inc. Printed in U.S.A.

SERIES TWO

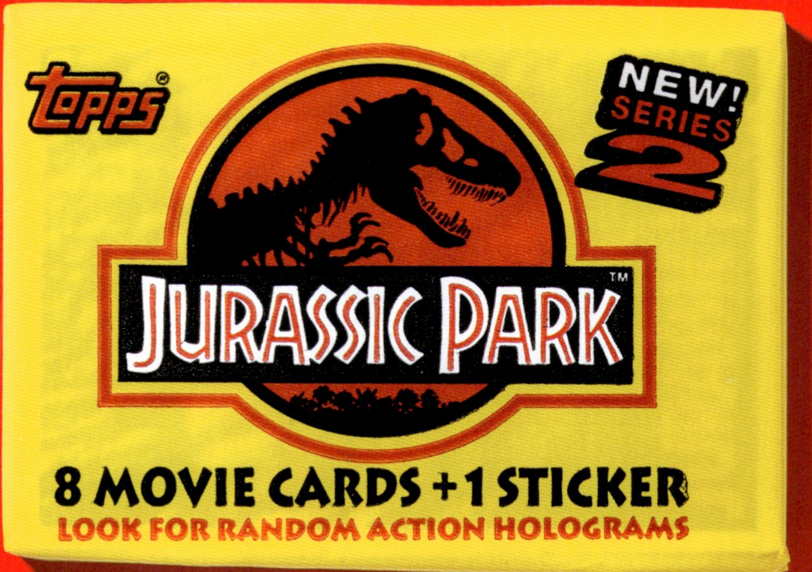
topps
NEW! SERIES 2
JURASSIC PARK
8 MOVIE CARDS + 1 STICKER
LOOK FOR RANDOM ACTION HOLOGRAMS

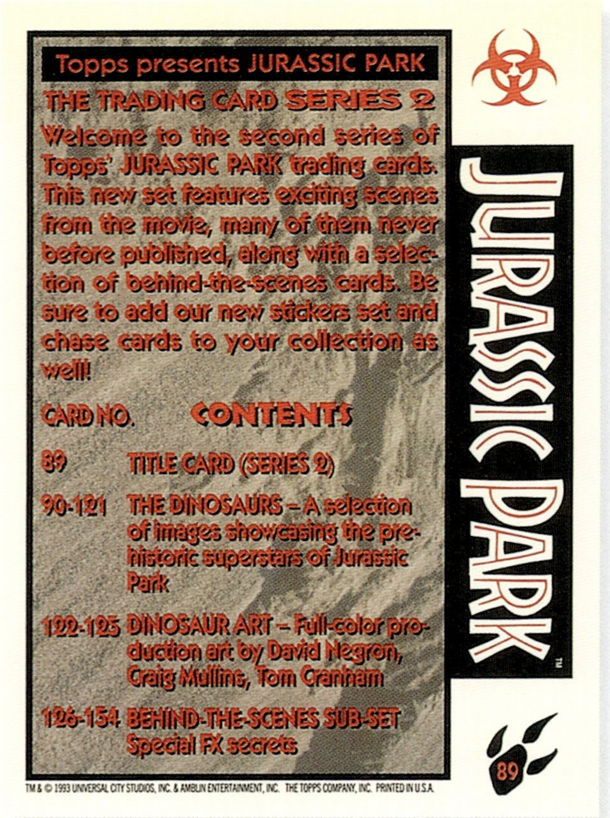
Topps presents JURASSIC PARK
THE TRADING CARD SERIES 2
Welcome to the second series of Topps' JURASSIC PARK trading cards. This new set features exciting scenes from the movie, many of them never before published, along with a selection of behind-the-scenes cards. Be sure to add our new stickers set and chase cards to your collection as well!
CARD NO. CONTENTS
89 TITLE CARD (SERIES 2)
90-121 THE DINOSAURS – A selection of images showcasing the prehistoric superstars of Jurassic Park
122-125 DINOSAUR ART – Full-color production art by David Negron, Craig Mullins, Tom Cranham
126-154 BEHIND-THE-SCENES SUB-SET Special FX secrets
JURASSIC PARK™
89
TM & © 1993 UNIVERSAL CITY STUDIOS, INC. & AMBLIN ENTERTAINMENT, INC. THE TOPPS COMPANY, INC. PRINTED IN U.S.A.

JURASSIC PARK
Topps
ALL NEW
SECOND SERIES

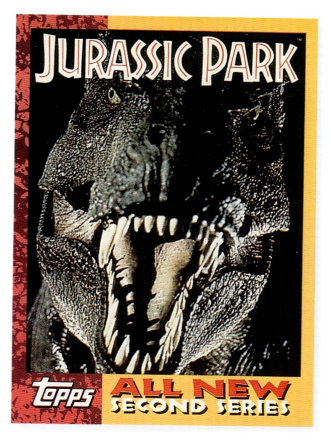

Series 2, released several months after Series 1, is once again set up by the Title Card. Topps's main card product included fewer subjects than Series 1 (66 instead of 88 cards). The listed contents, while somewhat simplified, offered a variation of the kind of exciting material we provided the first time around.

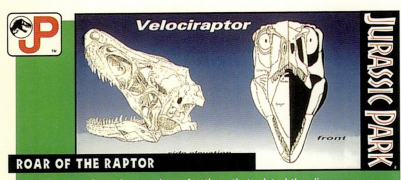

Velociraptor
front
JURASSIC PARK
ROAR OF THE RAPTOR
"We went through a number of actions that related the dinosaurs to the physical world. So we took into account things like the specific gravity of the Earth, and how much a particular dinosaur might weigh. If a creature weighed 400 to 600 pounds, like the Raptor, the character had to convey that sense of weight and presence."
PHIL TIPPETT, DINOSAUR SUPERVISOR
90
TM & © 1993 UNIVERSAL CITY STUDIOS, INC. & AMBLIN ENTERTAINMENT, INC.
THE TOPPS COMPANY, INC. PRINTED IN U.S.A.

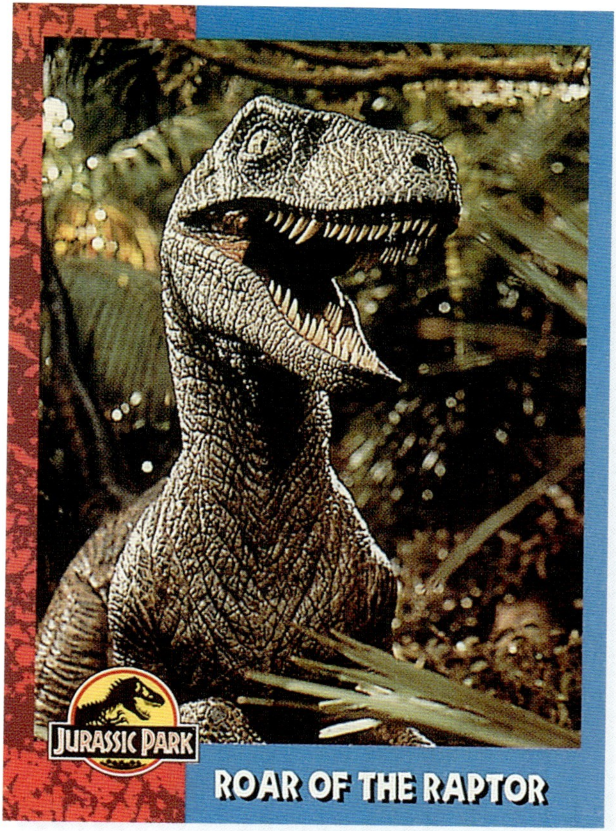
JURASSIC PARK
ROAR OF THE RAPTOR

Alliteration works especially well for trading card captions. Here, an especially fearsome raptor is given the classic title treatment. The card includes a great shot of the deadly dinosaur, one of Stan Winston's full-size articulated props.

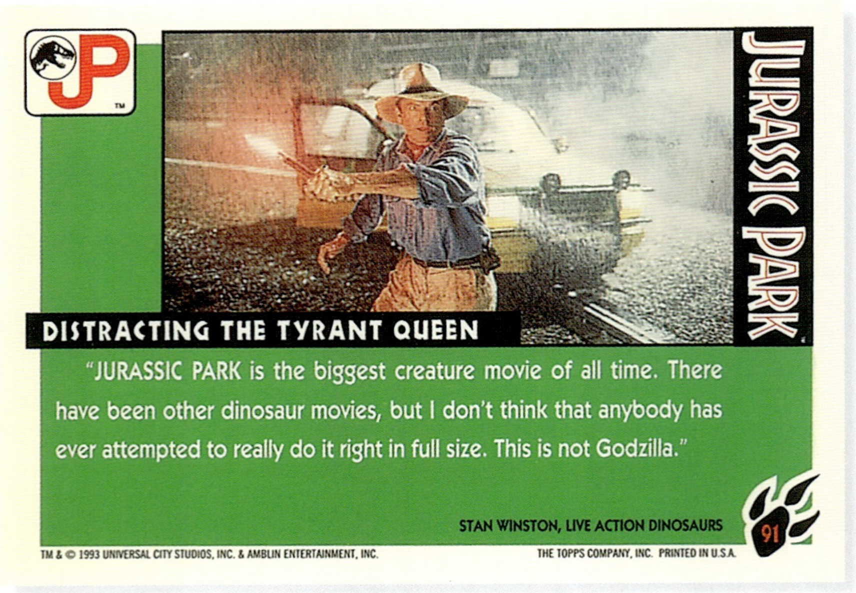
JP
JURASSIC PARK
DISTRACTING THE TYRANT QUEEN
"JURASSIC PARK is the biggest creature movie of all time. There have been other dinosaur movies, but I don't think that anybody has ever attempted to really do it right in full size. This is not Godzilla."
STAN WINSTON, LIVE ACTION DINOSAURS
91
TM & © 1993 UNIVERSAL CITY STUDIOS, INC. & AMBLIN ENTERTAINMENT, INC.
THE TOPPS COMPANY, INC. PRINTED IN U.S.A.

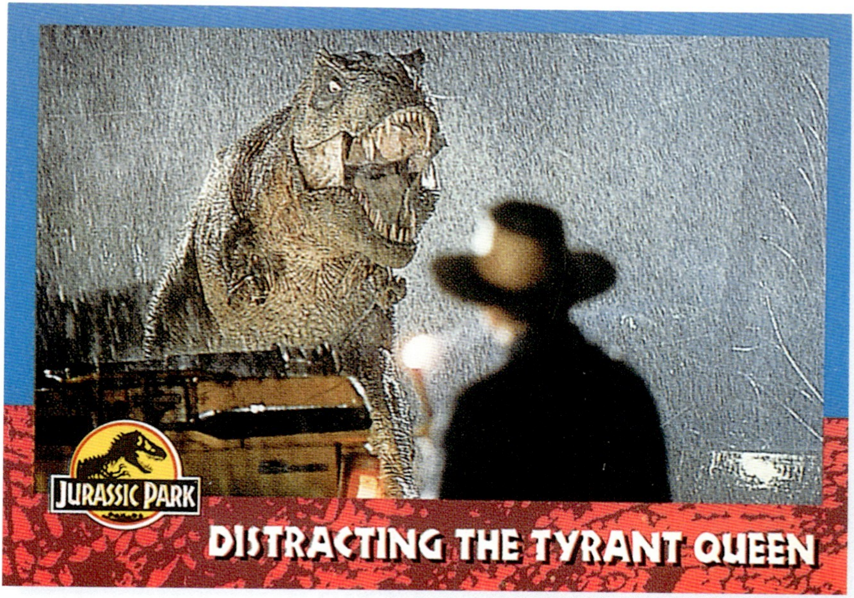
JURASSIC PARK
DISTRACTING THE TYRANT QUEEN

LIKEABLE BUT LETHAL
"The Spitter is one character who's small enough that we didn't have to stick to the storyboards completely. I liked being able to go from fast to slow (in its neck operation), like a cobra. There wasn't any of that sharp stopping as it slowed its movement to a stop."
STEVEN SPIELBERG, DIRECTOR
JURASSIC PARK
92
TM & © 1993 UNIVERSAL CITY STUDIOS, INC. & AMBLIN ENTERTAINMENT, INC.
THE TOPPS COMPANY, INC. PRINTED IN U.S.A.

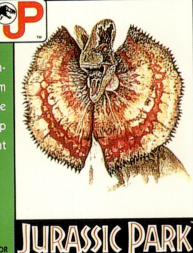

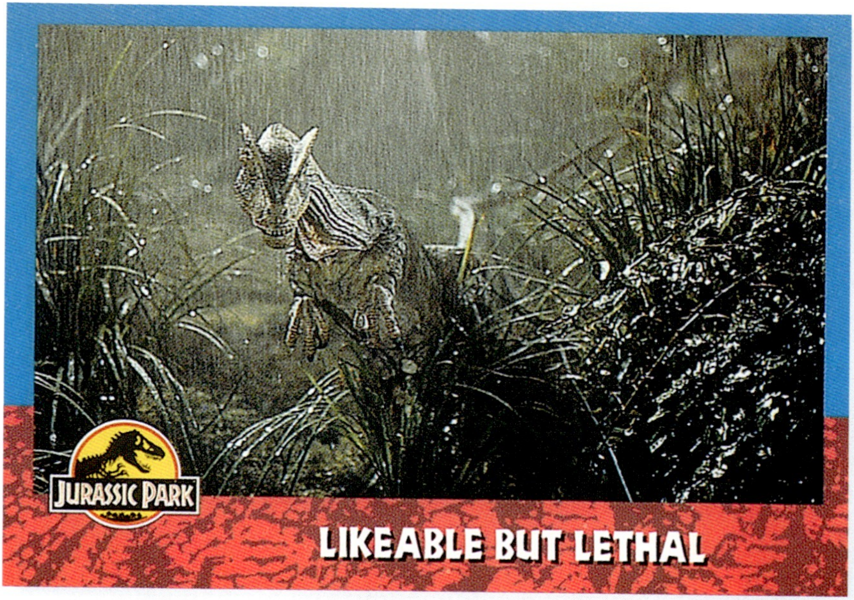
JURASSIC PARK
LIKEABLE BUT LETHAL

Say hi to the friendly-looking *Dilophosaurus* . . . and then duck, as it spits deadly venom right at you! Notice how we established an interesting design format for quotes on the card backs, this one provided by director Steven Spielberg. Since we weren't tracking visuals for a sequential storyline again, filmmaker quotes seemed like a satisfying substitute.

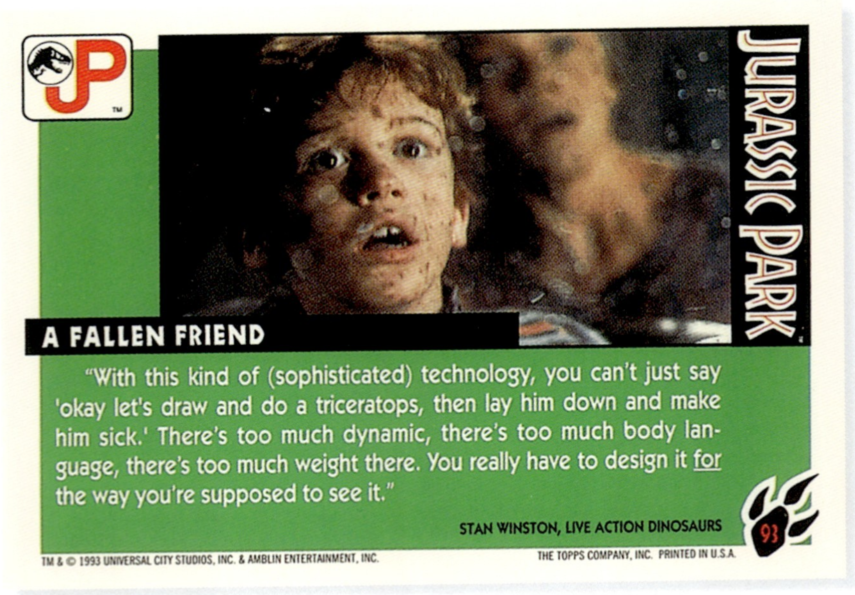
JP
JURASSIC PARK
A FALLEN FRIEND
"With this kind of (sophisticated) technology, you can't just say 'okay let's draw and do a triceratops, then lay him down and make him sick.' There's too much dynamic, there's too much body language, there's too much weight there. You really have to design it for the way you're supposed to see it."
STAN WINSTON, LIVE ACTION DINOSAURS
93
TM & © 1993 UNIVERSAL CITY STUDIOS, INC. & AMBLIN ENTERTAINMENT, INC.
THE TOPPS COMPANY, INC. PRINTED IN U.S.A.

JURASSIC PARK
A FALLEN FRIEND

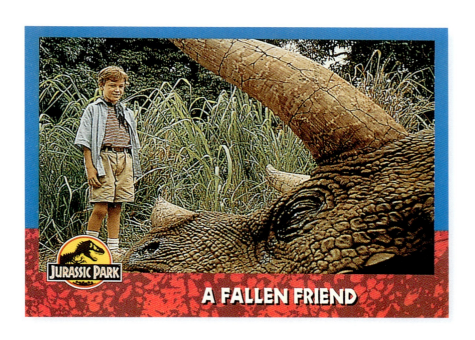

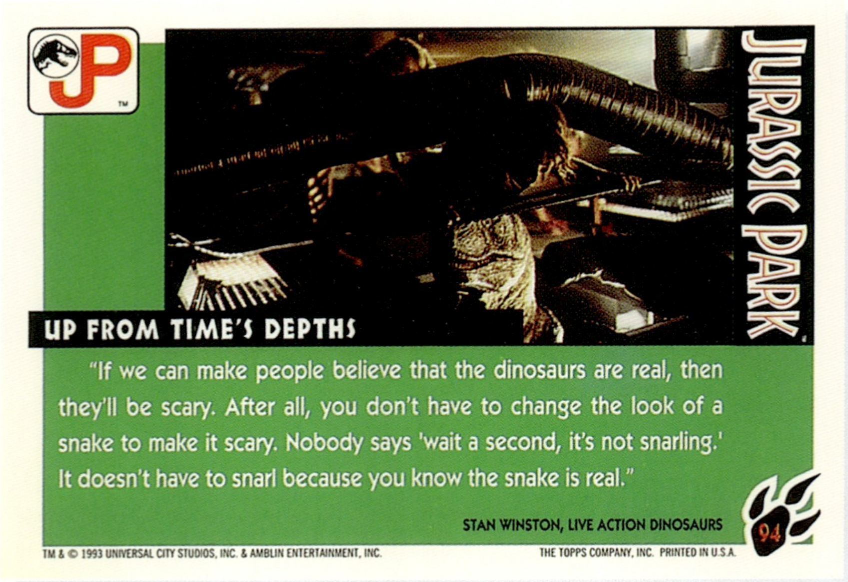
JP
JURASSIC PARK
UP FROM TIME'S DEPTHS
"If we can make people believe that the dinosaurs are real, then they'll be scary. After all, you don't have to change the look of a snake to make it scary. Nobody says 'wait a second, it's not snarling.' It doesn't have to snarl because you know the snake is real."
STAN WINSTON, LIVE ACTION DINOSAURS
94
TM & © 1993 UNIVERSAL CITY STUDIOS, INC. & AMBLIN ENTERTAINMENT, INC.
THE TOPPS COMPANY, INC. PRINTED IN U.S.A.

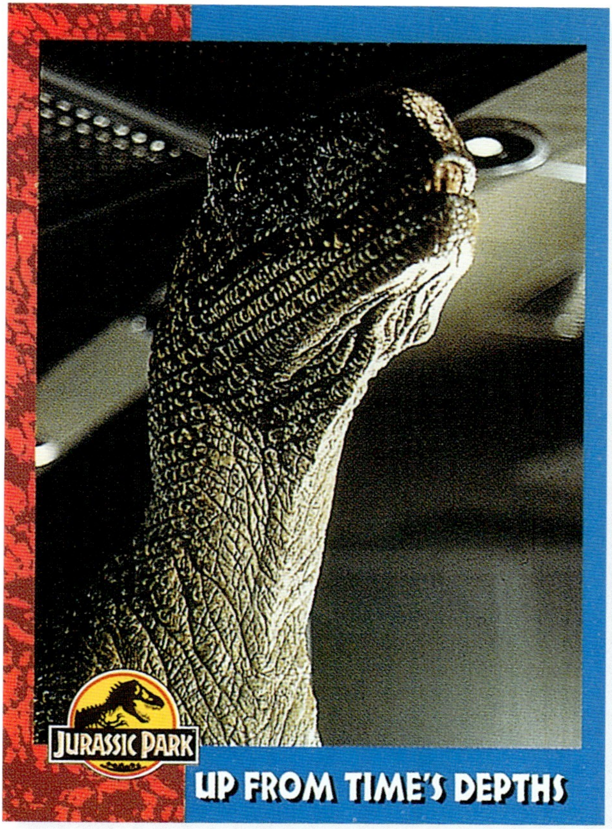
JURASSIC PARK
UP FROM TIME'S DEPTHS

This caption tried to be literal and figurative at the same time, with "up" having meaning for both photos. Special effects master Stan Winston provided the card back quote.

FIRST SIGHTING OF A BRACH
"For something as simple as the way a dinosaur walks, there may be 30 or 40 different axes of movement that are weaving in and out of each other. We tried to find the boundary between what these animals might have been like realistically, in the wild, and what they needed to be like as dramatic entities."
PHIL TIPPETT, DINOSAUR SUPERVISOR
95
JURASSIC PARK
TM & © 1993 UNIVERSAL CITY STUDIOS, INC. & AMBLIN ENTERTAINMENT, INC.
THE TOPPS COMPANY, INC. PRINTED IN U.S.A.

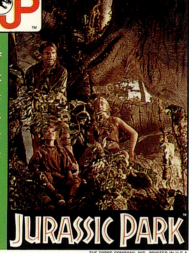

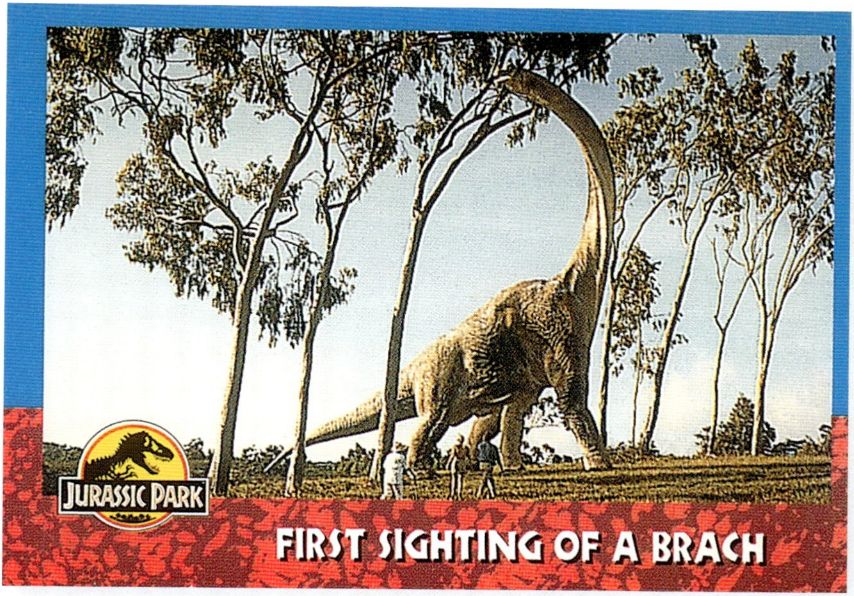
JURASSIC PARK
FIRST SIGHTING OF A BRACH

This is the first CGI (computer generated imagery) photo in our *Jurassic Park* card sets, from either Series 1 or 2. Digital special effects work is always handled separately from a movie's regular on-set shooting, and very often these beautiful images come through weeks, sometimes only days, before the film's release (which was well after our deadline at Topps to get the first set produced).

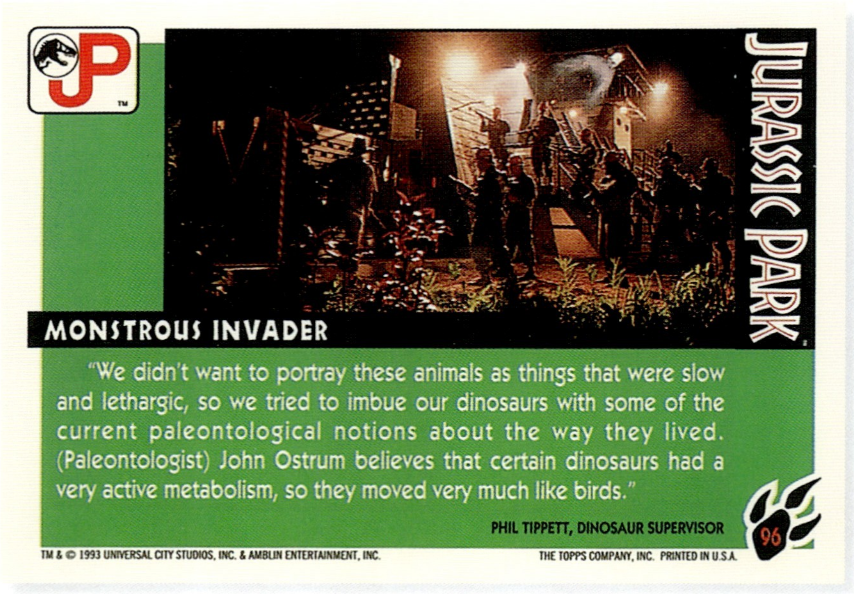
JP
JURASSIC PARK
MONSTROUS INVADER
"We didn't want to portray these animals as things that were slow and lethargic, so we tried to imbue our dinosaurs with some of the current paleontological notions about the way they lived. (Paleontologist) John Ostrum believes that certain dinosaurs had a very active metabolism, so they moved very much like birds."
PHIL TIPPETT, DINOSAUR SUPERVISOR
96
TM & © 1993 UNIVERSAL CITY STUDIOS, INC. & AMBLIN ENTERTAINMENT, INC.
THE TOPPS COMPANY, INC. PRINTED IN U.S.A.

PELIGRO
ALTO VOLTAJE
DANGER
HIGH VOLTAGE
JURASSIC PARK
MONSTROUS INVADER

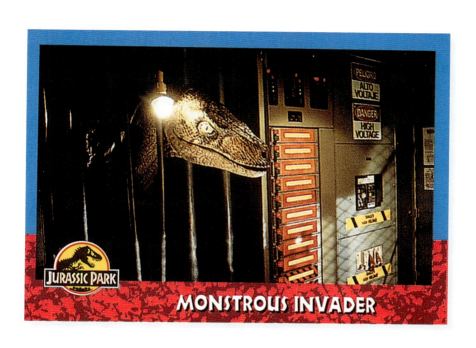

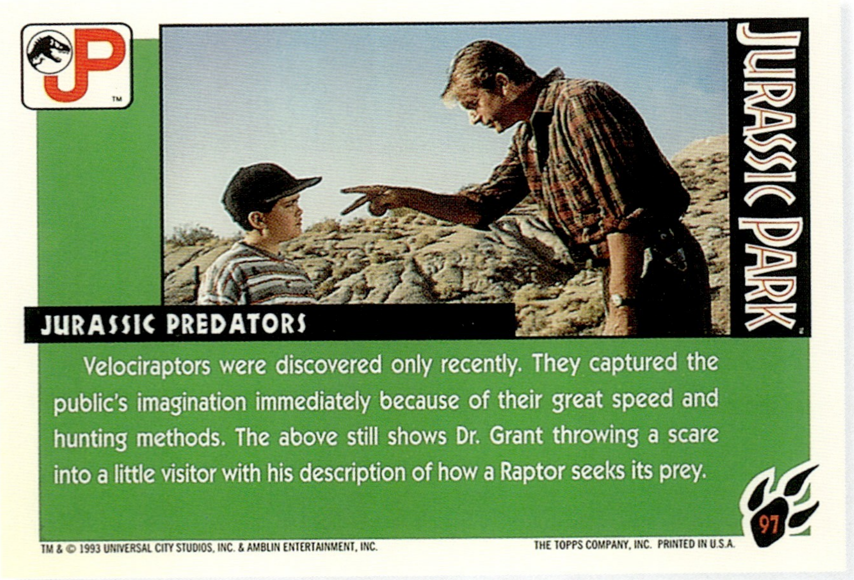
JP
JURASSIC PARK
JURASSIC PREDATORS
Velociraptors were discovered only recently. They captured the public's imagination immediately because of their great speed and hunting methods. The above still shows Dr. Grant throwing a scare into a little visitor with his description of how a Raptor seeks its prey.
97
TM & © 1993 UNIVERSAL CITY STUDIOS, INC. & AMBLIN ENTERTAINMENT, INC.
THE TOPPS COMPANY, INC. PRINTED IN U.S.A.

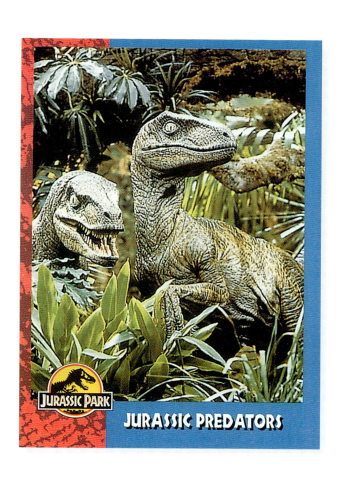

JURASSIC PARK

JURASSIC PREDATORS

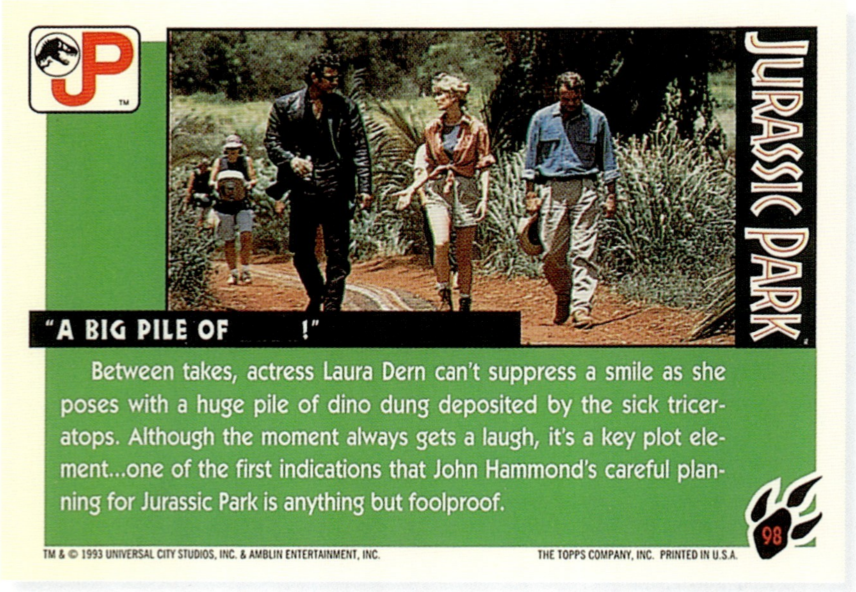
JP
JURASSIC PARK
"A BIG PILE OF [redacted]!"
Between takes, actress Laura Dern can't suppress a smile as she poses with a huge pile of dino dung deposited by the sick triceratops. Although the moment always gets a laugh, it's a key plot element...one of the first indications that John Hammond's careful planning for Jurassic Park is anything but foolproof.
98
TM & © 1993 UNIVERSAL CITY STUDIOS, INC. & AMBLIN ENTERTAINMENT, INC.
THE TOPPS COMPANY, INC. PRINTED IN U.S.A.

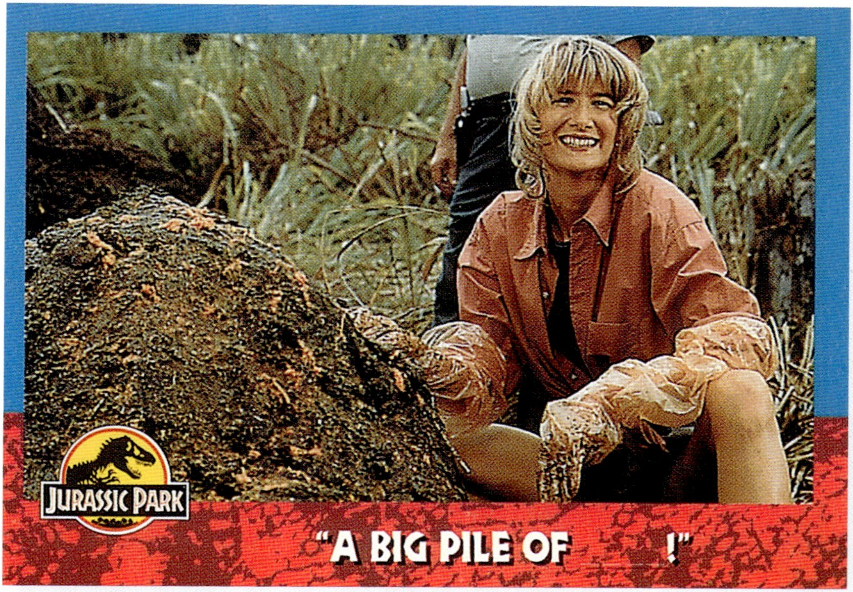
JURASSIC PARK
"A BIG PILE OF !"

How does an editor for a youth-oriented product handle a funky line of dialogue like this? Usually you take the easy way out and simply ignore it. But given how much fun youngsters had with this moment in the movie, and considering what a funny photo we were given (Laura Dern's expression is priceless), I believe we found a simple, rather amusing solution.

DEATH IN A DOORWAY
"I was lucky enough to work with a very talented artist named Randy Dutra, who is also a wildlife expert. Randy understands very well the behavioral aspects of animals. Together we built up a series of motions and movements applicable to the various dinosaur characters in the script."
PHIL TIPPETT, DINOSAUR SUPERVISOR
JP
JURASSIC PARK
99
TM & © 1993 UNIVERSAL CITY STUDIOS, INC. & AMBLIN ENTERTAINMENT, INC.
THE TOPPS COMPANY, INC. PRINTED IN U.S.A.

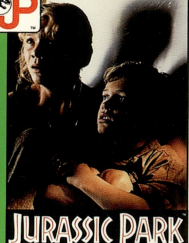

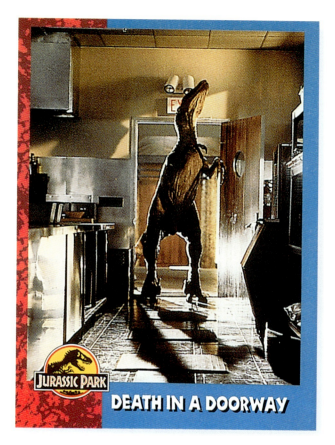

DEATH IN A DOORWAY

Great shot! The raptor truly makes a terrifying foe. Even the score by John Williams, rousingly upbeat when covering the magnificent park itself, gets eerie and strange as raptors prowl about, relentlessly seeking prey (like the scared kids on our card back).

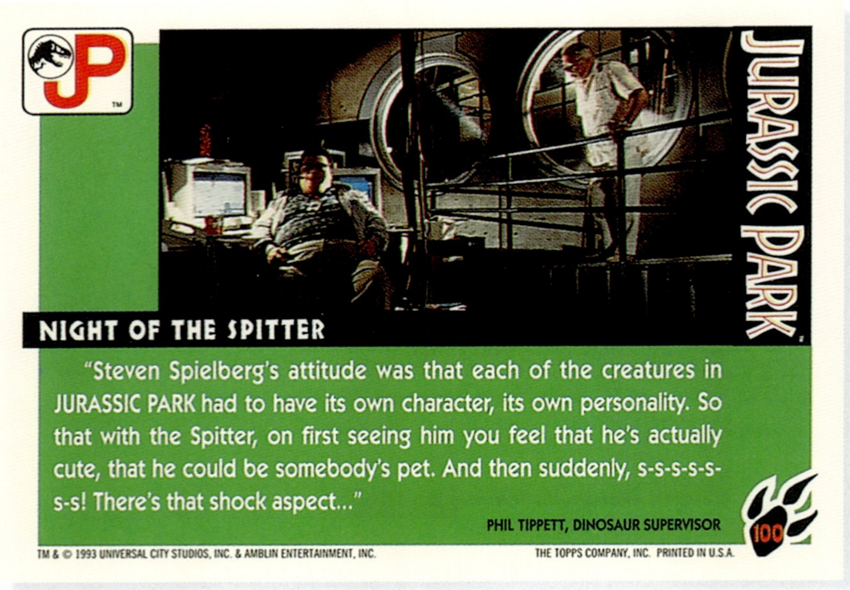
JURASSIC PARK
NIGHT OF THE SPITTER
"Steven Spielberg's attitude was that each of the creatures in JURASSIC PARK had to have its own character, its own personality. So that with the Spitter, on first seeing him you feel that he's actually cute, that he could be somebody's pet. And then suddenly, s-s-s-s-s-s-s! There's that shock aspect..."
PHIL TIPPETT, DINOSAUR SUPERVISOR
100
TM & © 1993 UNIVERSAL CITY STUDIOS, INC. & AMBLIN ENTERTAINMENT, INC.
THE TOPPS COMPANY, INC. PRINTED IN U.S.A.

JURASSIC PARK
NIGHT OF THE SPITTER

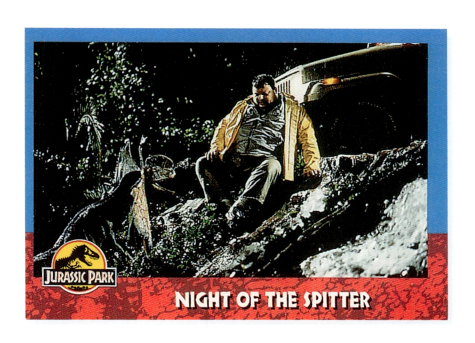

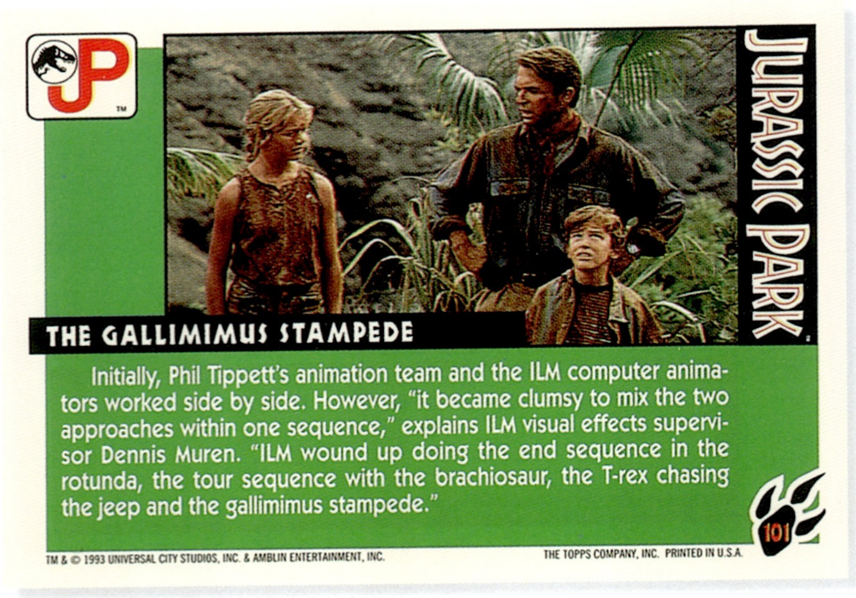
JURASSIC PARK
THE GALLIMIMUS STAMPEDE
Initially, Phil Tippett's animation team and the ILM computer animators worked side by side. However, "it became clumsy to mix the two approaches within one sequence," explains ILM visual effects supervisor Dennis Muren. "ILM wound up doing the end sequence in the rotunda, the tour sequence with the brachiosaur, the T-rex chasing the jeep and the gallimimus stampede."
101
TM & © 1993 UNIVERSAL CITY STUDIOS, INC. & AMBLIN ENTERTAINMENT, INC.
THE TOPPS COMPANY, INC. PRINTED IN U.S.A.

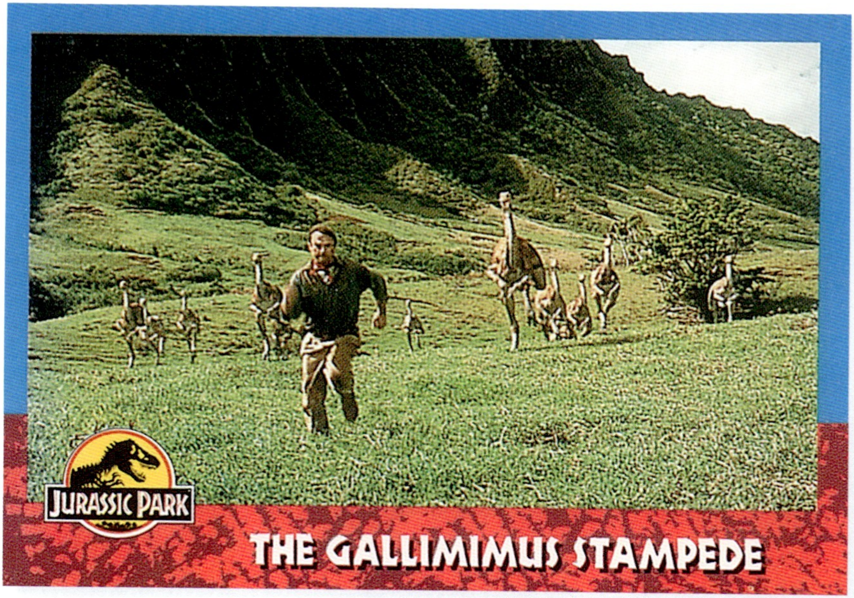
JURASSIC PARK
THE GALLIMIMUS STAMPEDE

Obviously, this front image is another computer-generated shot, as there'd be no way in the world a stampede of on-set dinosaur puppets or even extras in dinosaur costumes could be feasible for filming.

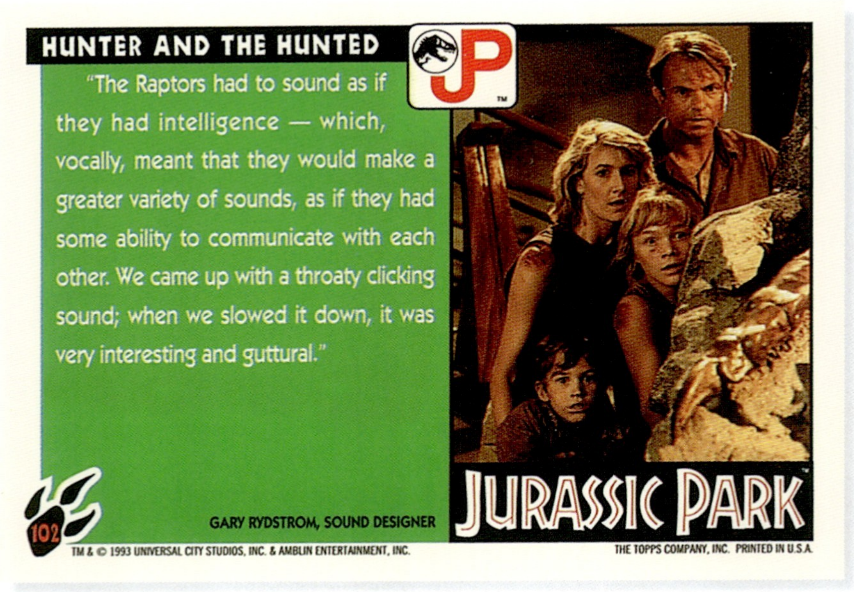
HUNTER AND THE HUNTED
"The Raptors had to sound as if they had intelligence — which, vocally, meant that they would make a greater variety of sounds, as if they had some ability to communicate with each other. We came up with a throaty clicking sound; when we slowed it down, it was very interesting and guttural."
GARY RYDSTROM, SOUND DESIGNER
102
JURASSIC PARK
TM & © 1993 UNIVERSAL CITY STUDIOS, INC. & AMBLIN ENTERTAINMENT, INC.
THE TOPPS COMPANY, INC. PRINTED IN U.S.A.

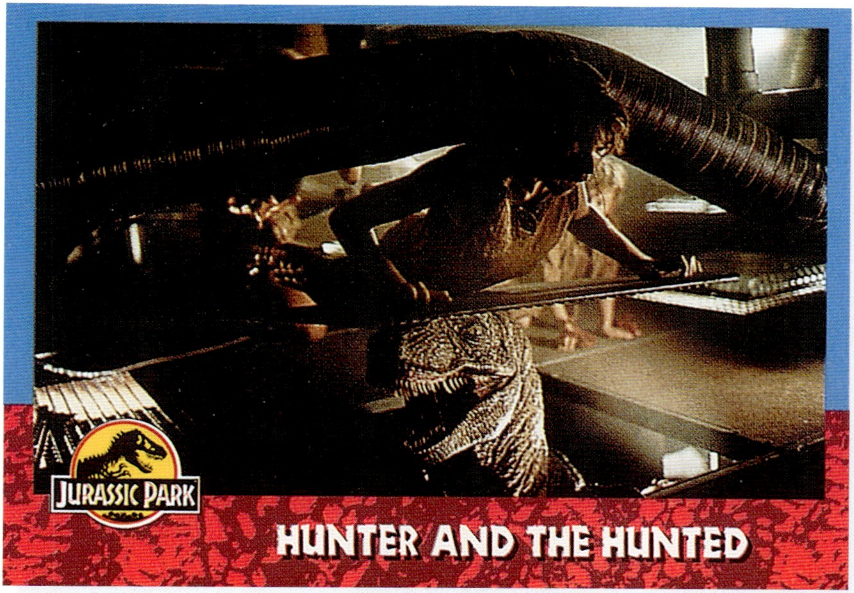
JURASSIC PARK
HUNTER AND THE HUNTED

THE PAST COMES ALIVE

At Stan Winston's studio, Steven Spielberg looked up at the full-size Tyrannosaurus rex and gasped. "I think my kids are gonna love to come to the set," he remarked. "...Until they see this guy. Then they're gonna want to go home." Unlike most of us, the T-rex actually likes lawyers...for a snack.

JURASSIC PARK

TM & © 1993 UNIVERSAL CITY STUDIOS, INC. & AMBLIN ENTERTAINMENT, INC.   THE TOPPS COMPANY, INC. PRINTED IN U.S.A.

103

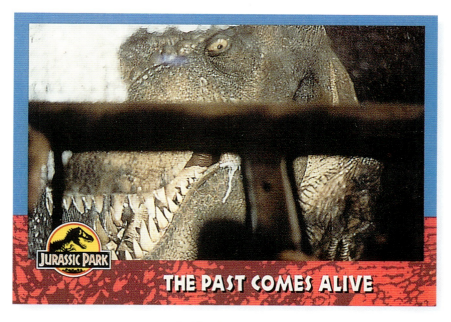

THE PAST COMES ALIVE

Something of an in-joke, the caption "The Past Comes Alive" was used in Topps's funky *Dinosaurs Attack!* trading card set in 1988. Even the bathroom-themed back photo has a satiric, and borderline distasteful, *DA!*-like sensibility about it.

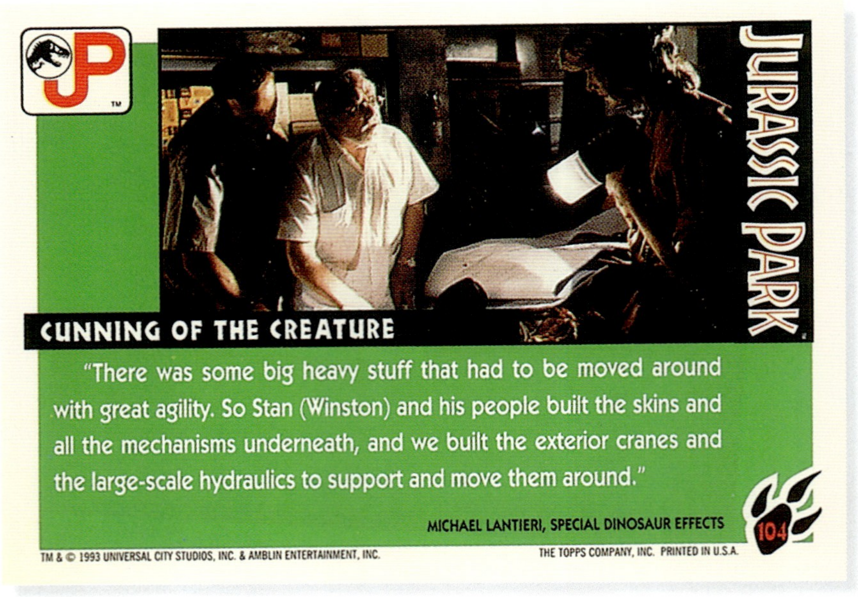
JP
JURASSIC PARK
CUNNING OF THE CREATURE
"There was some big heavy stuff that had to be moved around with great agility. So Stan (Winston) and his people built the skins and all the mechanisms underneath, and we built the exterior cranes and the large-scale hydraulics to support and move them around."
MICHAEL LANTIERI, SPECIAL DINOSAUR EFFECTS
104
TM & © 1993 UNIVERSAL CITY STUDIOS, INC. & AMBLIN ENTERTAINMENT, INC.
THE TOPPS COMPANY, INC. PRINTED IN U.S.A.

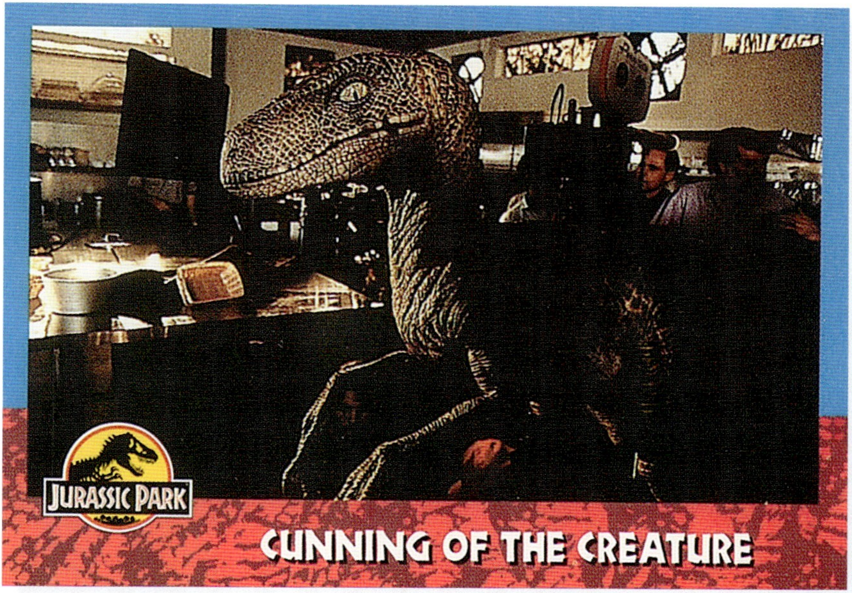
JURASSIC PARK
CUNNING OF THE CREATURE

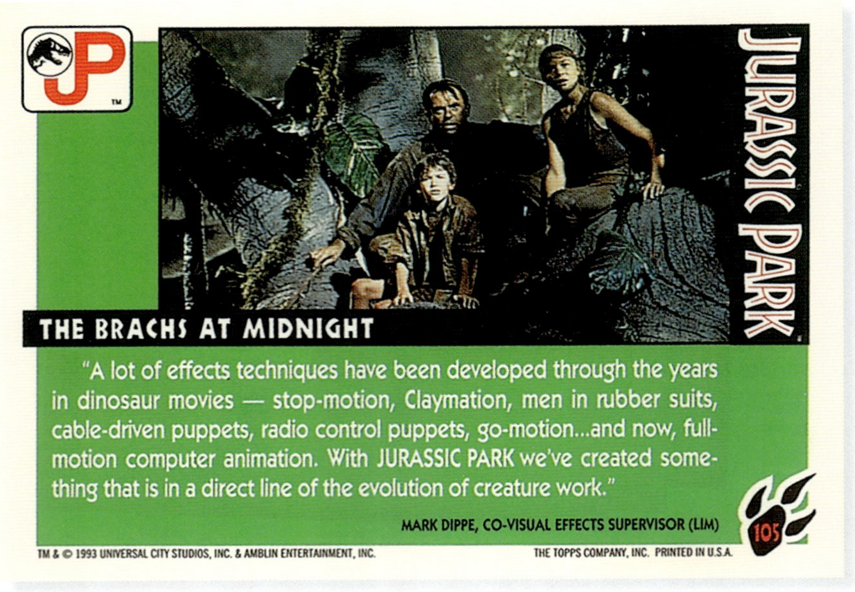
JURASSIC PARK
THE BRACHS AT MIDNIGHT
"A lot of effects techniques have been developed through the years in dinosaur movies — stop-motion, Claymation, men in rubber suits, cable-driven puppets, radio control puppets, go-motion...and now, full-motion computer animation. With JURASSIC PARK we've created something that is in a direct line of the evolution of creature work."
MARK DIPPE, CO-VISUAL EFFECTS SUPERVISOR (LIM)
105
TM & © 1993 UNIVERSAL CITY STUDIOS, INC. & AMBLIN ENTERTAINMENT, INC.
THE TOPPS COMPANY, INC. PRINTED IN U.S.A.

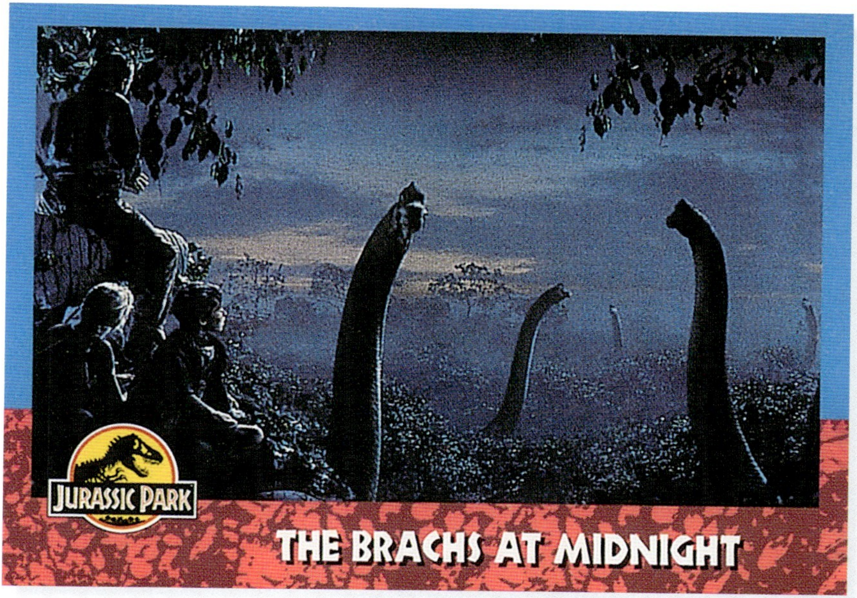
JURASSIC PARK
THE BRACHS AT MIDNIGHT

Wow, what an absolutely breathtaking CGI shot: a nighttime vista of massive, graceful *Brachio-sauruses*, a kind of sauropod. The screenplay is careful to make clear that these giant animals, in spite of their intimidating appearance, are not monsters, but rather beautiful creatures of the earth.

A DINOSAUR DOWN BELOW
"We used an insert head for the Raptor attack shots," explains Live Action Dinosaur Supervisor Stan Winston. "We also used a full-body, locking-joint version that had an articulated head. Finally, there were walking Raptor legs for the maintenance shed sequence, and we were able to get a wonderfully dynamic looking run."
PHIL TIPPETT, DINOSAUR SUPERVISOR
106
JURASSIC PARK
TM & © 1993 UNIVERSAL CITY STUDIOS, INC. & AMBLIN ENTERTAINMENT, INC.
THE TOPPS COMPANY, INC. PRINTED IN U.S.A.

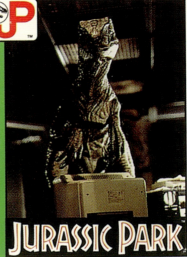

JURASSIC PARK

A DINOSAUR DOWN BELOW

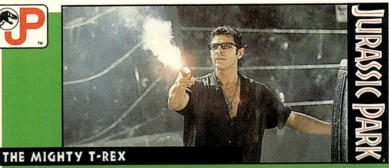

JURASSIC PARK
THE MIGHTY T-REX
"Size quadruples the problems. You take something and you make it twice as big, you add four times as many problems, you have weight factors, you have the amount of stress on every joint, mechanically. So everything has to be figured out and engineered..."
STAN WINSTON, LIVE ACTION DINOSAURS
107
TM & © 1993 UNIVERSAL CITY STUDIOS, INC. & AMBLIN ENTERTAINMENT, INC.
THE TOPPS COMPANY, INC. PRINTED IN U.S.A.

JURASSIC PARK
THE MIGHTY T-REX

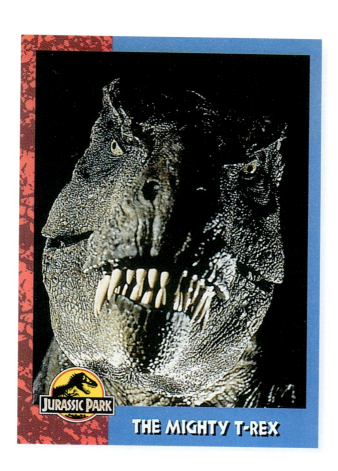

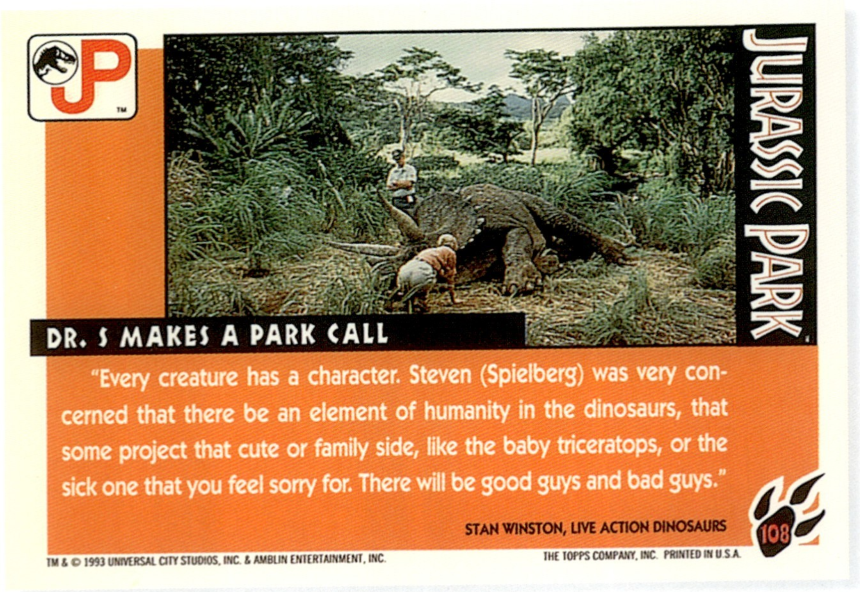
JURASSIC PARK
DR. S MAKES A PARK CALL
"Every creature has a character. Steven (Spielberg) was very concerned that there be an element of humanity in the dinosaurs, that some project that cute or family side, like the baby triceratops, or the sick one that you feel sorry for. There will be good guys and bad guys."
STAN WINSTON, LIVE ACTION DINOSAURS
108
TM & © 1993 UNIVERSAL CITY STUDIOS, INC. & AMBLIN ENTERTAINMENT, INC.
THE TOPPS COMPANY, INC. PRINTED IN U.S.A.

JURASSIC PARK
DR. S MAKES A PARK CALL

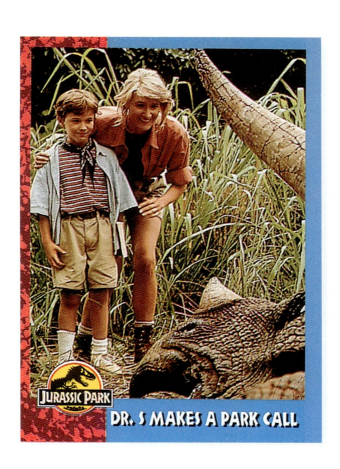

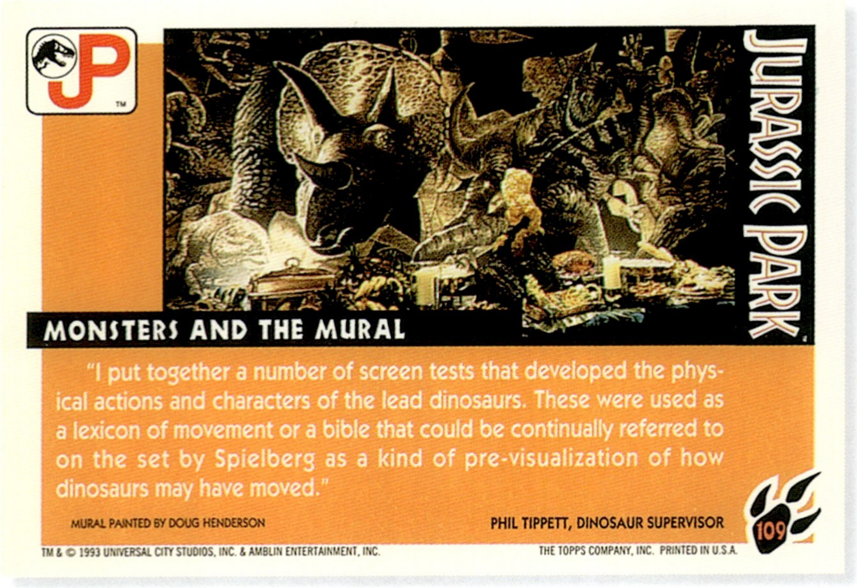
JURASSIC PARK
MONSTERS AND THE MURAL
"I put together a number of screen tests that developed the physical actions and characters of the lead dinosaurs. These were used as a lexicon of movement or a bible that could be continually referred to on the set by Spielberg as a kind of pre-visualization of how dinosaurs may have moved."
MURAL PAINTED BY DOUG HENDERSON
PHIL TIPPETT, DINOSAUR SUPERVISOR
109
TM & © 1993 UNIVERSAL CITY STUDIOS, INC. & AMBLIN ENTERTAINMENT, INC.
THE TOPPS COMPANY, INC. PRINTED IN U.S.A.

JURASSIC PARK
MONSTERS AND THE MURAL

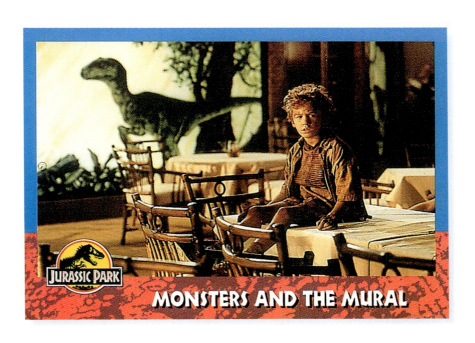

THE RAPTOR'S REVENGE

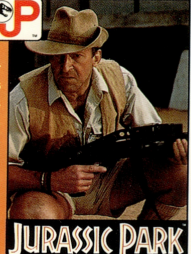

"Well, my God, the change between 1974 and 1992 is amazing," observes Steven Spielberg, comparing JP to JAWS. "Stan Winston has taken the state of the art from the limited movements of the shark, which could hardly move at all, to a whole new level. It doesn't even really compare. And the best news was, we didn't have to make this movie underwater."

110

JURASSIC PARK

x

TM & © 1993 UNIVERSAL CITY STUDIOS, INC. & AMBLIN ENTERTAINMENT, INC.

THE TOPPS COMPANY, INC. PRINTED IN U.S.A.

JURASSIC PARK
THE RAPTOR'S REVENGE

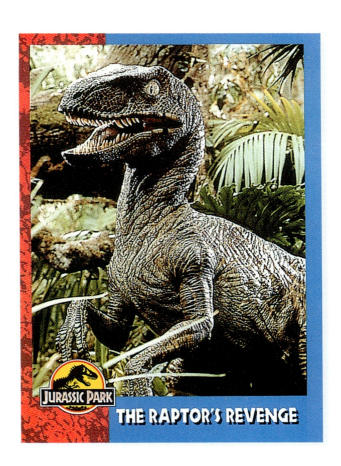

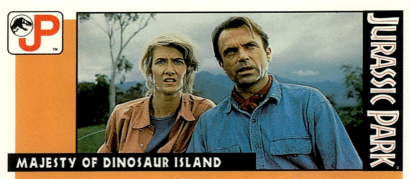

JP
JURASSIC PARK
MAJESTY OF DINOSAUR ISLAND
"I hadn't been very aware of CG (computer generated) technology until TERMINATOR 2 came out. I was so impressed with the work ILM had done on that film, I thought it was possible that someday they might be able to create three-dimensional, live-action characters through computer graphics. But I didn't think it would happen this soon!"
STEVEN SPIELBERG, DIRECTOR
111
TM & © 1993 UNIVERSAL CITY STUDIOS, INC. & AMBLIN ENTERTAINMENT, INC.
THE TOPPS COMPANY, INC. PRINTED IN U.S.A.

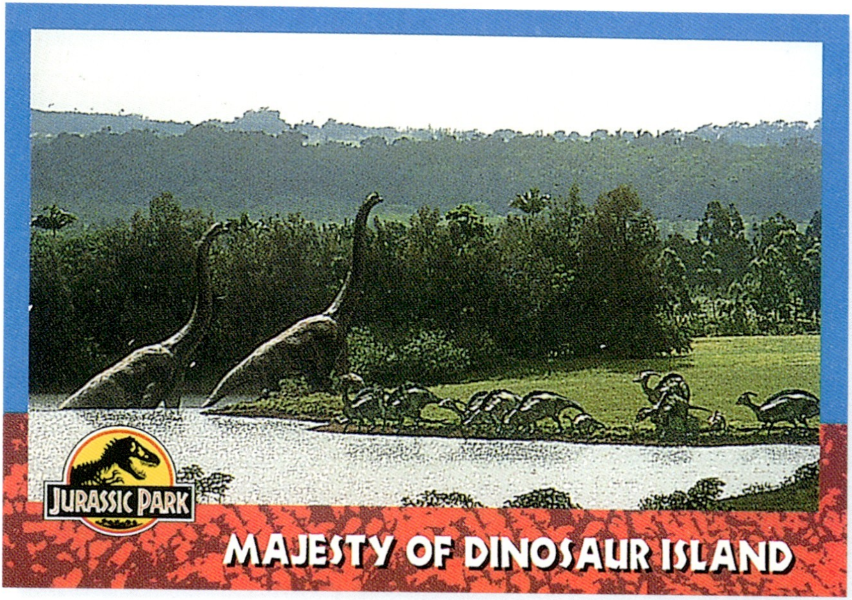
JURASSIC PARK
MAJESTY OF DINOSAUR ISLAND

You had to be there . . . but here's the next best thing, folks. This astonishing CGI vista blew viewers away back in 1993, as *Brachiosauruses* and other dinosaur species congregate near an inlet. I was so happy to get this picture in time for the second series of *Jurassic Park* cards.

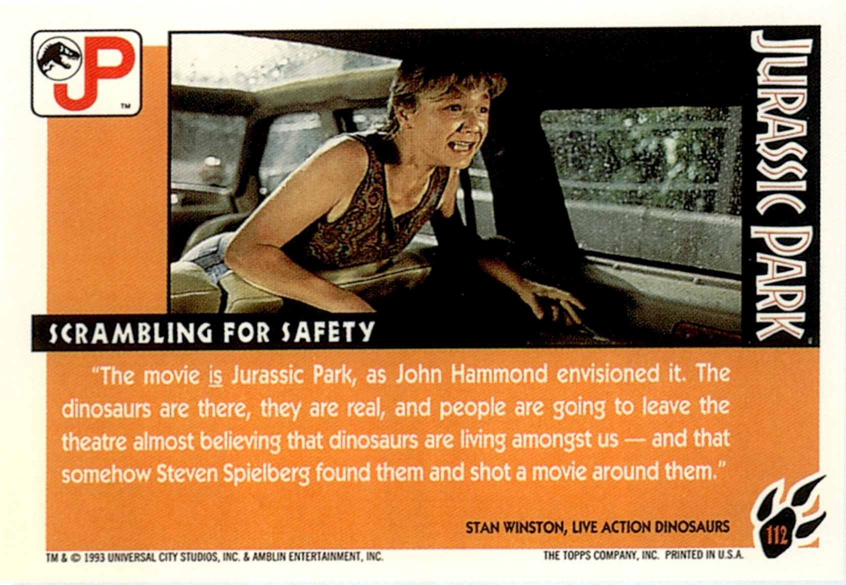
JURASSIC PARK
SCRAMBLING FOR SAFETY
"The movie is Jurassic Park, as John Hammond envisioned it. The dinosaurs are there, they are real, and people are going to leave the theatre almost believing that dinosaurs are living amongst us — and that somehow Steven Spielberg found them and shot a movie around them."
STAN WINSTON, LIVE ACTION DINOSAURS
112
TM & © 1993 UNIVERSAL CITY STUDIOS, INC. & AMBLIN ENTERTAINMENT, INC.
THE TOPPS COMPANY, INC. PRINTED IN U.S.A.

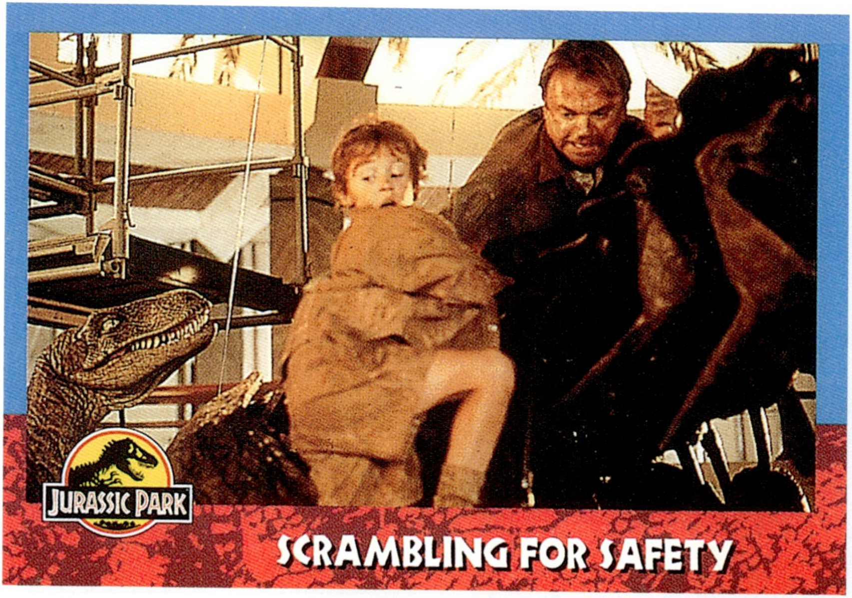
JURASSIC PARK
SCRAMBLING FOR SAFETY

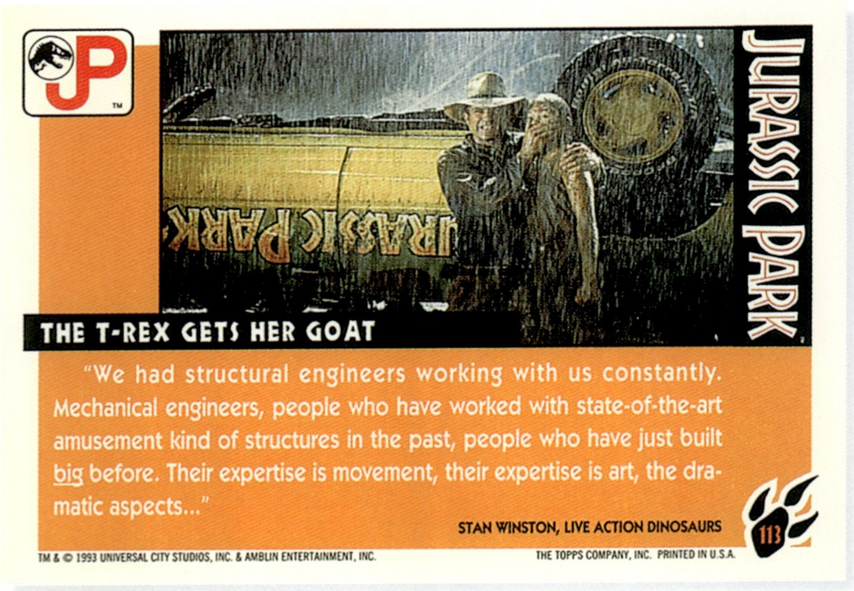
JURASSIC PARK
THE T-REX GETS HER GOAT
"We had structural engineers working with us constantly. Mechanical engineers, people who have worked with state-of-the-art amusement kind of structures in the past, people who have just built big before. Their expertise is movement, their expertise is art, the dramatic aspects..."
STAN WINSTON, LIVE ACTION DINOSAURS
113
TM & © 1993 UNIVERSAL CITY STUDIOS, INC. & AMBLIN ENTERTAINMENT, INC.
THE TOPPS COMPANY, INC. PRINTED IN U.S.A.

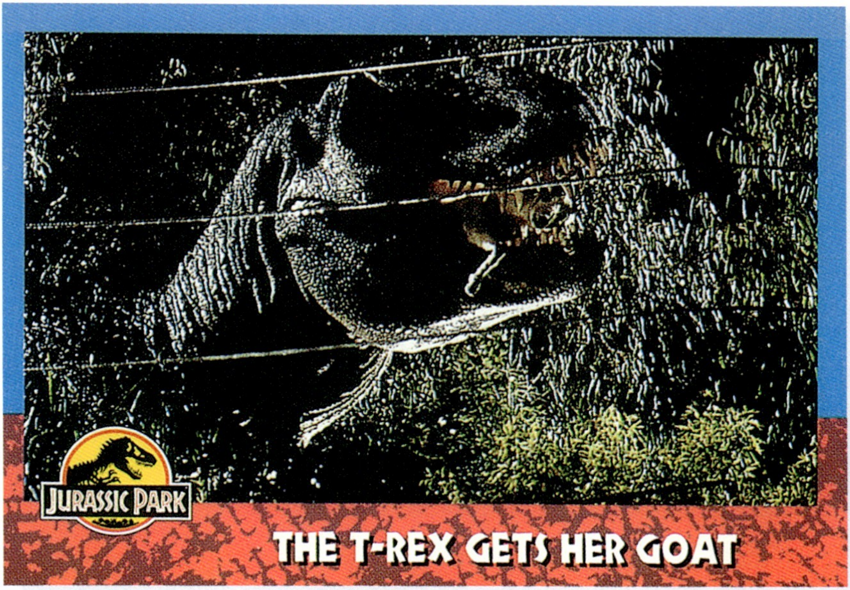
JURASSIC PARK
THE T-REX GETS HER GOAT

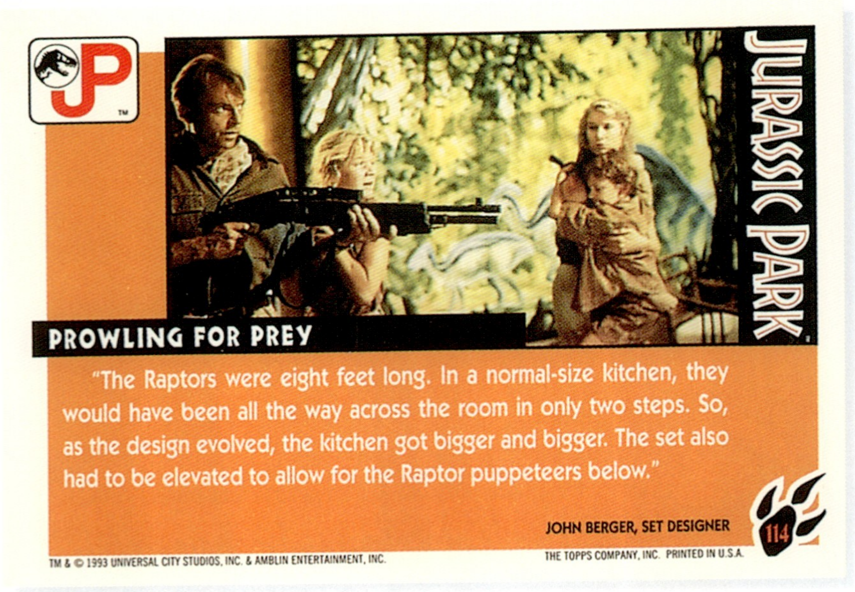
JP
JURASSIC PARK
PROWLING FOR PREY
"The Raptors were eight feet long. In a normal-size kitchen, they would have been all the way across the room in only two steps. So, as the design evolved, the kitchen got bigger and bigger. The set also had to be elevated to allow for the Raptor puppeteers below."
JOHN BERGER, SET DESIGNER
114
TM & © 1993 UNIVERSAL CITY STUDIOS, INC. & AMBLIN ENTERTAINMENT, INC.
THE TOPPS COMPANY, INC. PRINTED IN U.S.A.

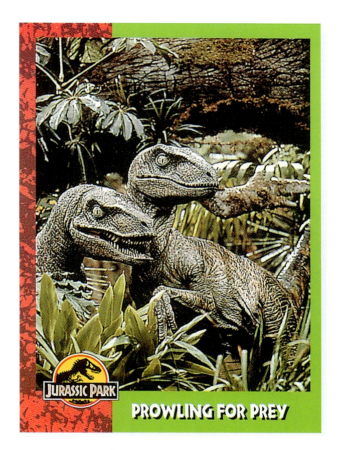

PROWLING FOR PREY

An interesting quote from set designer John Berger is featured on the card back. Often on these backs, we'll talk about the special effects that are required to make a scene convincing. But rarely do we cover the designing of environments that these exotic FX creations dwell in. Surroundings must be both realistic and large enough to accommodate on-set fantasy characters, like these raptors.

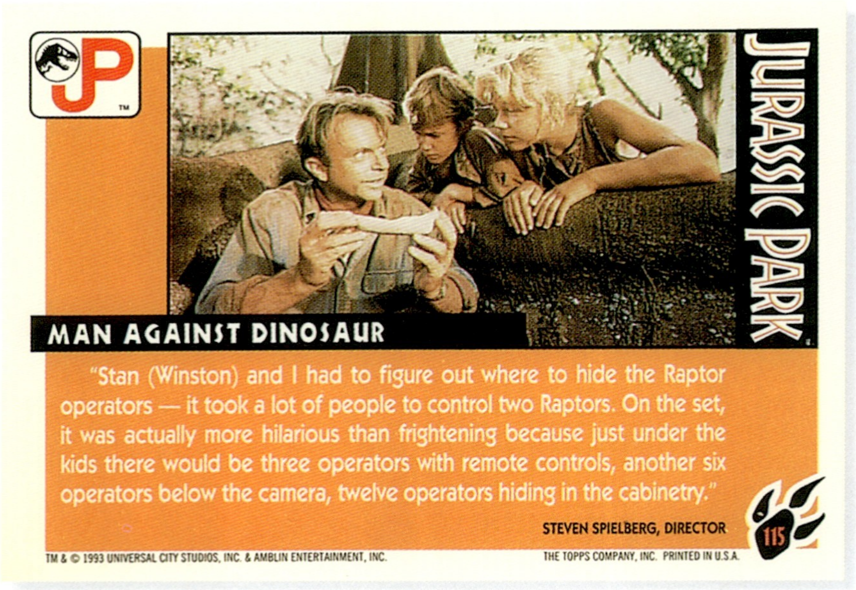
JURASSIC PARK
MAN AGAINST DINOSAUR
"Stan (Winston) and I had to figure out where to hide the Raptor operators — it took a lot of people to control two Raptors. On the set, it was actually more hilarious than frightening because just under the kids there would be three operators with remote controls, another six operators below the camera, twelve operators hiding in the cabinetry."
STEVEN SPIELBERG, DIRECTOR
115
TM & © 1993 UNIVERSAL CITY STUDIOS, INC. & AMBLIN ENTERTAINMENT, INC.
THE TOPPS COMPANY, INC. PRINTED IN U.S.A.

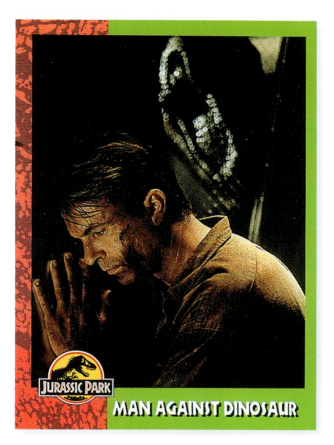

MAN AGAINST DINOSAUR

One of the biggest challenges of *Jurassic Park* was finding a way to hide all the puppeteers as they operated raptors and other on-set dinosaurs. Often they'd be crouched in lower areas of the set, directly below the actors.

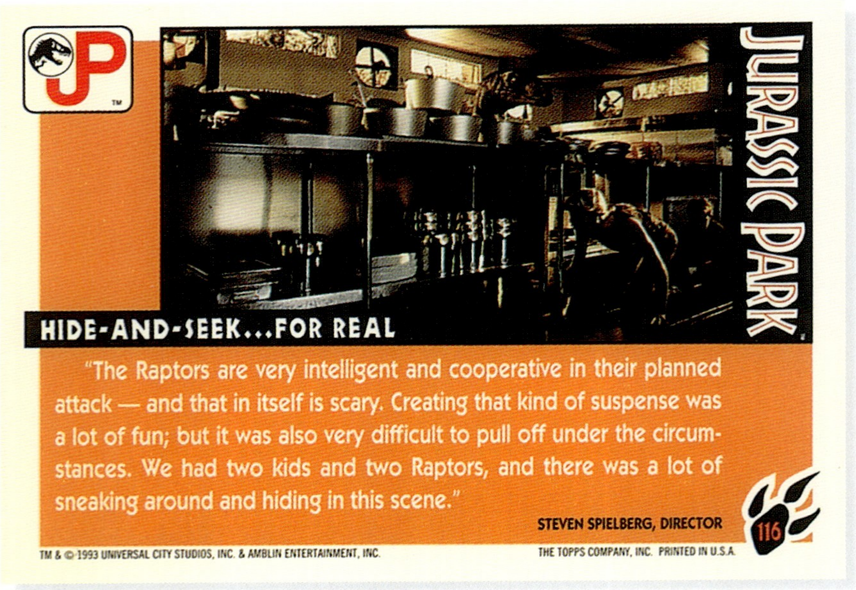
JP
TM
JURASSIC PARK
HIDE-AND-SEEK...FOR REAL
"The Raptors are very intelligent and cooperative in their planned attack — and that in itself is scary. Creating that kind of suspense was a lot of fun; but it was also very difficult to pull off under the circumstances. We had two kids and two Raptors, and there was a lot of sneaking around and hiding in this scene."
STEVEN SPIELBERG, DIRECTOR
116
TM & © 1993 UNIVERSAL CITY STUDIOS, INC. & AMBLIN ENTERTAINMENT, INC.
THE TOPPS COMPANY, INC. PRINTED IN U.S.A.

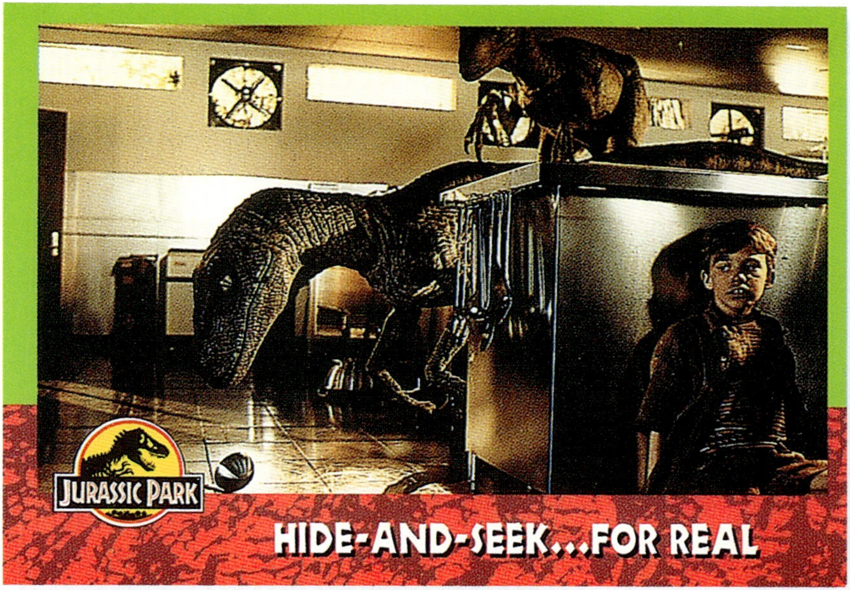
JURASSIC PARK
HIDE-AND-SEEK...FOR REAL

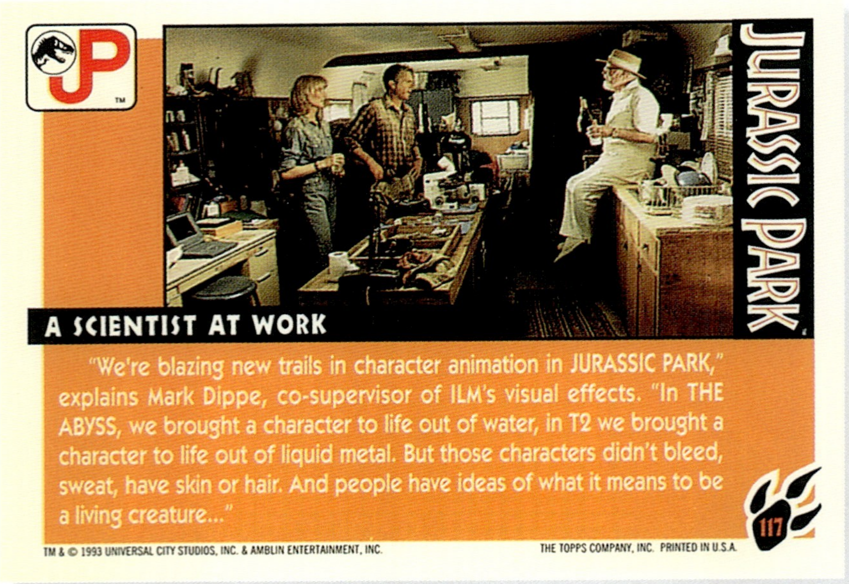
JURASSIC PARK
A SCIENTIST AT WORK
"We're blazing new trails in character animation in JURASSIC PARK," explains Mark Dippe, co-supervisor of ILM's visual effects. "In THE ABYSS, we brought a character to life out of water, in T2 we brought a character to life out of liquid metal. But those characters didn't bleed, sweat, have skin or hair. And people have ideas of what it means to be a living creature..."
117
TM & © 1993 UNIVERSAL CITY STUDIOS, INC. & AMBLIN ENTERTAINMENT, INC.
THE TOPPS COMPANY, INC. PRINTED IN U.S.A.

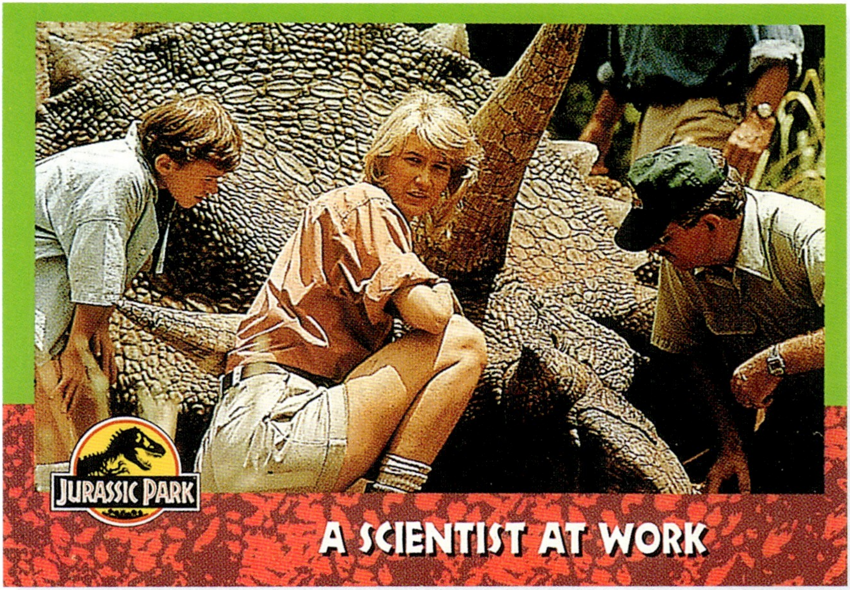
JURASSIC PARK
A SCIENTIST AT WORK

Here's a nice view of the downed *Triceratops*, featured briefly in *Jurassic Park*. The accepted appearance of this iconic dinosaur hasn't changed much from what scientists initially theorized a couple of centuries ago. Now, as then, we're talking about two formidable horns, another one on the snout, and a powerful head shield—but no feathers, please!

AHEAD OF HER GAME
"I know that Stan Winston's crew are people who are dinosaur enthusiasts, like myself. And they kept the dinosaur designs very paleontologically correct. JURASSIC PARK should be the dinosaur picture we've always wanted to see."
PHIL TIPPETT, DINOSAUR SUPERVISOR
118
JURASSIC PARK
TM & © 1993 UNIVERSAL CITY STUDIOS, INC. & AMBLIN ENTERTAINMENT, INC.
THE TOPPS COMPANY, INC. PRINTED IN U.S.A.

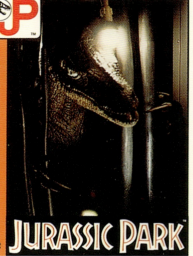

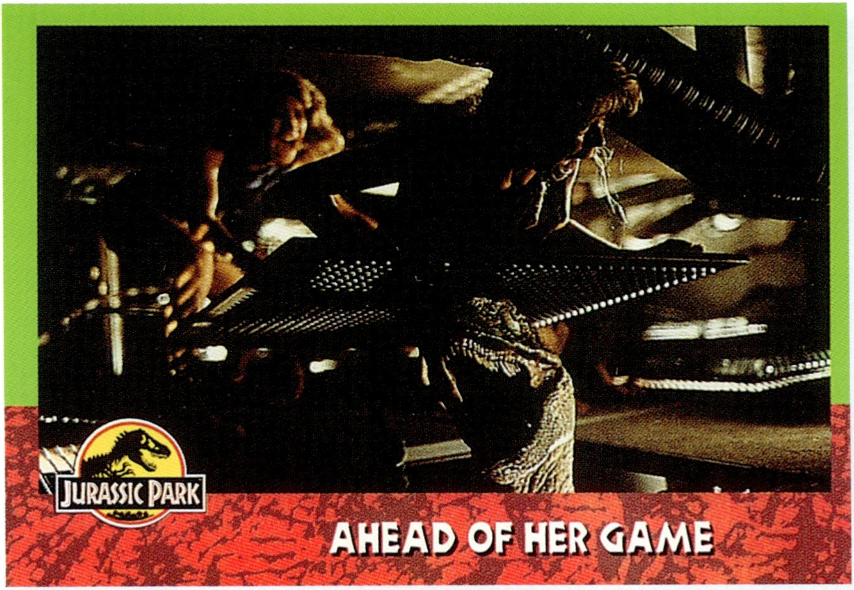
JURASSIC PARK
AHEAD OF HER GAME

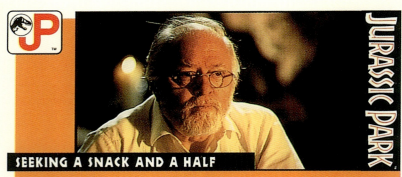

JURASSIC PARK
SEEKING A SNACK AND A HALF
In pre-production, Steven Spielberg was concerned about how much movement there would be in the Rex's forepaws. "We had a telemetry suit,' explained Stan Winston. "We had a technician connected to this device, so that whatever the technician's arms did, the T-Rex's arms would do."
119
TM & © 1993 UNIVERSAL CITY STUDIOS, INC. & AMBLIN ENTERTAINMENT, INC.
THE TOPPS COMPANY, INC. PRINTED IN U.S.A.

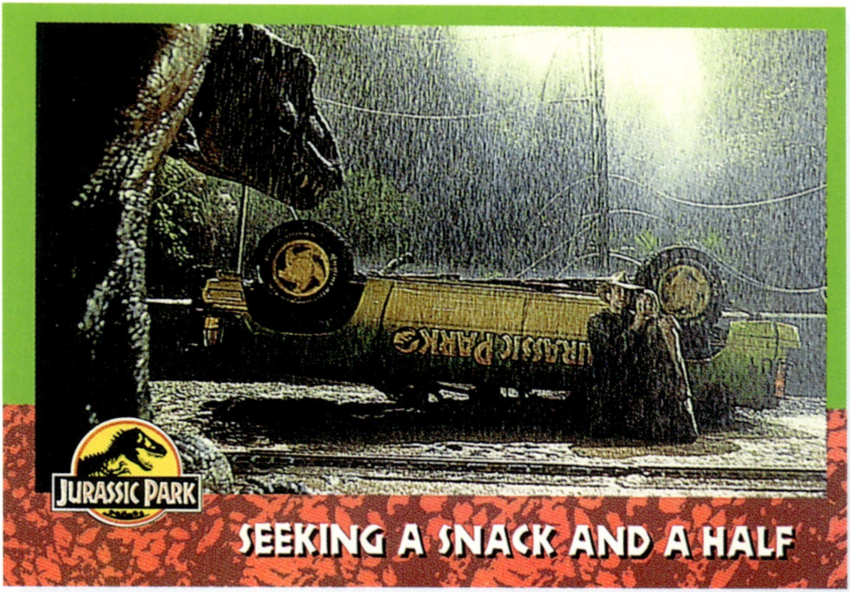
JURASSIC PARK
SEEKING A SNACK AND A HALF

Another example of "Hell, Upside-Down," recalling my Series 1 caption (card no. 38) for a very similar moment. Although *Jurassic Park*'s raptors were the new dinosaurs on the block, so to speak, the *Tyrannosaurus rex*, in truth a telemetrically controlled full-size puppet, cannot help but command our attention.

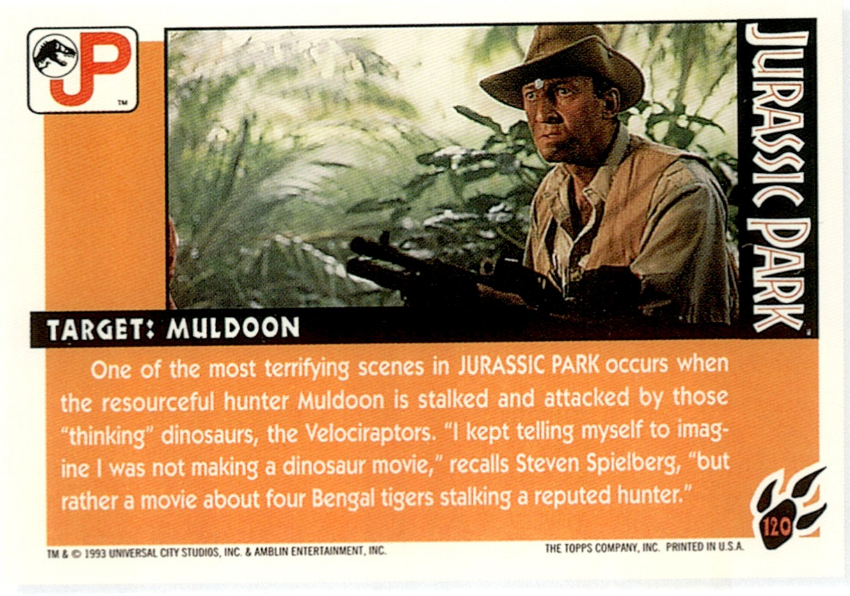
JP
TM
JURASSIC PARK
TARGET: MULDOON
One of the most terrifying scenes in JURASSIC PARK occurs when the resourceful hunter Muldoon is stalked and attacked by those "thinking" dinosaurs, the Velociraptors. "I kept telling myself to imagine I was not making a dinosaur movie," recalls Steven Spielberg, "but rather a movie about four Bengal tigers stalking a reputed hunter."
120
TM & © 1993 UNIVERSAL CITY STUDIOS, INC. & AMBLIN ENTERTAINMENT, INC.
THE TOPPS COMPANY, INC. PRINTED IN U.S.A.

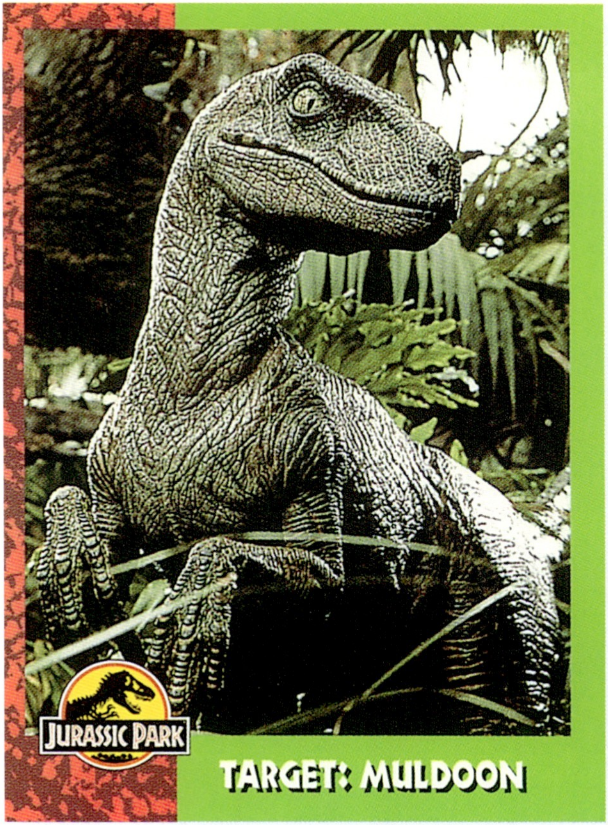
JURASSIC PARK
TARGET: MULDOON

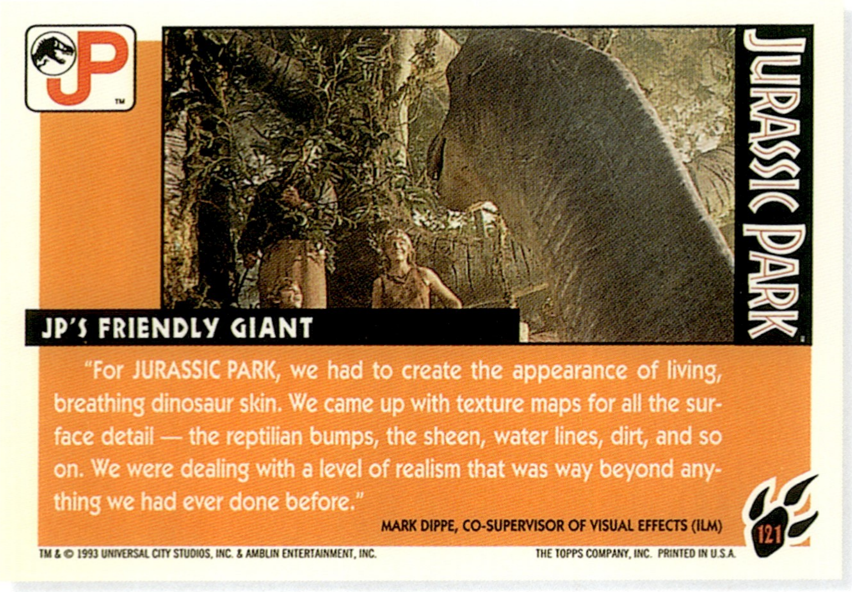
JP
JURASSIC PARK
JP'S FRIENDLY GIANT
"For JURASSIC PARK, we had to create the appearance of living, breathing dinosaur skin. We came up with texture maps for all the surface detail — the reptilian bumps, the sheen, water lines, dirt, and so on. We were dealing with a level of realism that was way beyond anything we had ever done before."
MARK DIPPE, CO-SUPERVISOR OF VISUAL EFFECTS (ILM)
121
TM & © 1993 UNIVERSAL CITY STUDIOS, INC. & AMBLIN ENTERTAINMENT, INC.
THE TOPPS COMPANY, INC. PRINTED IN U.S.A.

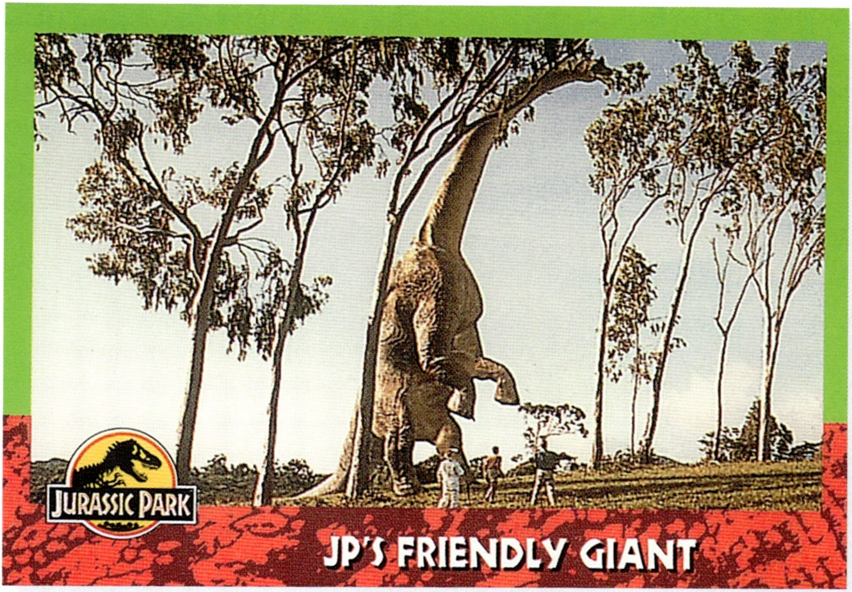
JURASSIC PARK
JP'S FRIENDLY GIANT

Incredible! The humans watch in awe as a living *Brachiosaurus* rises to full height so she can enjoy some leafy lunch. In years past, this kind of illusion would have been handled by the stop-motion animation process, as used in movies like *King Kong* and *Jason and the Argonauts*. CGI was initially viewed as perfected stop-motion—a more sophisticated special effects approach that eliminated the inherent jerkiness associated with frame-by-frame animation.

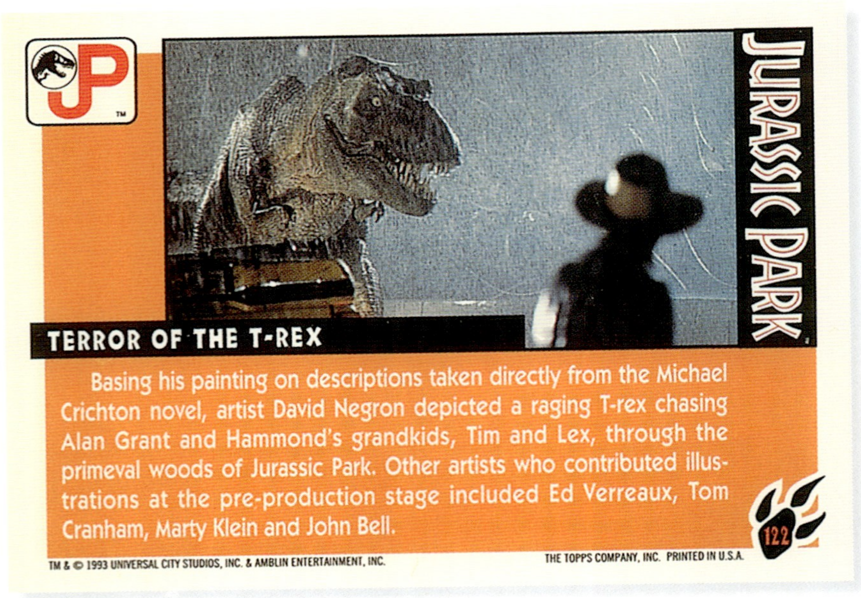
JURASSIC PARK
TERROR OF THE T-REX
Basing his painting on descriptions taken directly from the Michael Crichton novel, artist David Negron depicted a raging T-rex chasing Alan Grant and Hammond's grandkids, Tim and Lex, through the primeval woods of Jurassic Park. Other artists who contributed illustrations at the pre-production stage included Ed Verreaux, Tom Cranham, Marty Klein and John Bell.
122
TM & © 1993 UNIVERSAL CITY STUDIOS, INC. & AMBLIN ENTERTAINMENT, INC.
THE TOPPS COMPANY, INC. PRINTED IN U.S.A.

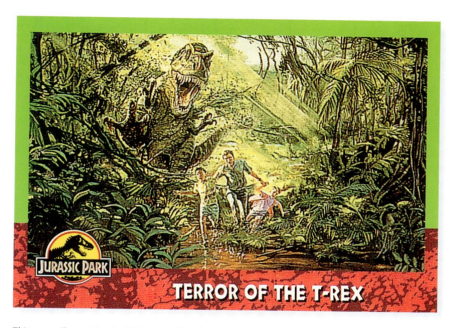

TERROR OF THE T-REX

This compelling mini-set within a set offers four colorful production paintings, some created for scenes that were planned but never filmed. Artist David Negrón based his illustration on descriptions from Crichton's book, as dutifully noted in the copy on the back of the card.

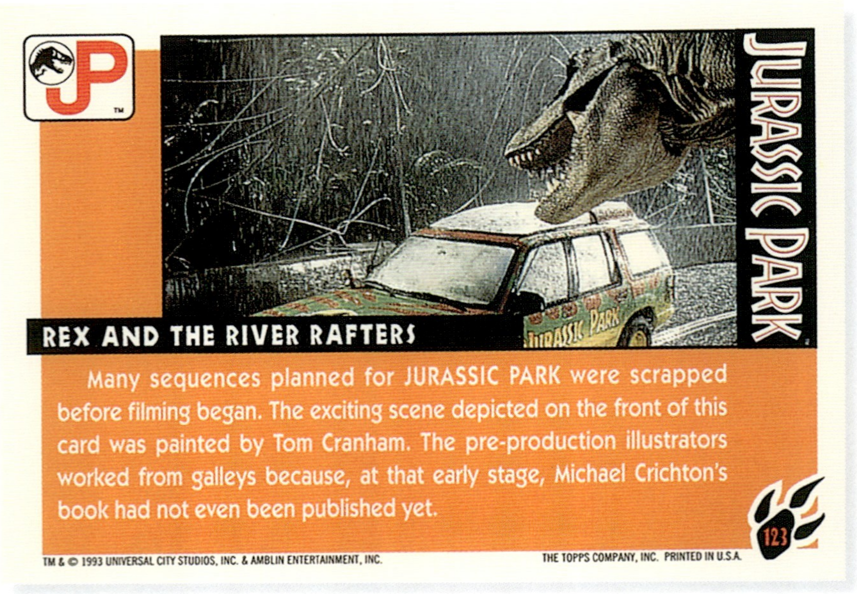
JP™
JURASSIC PARK
REX AND THE RIVER RAFTERS
Many sequences planned for JURASSIC PARK were scrapped before filming began. The exciting scene depicted on the front of this card was painted by Tom Cranham. The pre-production illustrators worked from galleys because, at that early stage, Michael Crichton's book had not even been published yet.
123
TM & © 1993 UNIVERSAL CITY STUDIOS, INC. & AMBLIN ENTERTAINMENT, INC.
THE TOPPS COMPANY, INC. PRINTED IN U.S.A.

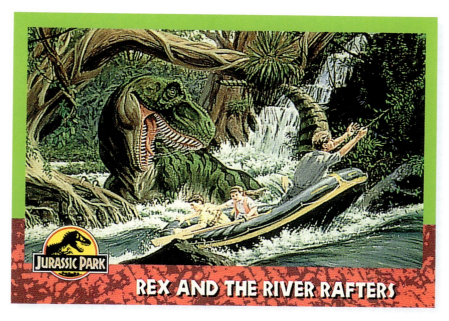

REX AND THE RIVER RAFTERS

You can't blame Topps for wanting to use these wonderful *Jurassic Park* production paintings as cards; they are so beautifully rendered. Here's another hungry *T. rex* in action, this time giving some hapless river rafters a ride they'll never forget—assuming they survive, of course. Art by Tom Cranham.

JURASSIC PARK

REX'S SAVAGE ASSAULT

"Crichton's best accomplishment was creating a basis of credibility that dinosaurs could return to the living today and walk amongst us. What I wanted to do is boil the book and choose my seven or eight favorite scenes and base the script around those. So we 'crunched' the book."

PRE-PRODUCTION ART (CARD FRONT) BY CRAIG MULLINS

STEVEN SPIELBERG, DIRECTOR 124

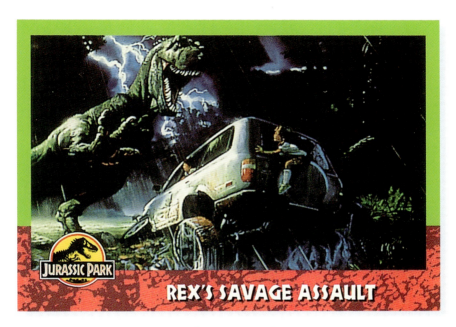

REX'S SAVAGE ASSAULT

It could be worse . . . it could be raining. CRACKA-BOOM! Thunderstorms always add delicious melodramatic texture to a scary movie scene. As if being attacked by a ferocious *Tyrannosaurus rex* weren't bad enough, the raging storm ups the ante, adding yet another layer of mystery and suspense. Artist Craig Mullins certainly delivered all the goods in this preproduction painting (front). The back features an impressive take on the Jurassic Park main building.

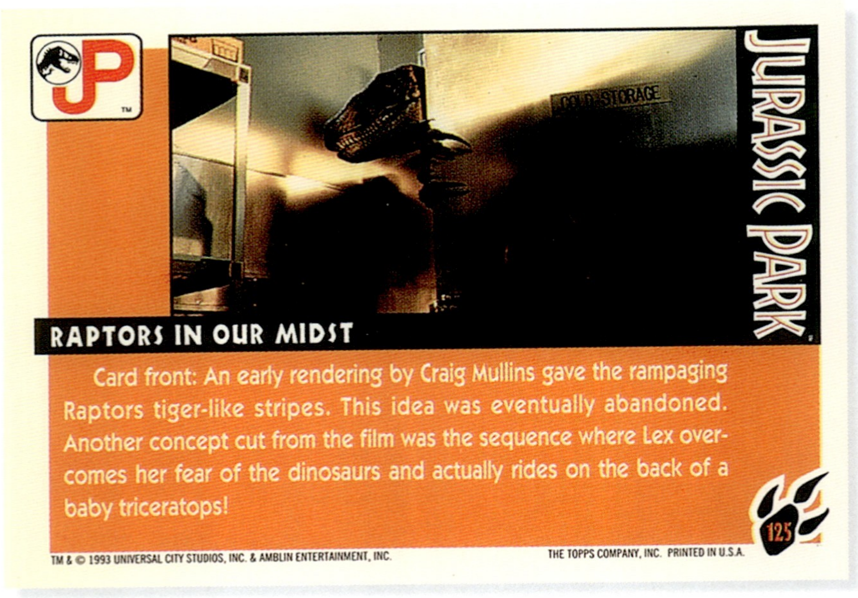
JP
JURASSIC PARK
COLD STORAGE
RAPTORS IN OUR MIDST
Card front: An early rendering by Craig Mullins gave the rampaging Raptors tiger-like stripes. This idea was eventually abandoned. Another concept cut from the film was the sequence where Lex overcomes her fear of the dinosaurs and actually rides on the back of a baby triceratops!
125
TM & © 1993 UNIVERSAL CITY STUDIOS, INC. & AMBLIN ENTERTAINMENT, INC.
THE TOPPS COMPANY, INC. PRINTED IN U.S.A.

JURASSIC PARK
RAPTORS IN OUR MIDST

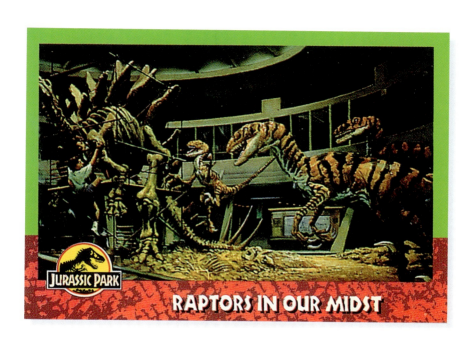

BEHIND-THE-SCENES SUB-SET
"The first big words I ever learned were different dinosaur species," reveals Steven Spielberg, world-class director of Universal's JURASSIC PARK, "and when my son Max was two years old, he could not only identify, but pronounce 'iguanadon.' I think one of the things that interests kids is that dinosaurs are so mysterious..."
126
JURASSIC PARK
SPECIAL FX SECRETS
TM & © 1993 UNIVERSAL CITY STUDIOS, INC. & AMBLIN ENTERTAINMENT, INC.
THE TOPPS COMPANY, INC. PRINTED IN U.S.A.

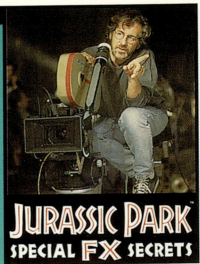

BEHIND THE SCENES SUB-SET
JP
JURASSIC PARK
SPECIAL FX SECRETS

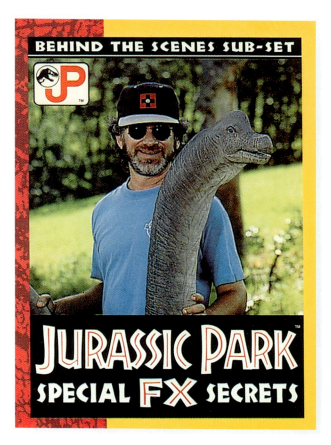

Once again, our Title Card design was rolled out for a subset within an overall series. I have to say, this photo of Steven Spielberg posing with a *Brachiosaurus* model is a real hoot, and a fun way to launch this group of cards.

SPIELBERG, KENNEDY AND FRIEND

"Steven and I had talked about every detail of the production by the time the cameras rolled, which gave me a huge advantage from a producing standpoint. By the time we got to shooting JURASSIC PARK, we knew exactly where we were going with this movie; and we knew exactly how much it was going to cost."

KATHLEEN KENNEDY, PRODUCER

JURASSIC PARK™
SPECIAL FX SECRETS

127

TM & © 1993 UNIVERSAL CITY STUDIOS, INC. & AMBLIN ENTERTAINMENT, INC.

THE TOPPS COMPANY, INC. PRINTED IN U.S.A.

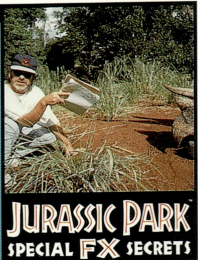

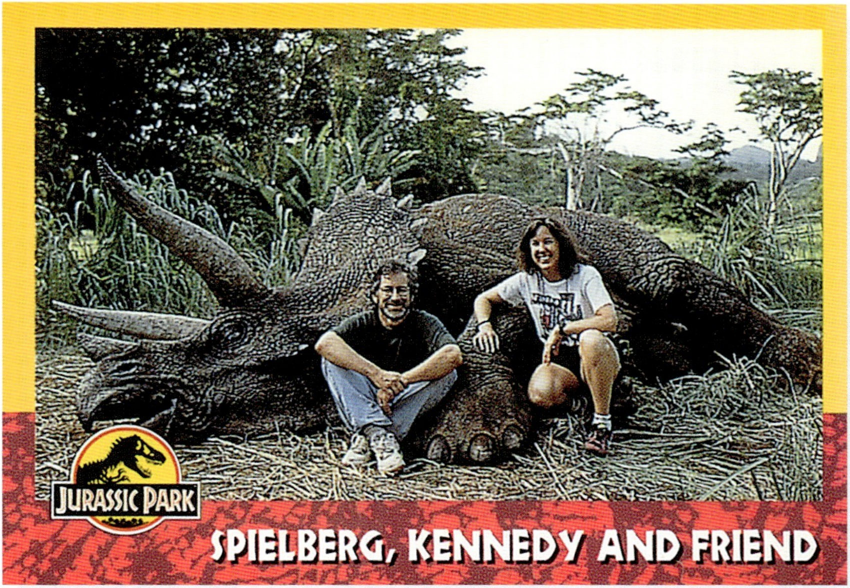
JURASSIC PARK
SPIELBERG, KENNEDY AND FRIEND

Here's a quote from Kathleen Kennedy, longtime producer and current president of Lucasfilm. The downed *Triceratops* served as a striking background prop in this promotional photo of both Spielberg and Kennedy, who seem delighted by it all.

WINSTON'S BRACHIOSAUR
"We built everything first in one fifth scale, to make sure the animal worked mechanically. Then, we used actual aerospace technology (for the full-sized creatures) to make big, lightweight molds. Because when you work this big everything is heavy."
STAN WINSTON, LIVE ACTION DINOSAURS
128
JURASSIC PARK™
SPECIAL FX SECRETS
TM & © 1993 UNIVERSAL CITY STUDIOS, INC. & AMBLIN ENTERTAINMENT, INC.
THE TOPPS COMPANY, INC. PRINTED IN U.S.A.

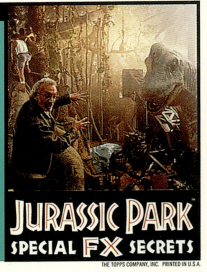

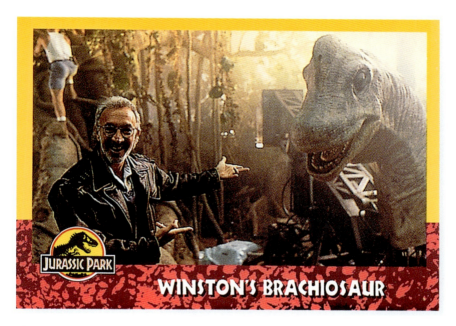

WINSTON'S BRACHIOSAUR

That's Stan (the Man) Winston again, the special effects wizard behind *Jurassic Park*'s ground-breaking and Oscar-winning special effects. Winston, who died in 2008, was regarded by Hollywood's top filmmakers, as were his remarkable FX creations, mostly of the practical on-set variety, which always enhanced their movies.

DAY OF THE RAPTORS
For the scene in which Muldoon meets his grisly end, Stan Winston team member John Rosengrant was required to perform inside a life-sized Raptor suit. The second Raptor featured in the scene (the one Muldoon spots directly in front of him) was simply an insert head, operated by Craig Caton.
JURASSIC PARK™
SPECIAL FX SECRETS
129
TM & © 1993 UNIVERSAL CITY STUDIOS, INC. & AMBLIN ENTERTAINMENT, INC.
THE TOPPS COMPANY, INC. PRINTED IN U.S.A.

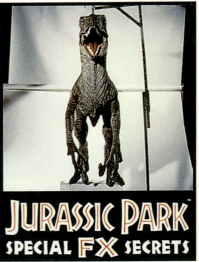

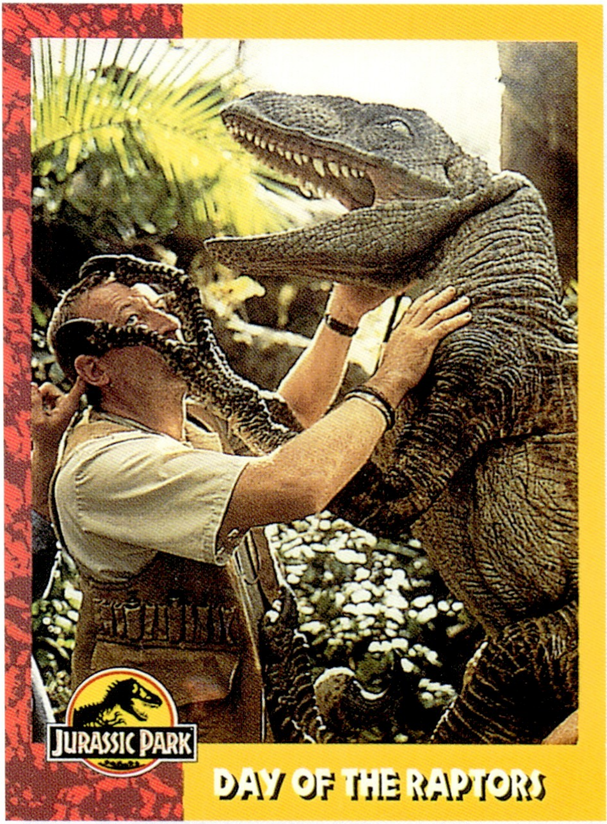
JURASSIC PARK
DAY OF THE RAPTORS

What a great picture! In the movie, self-assured hunter Muldoon (Bob Peck) meets a grisly demise, but it's mostly filmed out of camera range. This canny behind-the-scenes photo shows us the horrific potential of what this scene may have played like on-screen.

THE FANTASTIC REX HEAD
In previous dinosaur epics like KING KONG and BEAST FROM 20,000 FATHOMS, the prehistoric creatures were miniature models brought to cinematic life through stop-motion animation. For JURASSIC PARK, director Steven Spielberg and effects master Stan Winston wanted to "push the envelope" with life-sized, fully articulated animals.
130
TM & © 1993 UNIVERSAL CITY STUDIOS, INC. & AMBLIN ENTERTAINMENT, INC.
JURASSIC PARK™
SPECIAL FX SECRETS
THE TOPPS COMPANY, INC. PRINTED IN U.S.A.

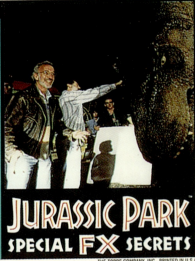

JURASSIC PARK
THE FANTASTIC REX HEAD

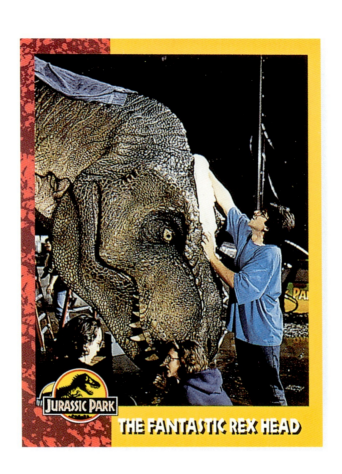

AILING TRICERATOPS SCENE
"Acting with the dinosaurs was wonderful," admits actress Laura Dern. "My favorite scene was the one where I was working with the sick triceratops — she was so beautiful and real, and I was truly moved, as I am in the scene, just by being with her. That creature actually helped me act in the scene and made me fall in love with her."
131
JURASSIC PARK™
SPECIAL FX SECRETS
TM & © 1993 UNIVERSAL CITY STUDIOS, INC. & AMBLIN ENTERTAINMENT, INC.
THE TOPPS COMPANY, INC. PRINTED IN U.S.A.

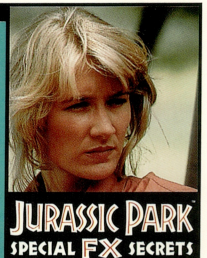

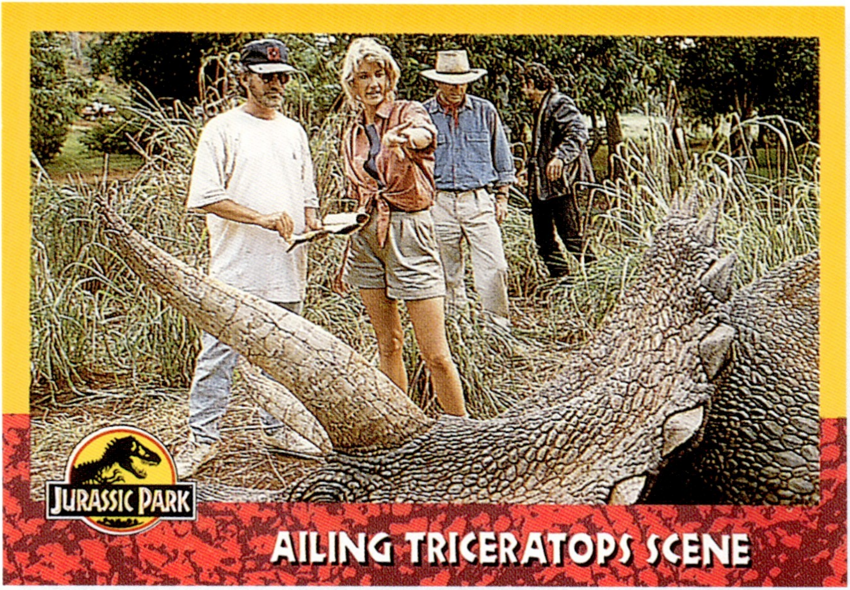
JURASSIC PARK
AILING TRICERATOPS SCENE

KING (QUEEN?) OF THE DINOS

As every schoolkid knows, the T-rex is the king of the dinosaurs...but since every dinosaur in Jurassic Park is a female, this King is actually a Queen! Either way, the Rex is a bonafide superstar. Director Steven Spielberg was so impressed with Rex's initial scene that he altered the film's climax to include a return appearance of the towering terror.

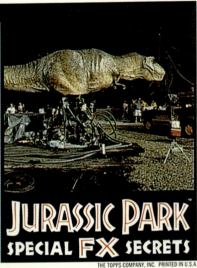

JURASSIC PARK™
SPECIAL FX SECRETS

132

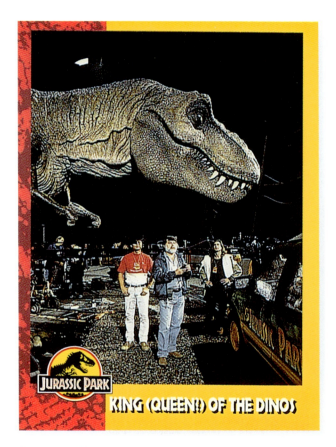

KING (QUEEN!) OF THE DINOS

The full-scale *Tyrannosaurus rex* puppet was truly a marvel to behold. This giant creature was so lifelike, it even scared some of the workers on set. And yes, the Tyrant King was actually a Queen, in keeping with a major plot point of *Jurassic Park*.

OF SCIENCE AND SAURIANS
The JURASSIC PARK storyline ventured into an area of growing controversy — biogenetics for the sake of profit. "It's a big moral question," comments Spielberg. "DNA cloning may be viable, but is it acceptable? Is it right for man to do this, or did dinosaurs have their shot a million years ago?"
133
JURASSIC PARK
SPECIAL FX SECRETS
TM & © 1993 UNIVERSAL CITY STUDIOS, INC. & AMBLIN ENTERTAINMENT, INC.
THE TOPPS COMPANY, INC. PRINTED IN U.S.A.

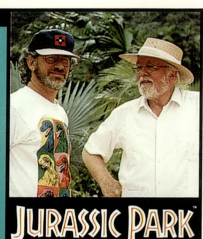

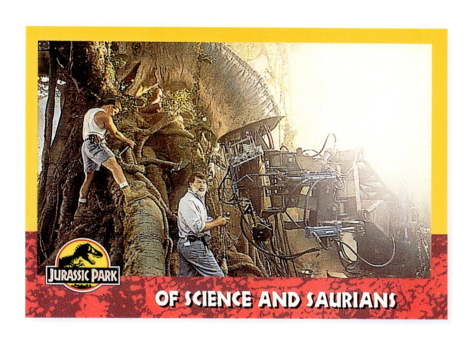

OF SCIENCE AND SAURIANS

THE MASTER DIRECTOR
"This is not science fiction," observes director Steven Spielberg. "It's science eventuality." Spielberg's films are among the most popular in movie history. They include JAWS, E.T., RAIDERS OF THE LOST ARK and CLOSE ENCOUNTERS OF THE THIRD KIND.
134
TM & © 1993 UNIVERSAL CITY STUDIOS, INC. & AMBLIN ENTERTAINMENT, INC.
JURASSIC PARK™
SPECIAL FX SECRETS
THE TOPPS COMPANY, INC. PRINTED IN U.S.A.

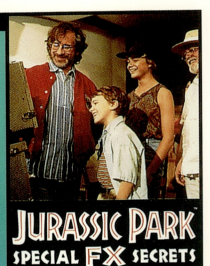

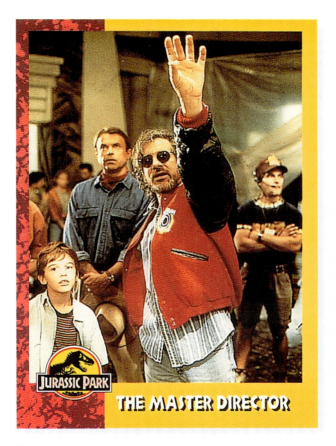

THE MASTER DIRECTOR

Director Steven Spielberg has massed quite a portfolio of now-classic films over the years, making memorable movies in all genres and for all different age groups. Science fiction has always been a favorite subject of his, with pictures like *Close Encounters of the Third Kind* (1977), *E.T. the Extra Terrestrial* (1982), and the 2005 remake of *War of the Worlds* demonstrating his versatility within the genre.

MAN-MADE MONSTERS
Special effects wizard Stan Winston (seen on the front of this card, posing with a Raptor) is no stranger to cinematic monsters: he created the famous "Queen Alien" for James Cameron's ALIENS, the extraterrestrial hunter for PREDATOR, and the elegant demon PUMPKINHEAD.
135
JURASSIC PARK™
SPECIAL FX SECRETS
TM & © 1993 UNIVERSAL CITY STUDIOS, INC. & AMBLIN ENTERTAINMENT, INC.
THE TOPPS COMPANY, INC. PRINTED IN U.S.A.

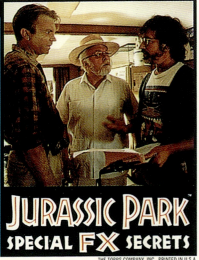

JURASSIC PARK

MAN-MADE MONSTERS

MULDOON AND THE RAPTORS

Director Steven Spielberg discusses a scene with British actor Bob Peck, who portrays Jurassic Park's serious-minded game warden, Robert Muldoon. It is Muldoon who first appreciates the deadliness of these creatures. Peck is an accomplished Shakespearian performer as well as a popular TV actor for the BBC.

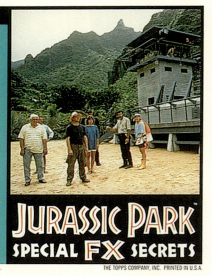

136

JURASSIC PARK™
SPECIAL FX SECRETS

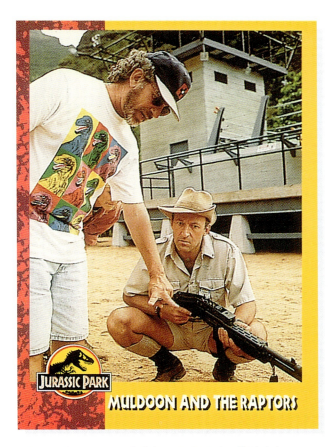

MULDOON AND THE RAPTORS

In *Jurassic Park*, Muldoon finds his weapons to be of little help. The movie is more about respecting these remarkable animals and treating them like an endangered species. In a more extreme sense, perhaps they might also be viewed as the innocent victims of man's uncontrollable hubris.

DIRECTING DINOS AND THEIR PREY
"I knew this was going to be a very difficult movie to make," admits JURASSIC PARK author Michael Crichton. "Steven Spielberg is arguably the most experienced and most successful director of these kinds of movies. And he's really terrific at running the technology rather than letting the technology run him."
137
JURASSIC PARK
SPECIAL FX SECRETS
TM & © 1993 UNIVERSAL CITY STUDIOS, INC. & AMBLIN ENTERTAINMENT, INC.
THE TOPPS COMPANY, INC. PRINTED IN U.S.A.

JURASSIC PARK

DIRECTING DINOS AND THEIR PREY

That's actually FX headman Stan Winston giving instructions to the person operating the dinosaur puppet, an effect that is 100% believable in the finished movie. For years and years, fans would groan about "men in suits" playing dinosaurs, as the superior technique of stop-motion animation was so clearly preferred. But state-of-the-art dinosaur puppets that have been made in recent years happen to be amazingly lifelike. The raptor, Blue, from *Jurassic World* became a popular attraction at Universal Studios Hollywood in 2015, and this realistic-looking puppet was inhabited by a very competent (and no doubt heavily perspiring) actor/athlete.

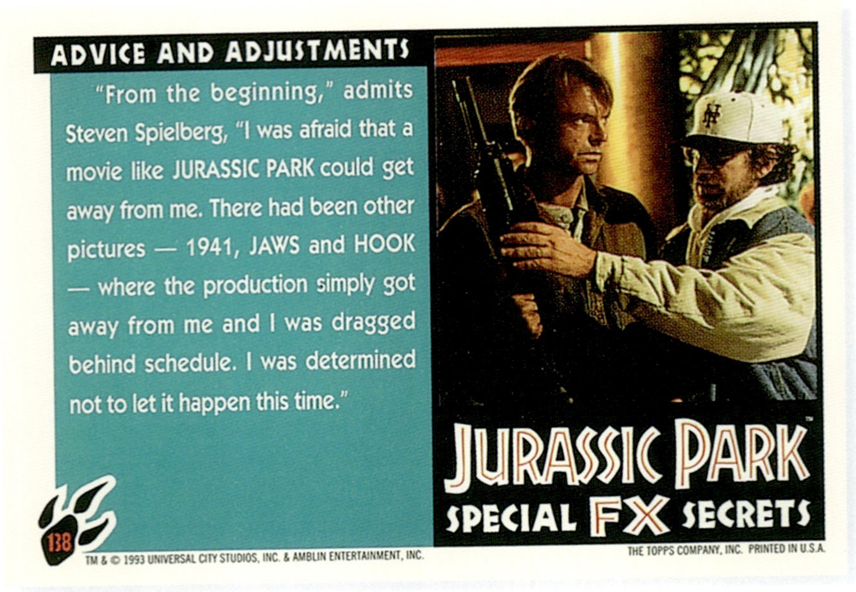

ADVICE AND ADJUSTMENTS
"From the beginning," admits Steven Spielberg, "I was afraid that a movie like JURASSIC PARK could get away from me. There had been other pictures — 1941, JAWS and HOOK — where the production simply got away from me and I was dragged behind schedule. I was determined not to let it happen this time."
138
TM & © 1993 UNIVERSAL CITY STUDIOS, INC. & AMBLIN ENTERTAINMENT, INC.
JURASSIC PARK™
SPECIAL FX SECRETS
THE TOPPS COMPANY, INC. PRINTED IN U.S.A.

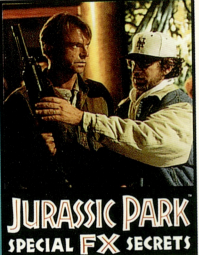

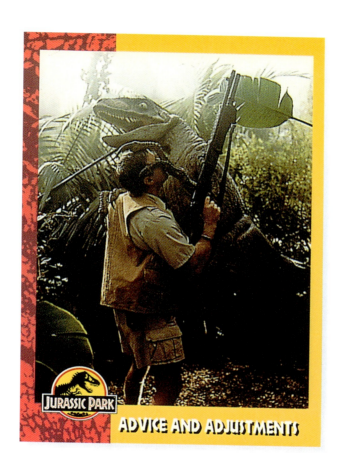

JURASSIC PARK

ADVICE AND ADJUSTMENTS

FILMING THE HATCHERY
Originally, the hatchery scene was to have featured two infant dinosaurs — a hatching triceratops and a somewhat older baby Raptor. "The baby triceratops was going to be a simple finger puppet," explained Stan Winston, "with just its head popping out from the egg."
139
TM & © 1993 UNIVERSAL CITY STUDIOS, INC. & AMBLIN ENTERTAINMENT, INC.
JURASSIC PARK™
SPECIAL FX SECRETS
THE TOPPS COMPANY, INC. PRINTED IN U.S.A.

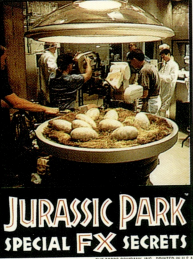

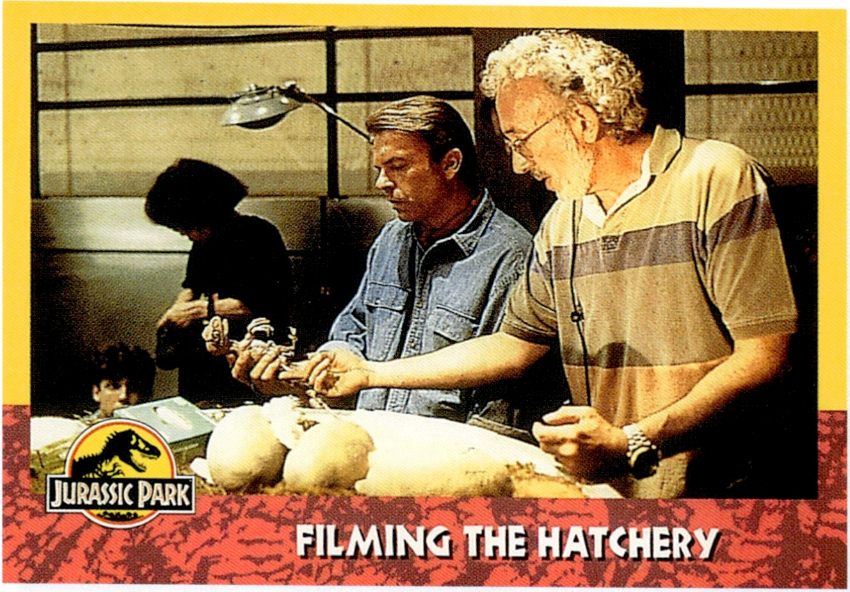
JURASSIC PARK
FILMING THE HATCHERY

INSIDE THE JAWS OF DEATH
Stan Winston art department supervisor John Rosengrant — who also portrayed a Raptor in Muldoon's death scene — airbrushes the inside of T-rex's enormous mouth (card front). The complete Tyrannosaurus prop weighed in at just under 4,000 pounds.
140
JURASSIC PARK™
SPECIAL FX SECRETS
TM & © 1993 UNIVERSAL CITY STUDIOS, INC. & AMBLIN ENTERTAINMENT, INC.
THE TOPPS COMPANY, INC. PRINTED IN U.S.A.

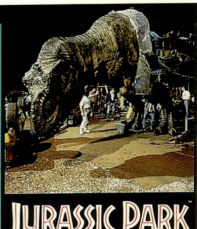

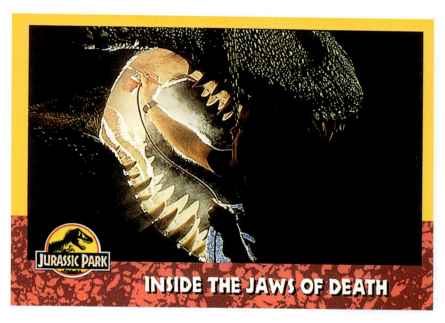

INSIDE THE JAWS OF DEATH

"Jaws of Death," huh? Could I have been subconsciously thinking of Steven Spielberg's other iconic movie, that gem from 1975?

SOOTHING THE SAVAGE BEAST

The exciting musical score for JURASSIC PARK was composed by John Williams, a longtime Spielberg collaborator (everything from the ominous JAWS theme to E.T.'s wondrous background music). "Steven could have been a composer himself," observes Williams. "He has that rhythmic sense in his whole being..."

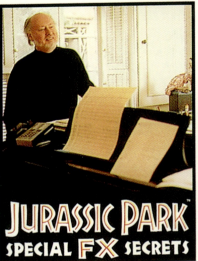

141

JURASSIC PARK
SPECIAL FX SECRETS

TM & © 1993 UNIVERSAL CITY STUDIOS, INC. & AMBLIN ENTERTAINMENT, INC.   THE TOPPS COMPANY, INC. PRINTED IN U.S.A.

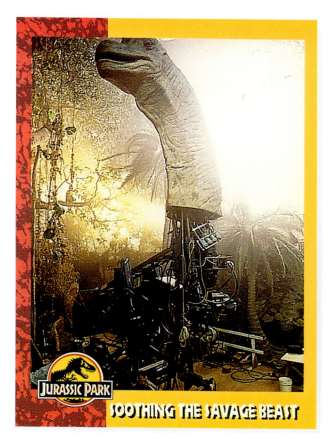

SOOTHING THE SAVAGE BEAST

Now here's a clever caption for you. What is it exactly that soothes these mighty animals? Music, of course. And who composed the memorable score for *Jurassic Park*? That would be the legendary John Williams. The theme for *Jurassic Park* is among Williams's most popular and hummable works, celebrating the wonder of scientific progress with just a hint of "pride before a fall" around the edges.

THE DIRECTOR'S DIRECTOR
Steven Spielberg admits being a fan of past dinosaur movies, but he hoped JP would wind up being something very different: "I never thought I wanted to do a dinosaur movie better than anyone else's, but I did want my dinosaur movie to be the most realistic of them all..."
JURASSIC PARK
JURASSIC PARK™
SPECIAL FX SECRETS
142
TM & © 1993 UNIVERSAL CITY STUDIOS, INC. & AMBLIN ENTERTAINMENT, INC.
THE TOPPS COMPANY, INC. PRINTED IN U.S.A.

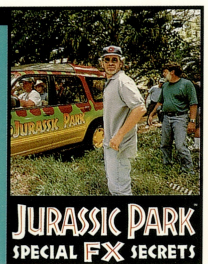

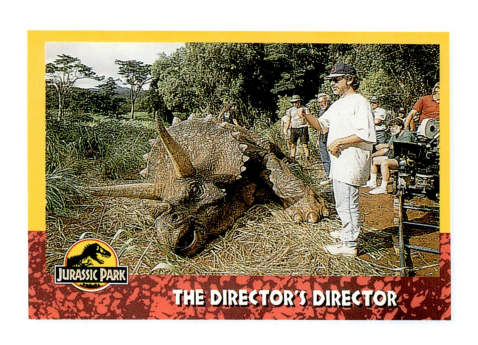

THE DIRECTOR'S DIRECTOR

BRINGING REX TO LIFE
After almost two years in the making, the full-size, hydraulically actuated T-rex was finally ready for the cameras. It was the largest creature prop the Stan Winston studio had ever built and the first — by Winston or anyone else — to be mounted on a motion simulator to achieve spectacular body movements.
143
TM & © 1993 UNIVERSAL CITY STUDIOS, INC. & AMBLIN ENTERTAINMENT, INC.
JURASSIC PARK™
SPECIAL FX SECRETS
THE TOPPS COMPANY, INC. PRINTED IN U.S.A.

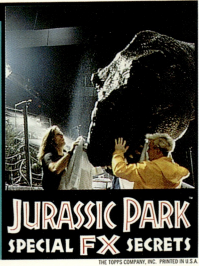

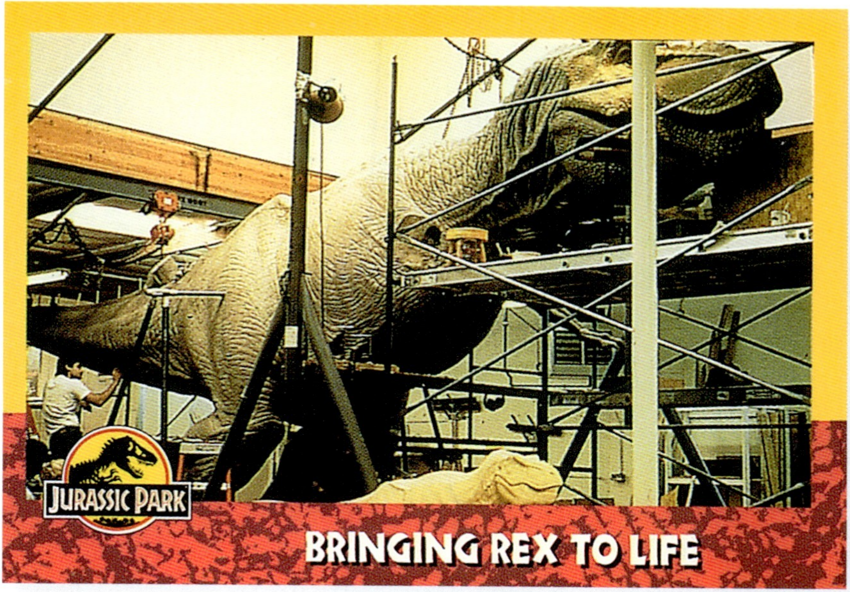
JURASSIC PARK
BRINGING REX TO LIFE

Here's the *T. rex* again, in a couple of different incarnations. As mentioned in my card copy on the back, this is the largest full-size puppet prop Stan Winston (or anyone) ever conceived. Notice the small-scale sculpted version directly below.

THIS PROJECT HAS LEGS...
To film the exciting T-rex attack sequence, Spielberg moved his crew to Stage 16 at Warner Brothers — one of the biggest sound stages in Hollywood. The flooring was built over a six foot deep concrete pit, which afforded a solid mounting place for the T-rex simulator platform.
JURASSIC PARK™
SPECIAL FX SECRETS
144
TM & © 1993 UNIVERSAL CITY STUDIOS, INC. & AMBLIN ENTERTAINMENT, INC.
THE TOPPS COMPANY, INC. PRINTED IN U.S.A.

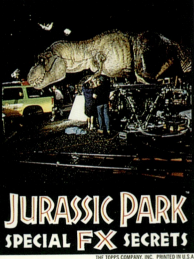

JURASSIC PARK

THIS PROJECT HAS LEGS...

Question: Can a trading card caption ever be too corny? At Topps we have been known to push the envelope in this department now and again, to a point where groaners are so stale and silly, they actually become hip. In any event, I'm very proud of this leggy gag of mine, which practically wrote itself.

MASSIVE UNDERTAKING
"We had to come up with a way to support the weight and all the g-forces that would be generated when the T-rex was moving," explains Michael Lantieri (Special Dinosaur Effects). "One of the things Steven had emphasized was that he wanted the Rex to move fast — and that meant that a tremendous amount of force was going to be generated."
145
TM & © 1993 UNIVERSAL CITY STUDIOS, INC. & AMBLIN ENTERTAINMENT, INC.
JURASSIC PARK™
SPECIAL FX SECRETS
THE TOPPS COMPANY, INC. PRINTED IN U.S.A.

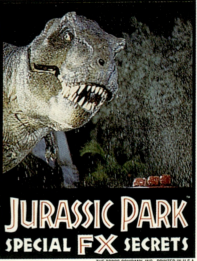

JURASSIC PARK
MASSIVE UNDERTAKING

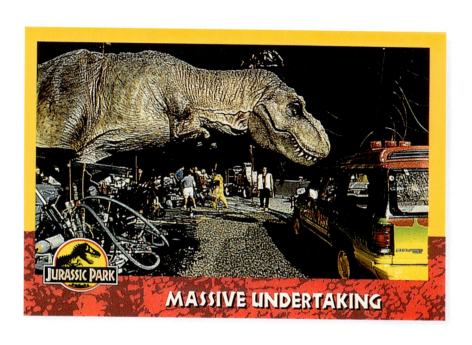

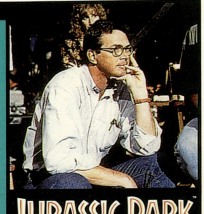

CRICHTON'S BRAINCHILD
"You decide you'll control nature, and from that moment on you're in deep trouble because you can't do it. You can make a boat, but you can't make the ocean. You can make an airplane, but you can't make the air. Your powers are much less than your dreams would have you believe."
MICHAEL CRICHTON, AUTHOR
146
JURASSIC PARK™
SPECIAL FX SECRETS
TM & © 1993 UNIVERSAL CITY STUDIOS, INC. & AMBLIN ENTERTAINMENT, INC.
THE TOPPS COMPANY, INC. PRINTED IN U.S.A.

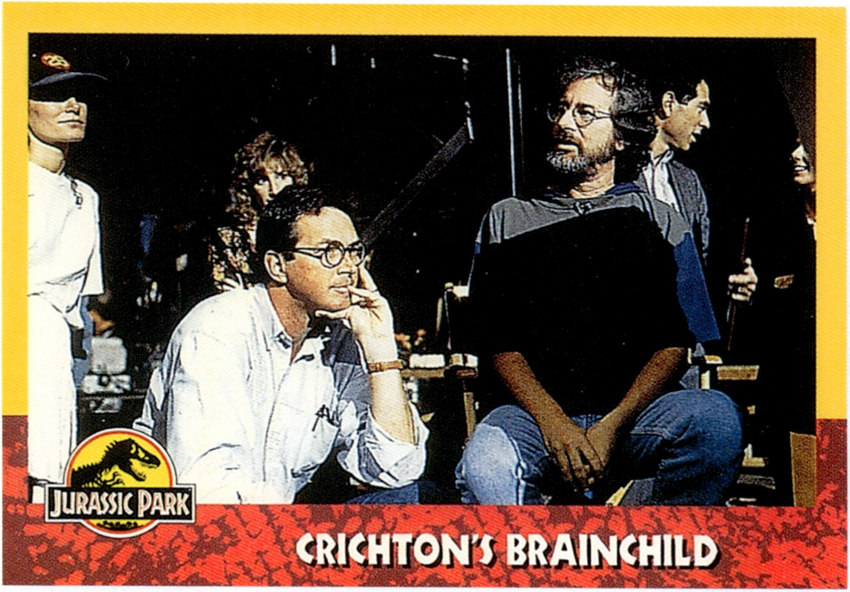
JURASSIC PARK
CRICHTON'S BRAINCHILD

Here's Michael Crichton, author of *Jurassic Park*, on set. Crichton happened to be a deft filmmaker in addition to being a bestselling author (e.g. *Westworld* in 1973, which features a familiar setting—theme parks that have the adverse intentions of their creators). Crichton was fully aware of the difficulties in making a sci-fi movie of this kind, however, and knew Steven Spielberg would be the right director for this particular challenge.

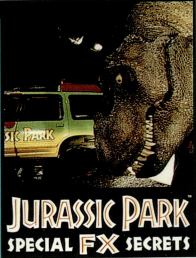

MORE THAN A MERE MONSTER
"We were afforded the luxury of being able to develop the dinosaur characters in extensive tests. Usually it's not so much of an issue because the filmmakers are just treating these characters as monsters. But for JP we had an opportunity to show dinosaurs as they really were, as living animals..."
PHIL TIPPETT, DINOSAUR SUPERVISOR
147
JURASSIC PARK™
SPECIAL FX SECRETS
TM & © 1993 UNIVERSAL CITY STUDIOS, INC. & AMBLIN ENTERTAINMENT, INC.
THE TOPPS COMPANY, INC. PRINTED IN U.S.A.

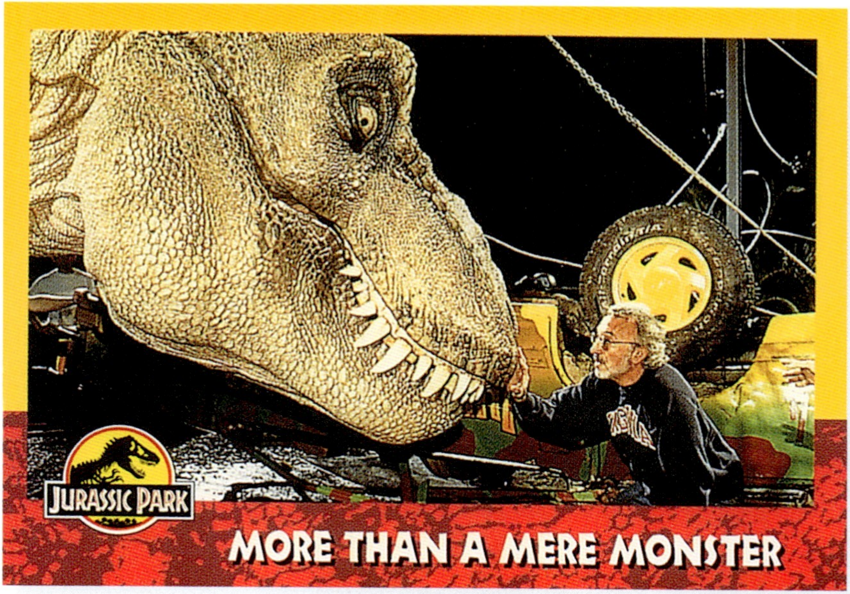
JURASSIC PARK
MORE THAN A MERE MONSTER

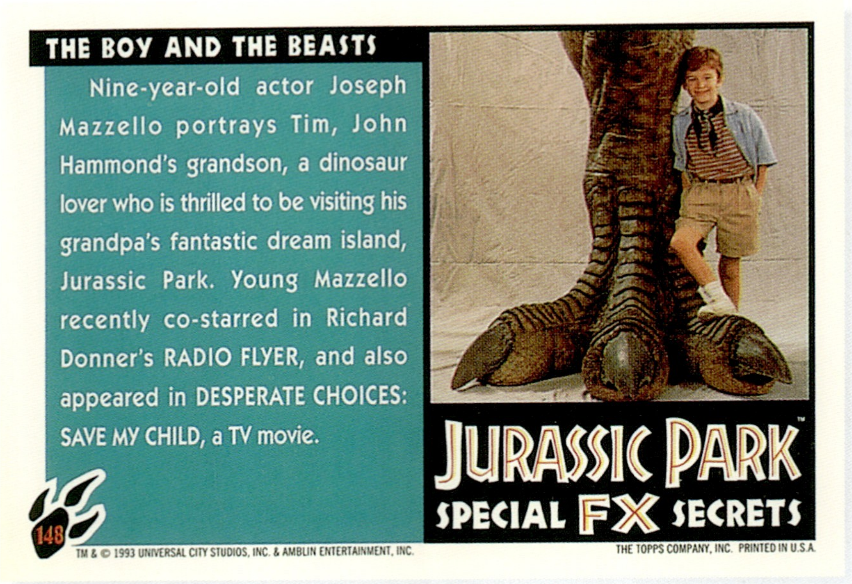
THE BOY AND THE BEASTS
Nine-year-old actor Joseph Mazzello portrays Tim, John Hammond's grandson, a dinosaur lover who is thrilled to be visiting his grandpa's fantastic dream island, Jurassic Park. Young Mazzello recently co-starred in Richard Donner's RADIO FLYER, and also appeared in DESPERATE CHOICES: SAVE MY CHILD, a TV movie.
JURASSIC PARK™
SPECIAL FX SECRETS
148
TM & © 1993 UNIVERSAL CITY STUDIOS, INC. & AMBLIN ENTERTAINMENT, INC.
THE TOPPS COMPANY, INC. PRINTED IN U.S.A.

JURASSIC PARK

THE BOY AND THE BEASTS

Time and again, filmmaker Steven Spielberg has demonstrated his facility for directing child actors. In *E.T.*, a young boy named Elliot became the focus of the story. *Jurassic Park* placed two likeable youngsters in an equally fantastic situation, but one fraught with more danger. Here, Spielberg has a helpful chat with actor Joseph Mazzello, who played John Hammond's soon to be imperiled grandson, Tim.

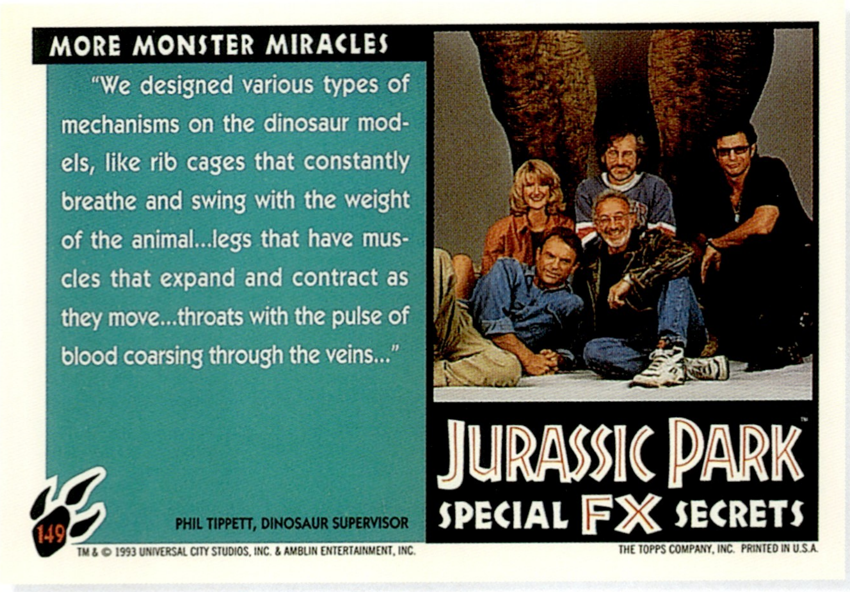
MORE MONSTER MIRACLES
"We designed various types of mechanisms on the dinosaur models, like rib cages that constantly breathe and swing with the weight of the animal...legs that have muscles that expand and contract as they move...throats with the pulse of blood coarsing through the veins..."
PHIL TIPPETT, DINOSAUR SUPERVISOR
149
JURASSIC PARK™
SPECIAL FX SECRETS
TM & © 1993 UNIVERSAL CITY STUDIOS, INC. & AMBLIN ENTERTAINMENT, INC.
THE TOPPS COMPANY, INC. PRINTED IN U.S.A.

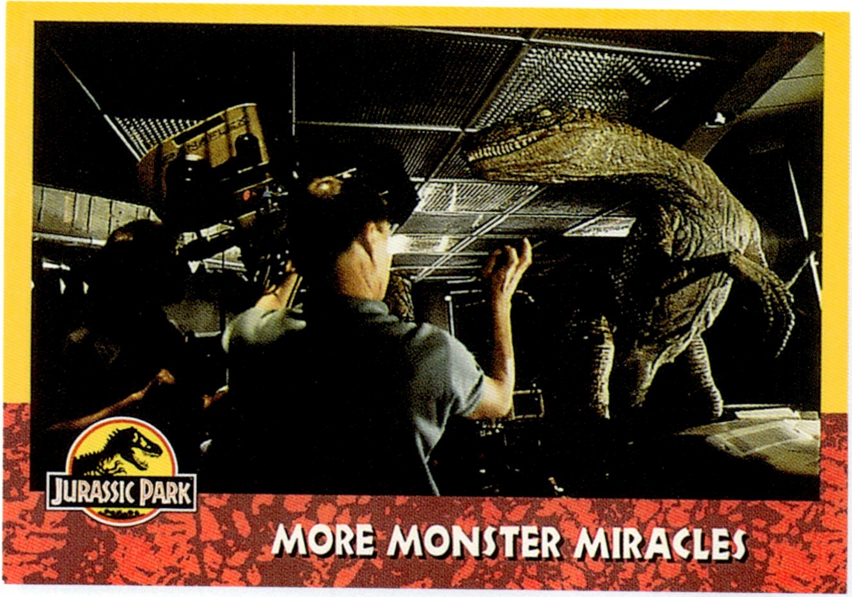
JURASSIC PARK
MORE MONSTER MIRACLES

LIGHTS! CAMERA! DINO-ACTION!

For Dennis Nedry's shocking death scene, Stan Winston's technicians developed a full-body Spitter puppet, with interchangeable heads to accommodate specific actions and the various configurations of the animal's cowl. Hopping insert legs were also constructed for the creature's initial approach.

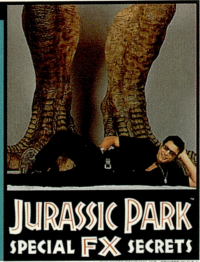

JURASSIC PARK™
SPECIAL FX SECRETS

150

TM & © 1993 UNIVERSAL CITY STUDIOS, INC. & AMBLIN ENTERTAINMENT, INC.   THE TOPPS COMPANY, INC. PRINTED IN U.S.A.

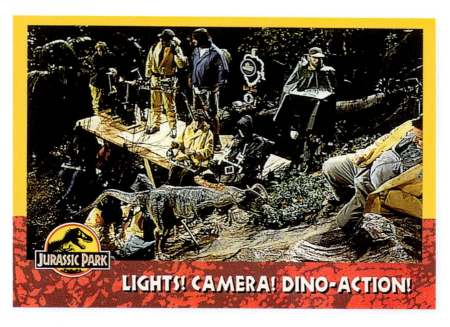

LIGHTS! CAMERA! DINO-ACTION!

It's so cool that we were able to include several shots of the "shocking" *Dilophosaurus* attack scene. It's hard to believe that this lifelike creature was not a computer-generated effect, but a brilliantly designed and manipulated puppet, occupying the same physical space as the actor.

BIGGER (AND NASTIER) THAN LIFE
"Short of the original KING KONG, which was a pure fantasy and done over 50 years ago, and some of the Ray Harryhausen films where the emphasis was on a thrashing, snarling, generic approach, no one's ever tried to do anything like JURASSIC PARK before."
PHIL TIPPET, DINOSAUR SUPERVISOR
151
JURASSIC PARK™
SPECIAL FX SECRETS
TM & © 1993 UNIVERSAL CITY STUDIOS, INC. & AMBLIN ENTERTAINMENT, INC.
THE TOPPS COMPANY, INC. PRINTED IN U.S.A.

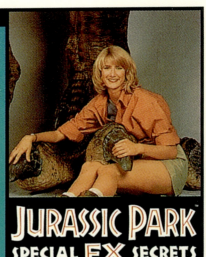

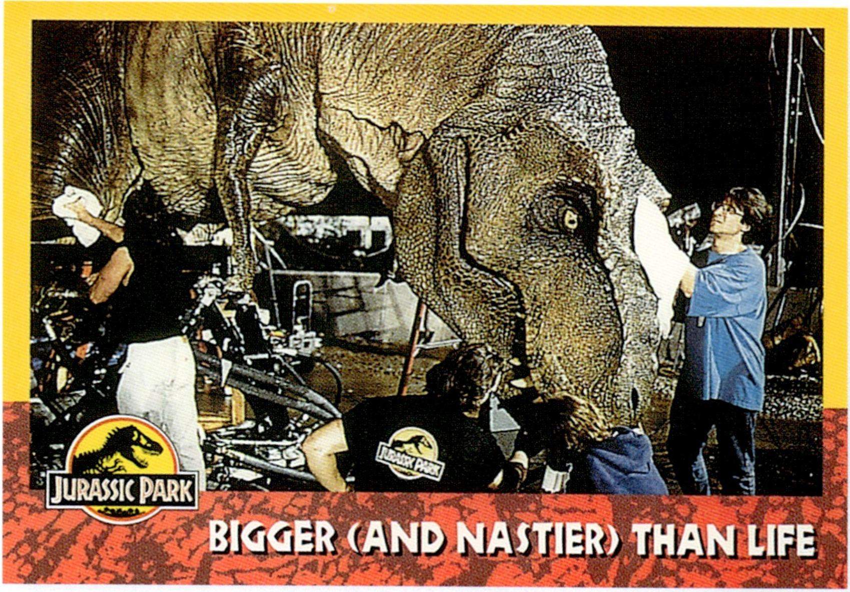
JURASSIC PARK
BIGGER (AND NASTIER) THAN LIFE

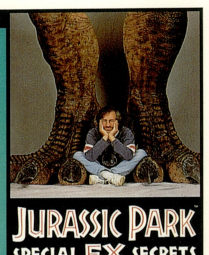

CINEMA'S GREATEST SHOWMAN
Director Steven Spielberg has earned a reputation as one of the world's most respected and successful talents. He has directed and/or produced six of the top twenty films of all time (JURASSIC PARK will make seven). His classic E.T. is still the biggest grossing film in the history of motion pictures.
152
TM & © 1993 UNIVERSAL CITY STUDIOS, INC. & AMBLIN ENTERTAINMENT, INC.
JURASSIC PARK™
SPECIAL FX SECRETS
THE TOPPS COMPANY, INC. PRINTED IN U.S.A.

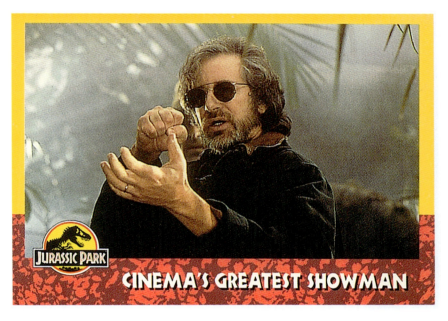

JURASSIC PARK

CINEMA'S GREATEST SHOWMAN

For those of us who came of age during the '70s and '80s, the name Steven Spielberg meant wonderment on the screen that very few filmmakers could match. When he and his good friend George Lucas collaborated to create the *Indiana Jones* franchise, it was an ideal blending of visionary talents. Spielberg continued to develop as a director as the years passed, tackling more-adult movie fare like *Schindler's List* (1993), which finally earned him Oscar recognition.

A WHALE OF A TAIL

Once sculpted, the T-rex was sliced into pieces for mold-making and the subsequent casting of foam rubber skins. An impressive assemblage of welded steel and hydraulics eventually served as both skeleton and muscles for the gigantic dinosaur.

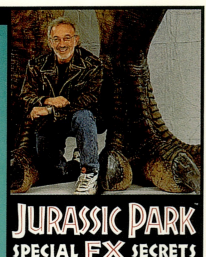

JURASSIC PARK™
SPECIAL FX SECRETS

153

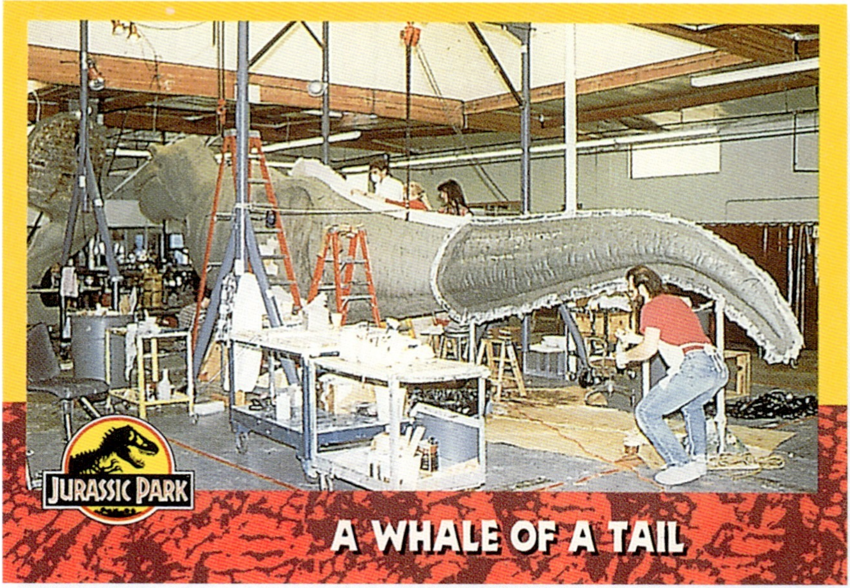
JURASSIC PARK
A WHALE OF A TAIL

Yikes! That really is some tail . . .

ANOTHER WALK IN THE PARK?
Will there be a sequel to JURASSIC PARK? At the time of this writing, no one connected with the project will say for sure. The film has been breaking box office records since the day it opened...it's earned over 200 million dollars domestically after only four weeks!
JURASSIC PARK
SPECIAL FX SECRETS
154
TM & © 1993 UNIVERSAL CITY STUDIOS, INC. & AMBLIN ENTERTAINMENT, INC.
THE TOPPS COMPANY, INC. PRINTED IN U.S.A.

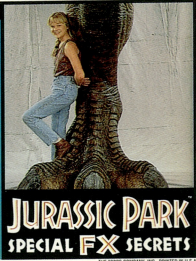

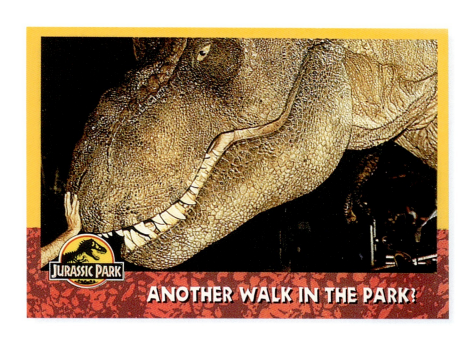

ANOTHER WALK IN THE PARK?

STICKER CARDS

JURASSIC PARK
T-REX
RAMPAGE
PEEL

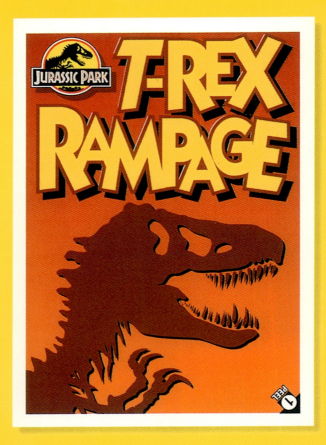

Topps would often get adventurous with its sticker designs, particularly when original lettering or slogans were involved. I can't exactly remember where "T-Rex Rampage" came from, although I suspect that it (and some of the others in this group) may have been lifted directly from the style guide.

2
PEEL
JURASSIC PARK

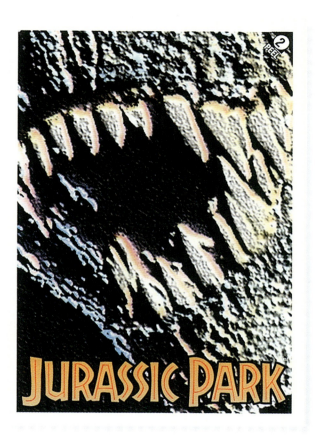

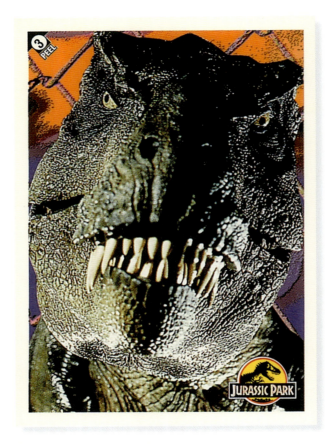

The expression "in your face" takes on terrifying new meaning, as an inquisitive *T. rex* stares directly at us.

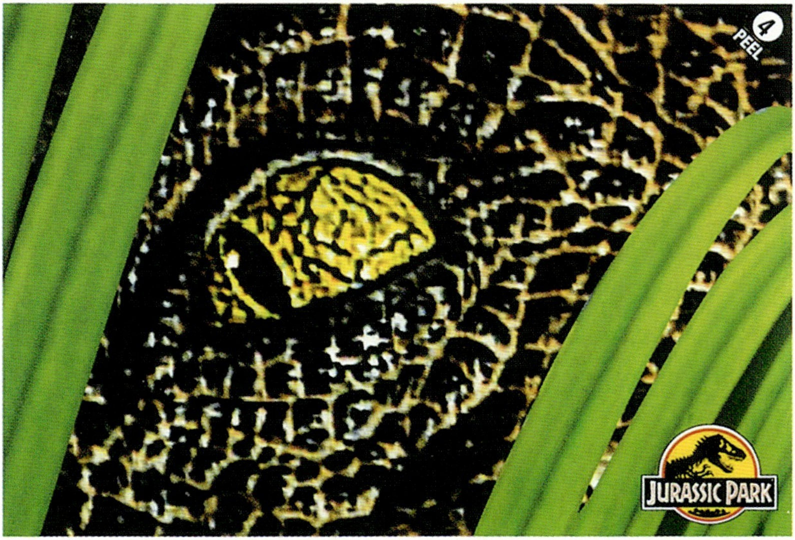
4
PEEL
JURASSIC PARK

JURASSIC PARK
CAUTION
KEEP WINDOWS UP!
PEEL
5

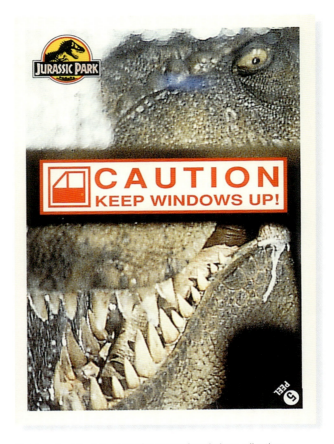

Here's a nice blending of graphic gimmick and photo, all rather artfully done.

6
PEEL
JURASSIC PARK

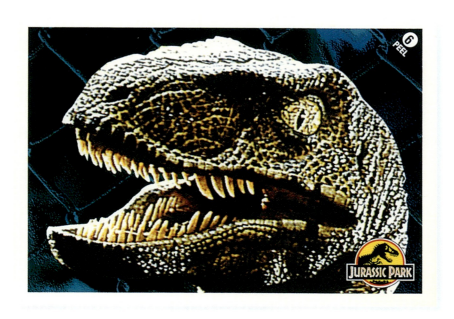

JURASSIC PARK
7
PEEL
RAP
ATTACK!

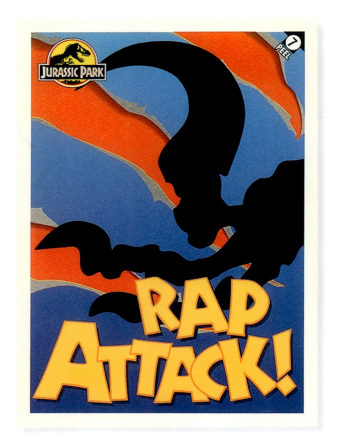

This foreboding image came from the official Universal style guide for *Jurassic Park*, which offered companies like Topps assorted images, designs, and other graphics to adorn their various products, creating a brand unity.

RAP
PACK
8
PEEL
JURASSIC PARK

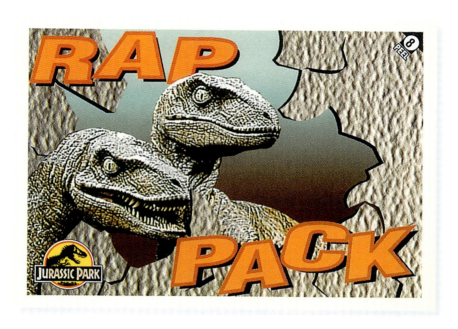

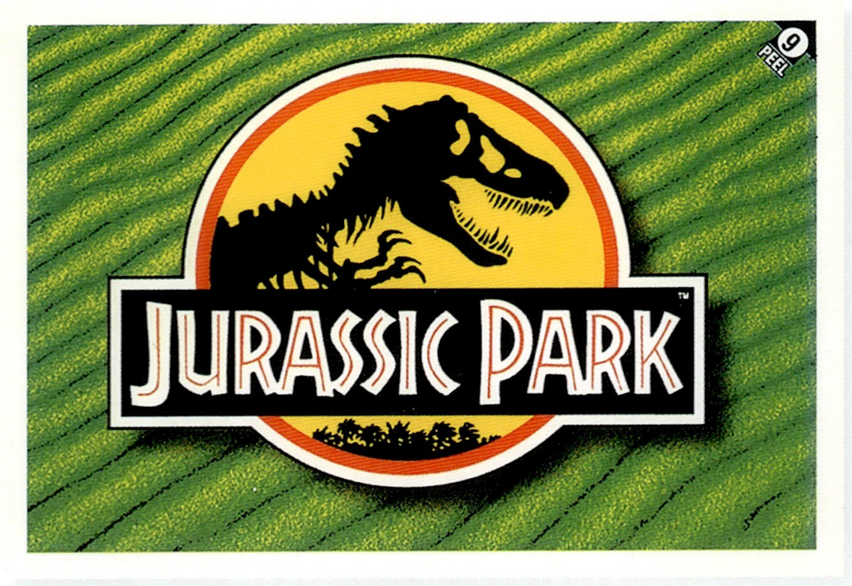
9
PEEL
JURASSIC PARK™

Sometimes simple is best. In the 1950s or '60s, *Jurassic Park* would have had a poster campaign with beautifully rendered dinosaurs tearing away at one another. Ironically, a simple but powerful and distinctive logo, like the *rex*-head silhouette by Chip Kidd from the cover of the bestselling book, would prove more effective.

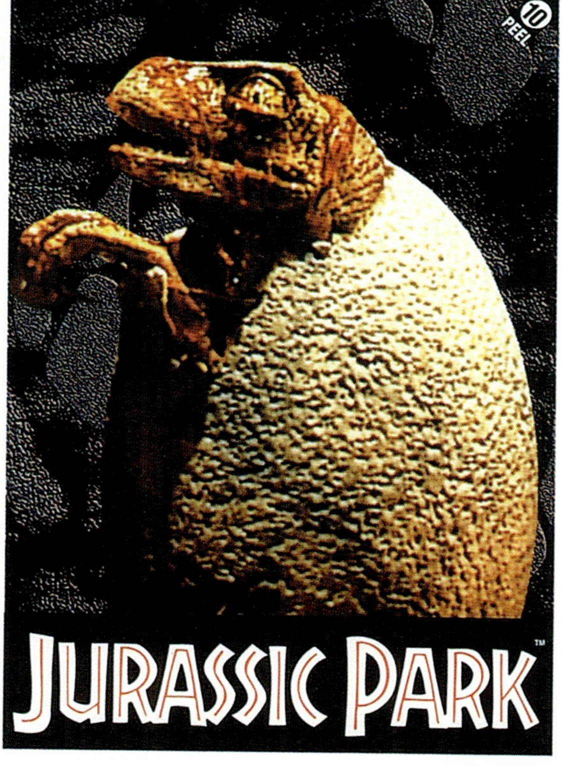
10
PEEL
JURASSIC PARK™

As with Series 1, Series 2 included eleven sticker cards: ten puzzle cards, plus a key showing the image the card backs formed when put together. This time around, the puzzle image comes from card no. 121, "JP's Friendly Giant."

JURASSIC PARK
SPITTER!
PEEL

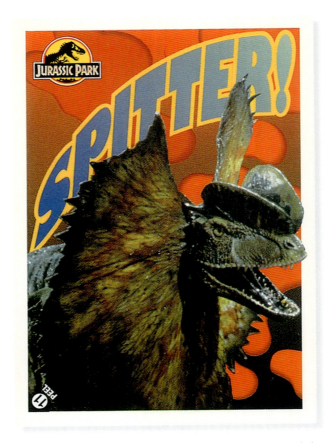

"Spitter" gets her own logo! I must say, she's earned it, having provided *Jurassic Park* with one of its most memorable sequences. Note the blood stains worked into our background design—a clue to this dinosaur's nature.

COLLECT ALL 10 CARDS OF PUZZLE A.
Topps
JP JURASSIC PARK
HERE IS WHAT YOUR COMPLETED
YELLOW BORDER PICTURE WILL LOOK LIKE:
TM & © 1993 UNIVERSAL CITY STUDIOS, INC. & AMBLIN ENTERTAINMENT, INC.
THE TOPPS COMPANY, INC. PRINTED IN U.S.A.

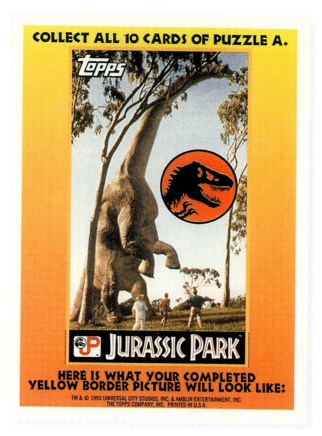

"Are you sure this image will take the huge blow-up?" I asked Ben Solomon while I was visiting Topps headquarters in New York. He looked at the file and nodded yes, which was rare for the highly critical veteran head of our art department. But I loved the shot and desperately wanted it for our puzzle gimmick. Unlike the celluloid blow-ups, which would become grainy, this digital frame wound up looking really good in its oversized form.

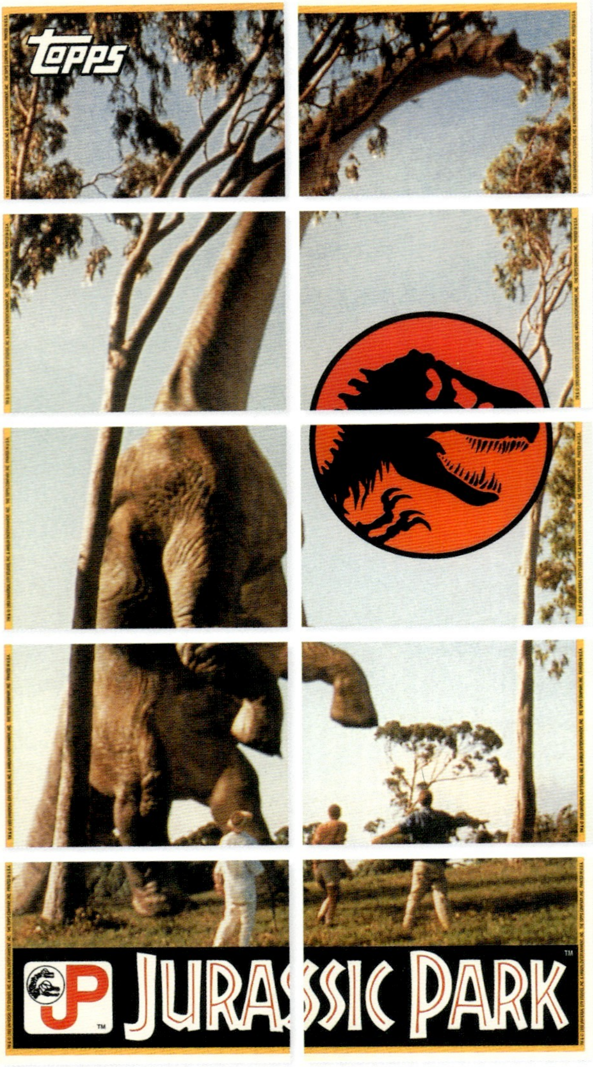
Topps
JP
JURASSIC PARK

DELUXE GOLD SERIES COMIC ART CARDS

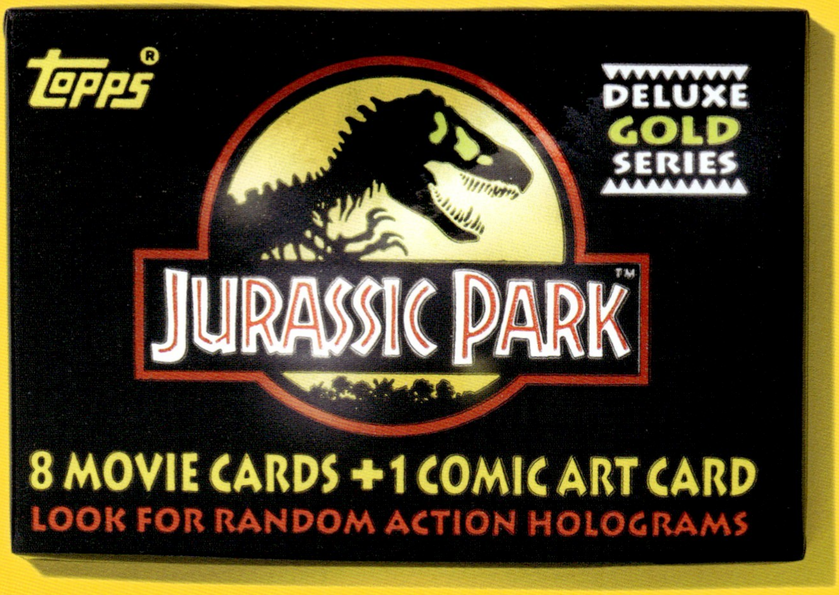
topps®
DELUXE
GOLD
SERIES
JURASSIC PARK™
8 MOVIE CARDS +1 COMIC ART CARD
LOOK FOR RANDOM ACTION HOLOGRAMS

In 1993, Topps released the Deluxe Gold Series. This follow-up set included the base cards from Series 1 and 2, now with the addition of gold foil logos, as well as the same four hologram cards. Unique to the box was a set of ten comic art cards in place of the sticker cards. Each of these ten cards, shown on the following pages, showcase *Jurassic Park*–inspired art by a different comics artist.

JURASSIC PARK

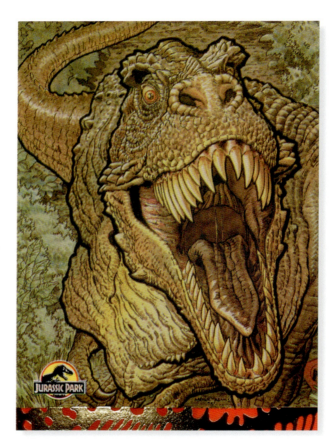

Art by Arthur Adams

BRUNNER
JURASSIC PARK

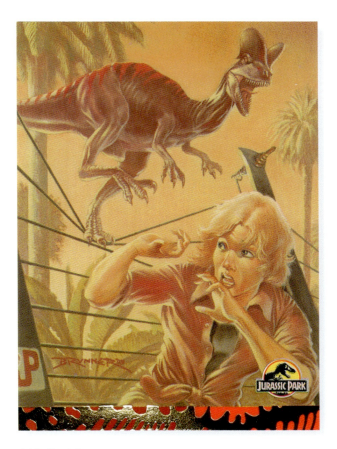

Art by Frank Brunner

WARNING
BIOLOGICAL
MATERIAL
JURASSIC PARK

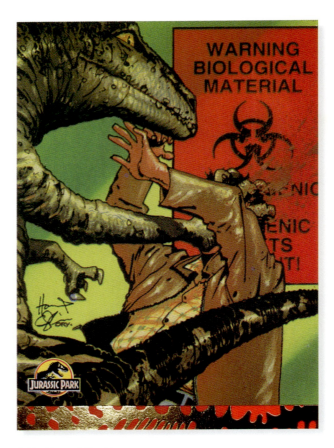

Art by Howard Chaykin

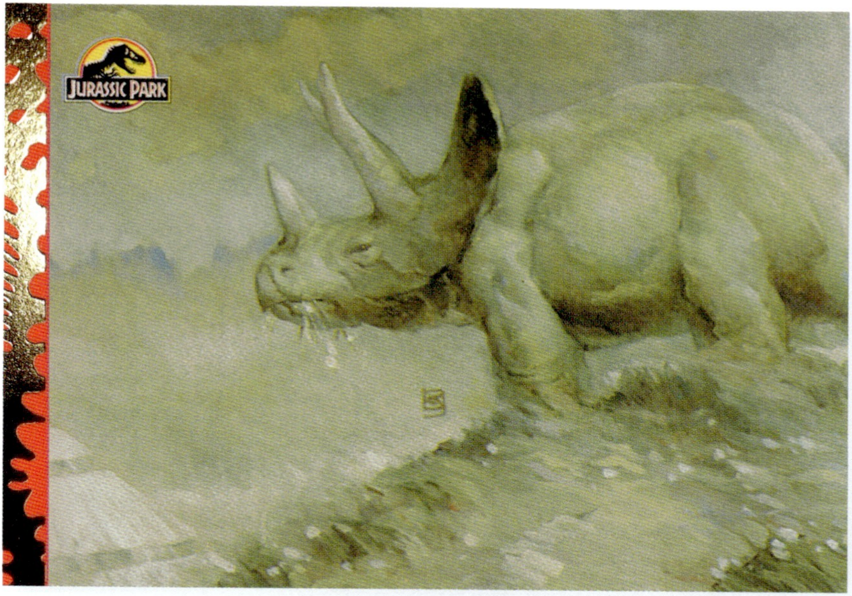
JURASSIC PARK

Art by Jeffrey Jones

Nelson
JURASSIC PARK

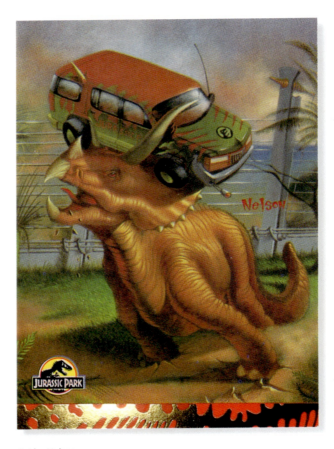

Art by Nelson

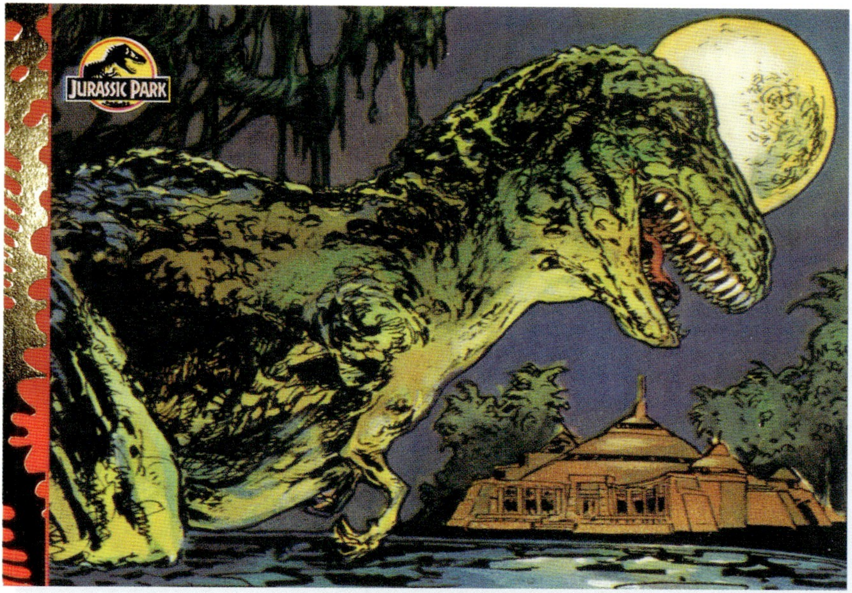
JURASSIC PARK

Art by Mark Pacella

JURASSIC PARK

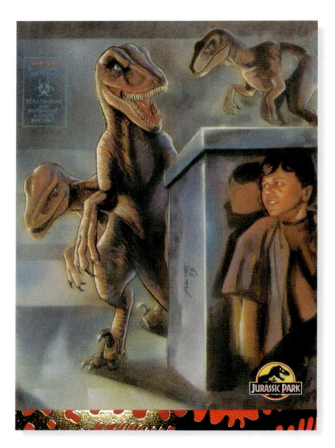

Art by Jason Palmer

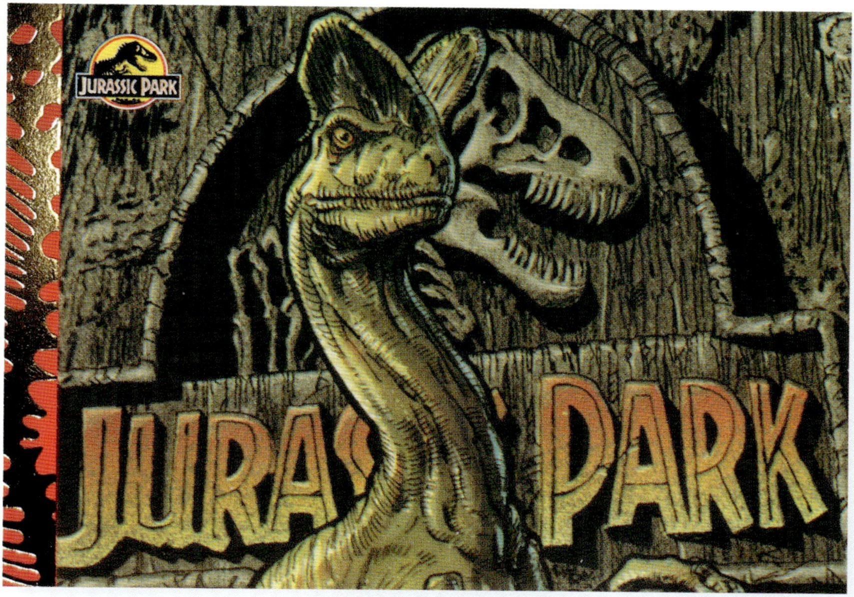
JURASSIC PARK
JURAS
PARK

Art by Joe Quesada

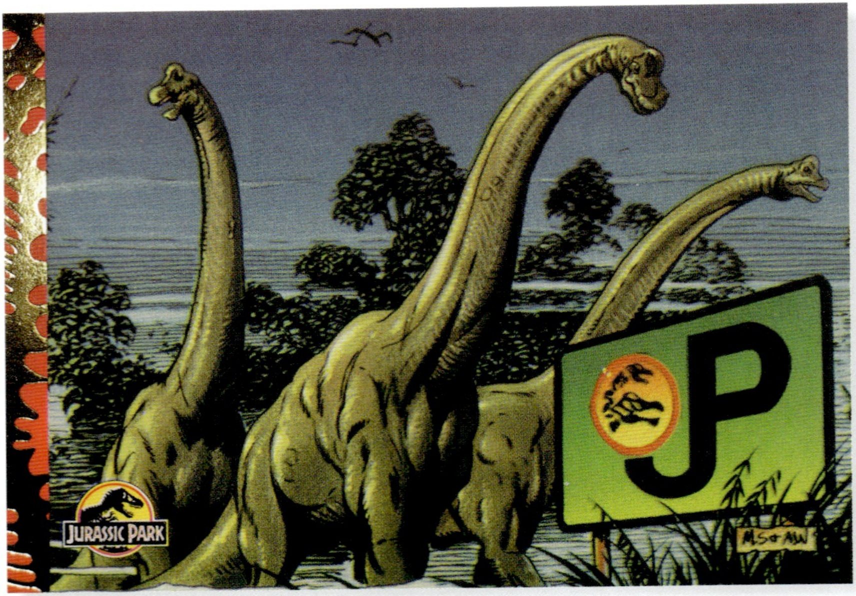
JURASSIC PARK
JP

Art by Mark Schultz and Al Williamson

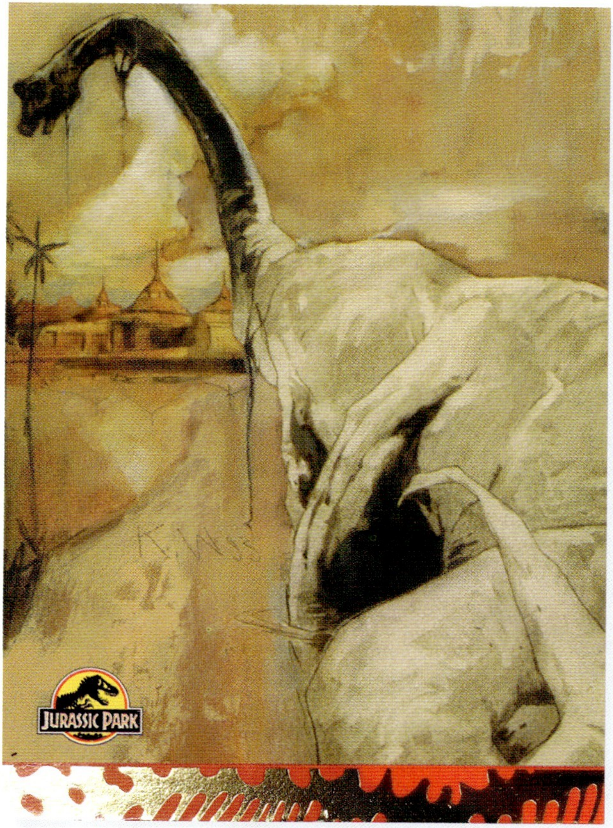
JURASSIC PARK

Art by Kent Williams

JUST THE HEAD?
(a)
po
prf
ps
n
sq
pm
qj
sa
(b)
(c)
pm
m
v
pal
prf
po
f
ect
j
qj
sq
p
q
bo
JURASSIC
PARK
MICHAEL CRICHTON

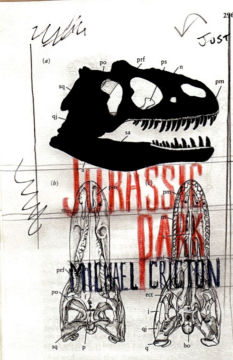

Figure 14-14. SKULL OF *ALLOSAURUS*. (*a*) Lateral, (*b*) dorsal, and (*c*) palatal views. Abbreviations as in Figure 8-3. *From Madsen, 1976.*

vertebrae and a single antorbital opening. The femur is slightly longer than the tibia.

The early megalosaurs radiated during the Jurassic and led to specialized forms that included *Spinosaurus* from the Upper Cretaceous and its relatives, which had neural spines of the trunk vertebrae that were 2 meters long, and the Upper Jurassic *Ceratosaurus,* which had a short "horn" that was borne on the nasal bones (Stromer, 1915; Gilmore, 1920).

Figure 14-15. THE GIGANTIC UPPER CRETACEOUS THEROPOD *TYRANNOSAURUS,* WHICH REACHED A HEIGHT OF 6 METERS. The forelimbs are much shorter than those of *Allosaurus* and have only two digits. *From Osborn, 1916.*

The upper Jurassic genus *Allosaurus* is the best-known representative of a conservative lineage that extends into the Upper Cretaceous. *Allosaurus* reached 12 meters in length and was among the most powerful carnivores of its time (Figure 14-13; see page 295). The body was strengthened to support the extra weight, and the sacrum had five fused vertebrae.

The skull is high and laterally compressed; the orbital opening is triangular and smaller than the principal antorbital fenestra (Figure 14-14). The teeth are long, laterally compressed, and recurved. In contrast with more primitive megalosaurs, the cervical vertebrae have well-ossified anterior condyles that contribute to well-defined ball-and-socket joints between the vertebrae. The more posterior trunk vertebrae retain a shallowly amphicoelous configuration. The tail is long, and the posterior prezygapophyses are considerably elongated.

The forelimb is considerably shorter than the rear limb and could not possibly have supported the body. Only three digits of the manus are retained. Each has a long recurved claw. Metatarsals II, III, and IV are closely integrated elements. The first digit, like that of birds, was oriented posteriorly.

Tyrannosaurids

The gigantic tyrannosaurids of the Upper Cretaceous were the largest of all theropods (Figure 14-15). Specializations of this family include the further reduction in the length of the forelimbs (which could not have reached the mouth) and the retention of only two functional digits, the first and second, which bear respectively two and three phalanges.

The skull is distinguished by the shape of the parietals, which form a sharp sagittal crest between the upper

OR UPPER ~~WHOLE~~ BODY?
JURASSIC
PARK
MICHAEL
CRICHTON

LOOK SHARP.

BY CHIP KIDD

"Think about what happened with *Jaws*. We need to do *that*."

Knopf editor in chief Sonny Mehta uttered this to me while exhaling a puff of smoke, elbow in arm, leaning back in his chair, staring out the window of his office (which was precisely twice the size of my apartment at the time). We were discussing the direction we should take with the book jacket of a new manuscript we had just received from Michael Crichton called *Jurassic Park*.

It was the summer of 1989. I was a junior staff book designer who had scarcely been working there for three years. I was twenty-five years old.

"Right," I said. Though I wanted to say, "I really don't know what you mean by that." The look on my face must have said it for me.

"The book jacket for *Jaws*," he continued, coolly (he said *everything* coolly), "became the image for the movie poster."

It did? I was familiar with the *Jaws* one-sheet for the film, of course, but I didn't realize it was a take on the original hardcover book jacket published by Doubleday in 1974. I had read the mass-market

Opposite: Jacket sketches by Chip Kidd drawn in colored pencil and ink on page 296 of *Vertebrate Paleontology and Evolution*, W. H. Freeman and company, 1989

paperback in junior high, and that had the image from the movie poster on the front. But a little digging proved that it was based on the jacket of the first edition hardcover.

Regardless, we already knew that the same director, Steven Spielberg, had optioned *Jurassic Park*, and it quickly sunk in what Sonny was asking me to do.

And *that* would be totally, utterly impossible.

There was just no way that, for this project, I would be able to make anything as iconic as that shark image. The idea was so ridiculous that I put it out of my mind, at least consciously.

So I set about approaching the cover the same way I had done for the handful of other books I had already designed. First, I read the manuscript. Wow. I was certainly familiar with Crichton's work, but this was the first book of his that I would actually be working on, and it was amazing to read it in its raw form of typescript. The by-now well-known conceit was ingenious: breeding dinosaurs by extracting their DNA from prehistoric mosquitoes preserved in amber. And then watching in horror as Dr. John Hammond's dream crumbles and the dinosaurs wreak havoc on the island.

But the novel was so much more than that—it was a *science* book. Science fiction, yes, but based on *real* science, nonetheless.

So, taking advantage of the luxury of both living and working in Manhattan, I decided to pay a call to that bastion of real science, the American Museum of Natural History, on the Upper West Side. I had seen their dinosaur displays before, of course, but now I'd be looking at them with an entirely new purpose.

What Crichton had done in the book was take what we actually know for sure, and then built on it. And what we know for sure about dinosaurs is what their skeletal remains look like. So I would try and build on *them*.

The AMNH has one of the only intact *Tyrannosaurus rex* skeletons on the continent, and as I sat studying it that afternoon, the sunlight from the ceiling-height window behind it gradually cast its profile in silhouette. The effect was kind of astounding, and as I took it in, I squinted and tried to imagine that it was, well, alive. I had not brought a camera with me (were photographs even allowed?), or a sketchbook, as I am actually not a good sketcher—I was terrible at drawing from models in school—I just did not have the eye-to-hand coordination gene.

So I got up and went to the bookshop. Eventually I chanced upon a large, thick, scholarly hardcover tome called *Vertebrate Paleontology and Evolution* by Robert L. Carroll. As dinosaur books go, this was about as dull and unsexy as you could possibly imagine, *but*, it had a ton of technical black-and-white drawings in it, however small. These I could use as reference. So I paid for it and took it back to my office.

The over 700-page book held a lot of possibilities, with diagrams of the bones

of just about every conceivable kind of dinosaur. But I kept coming back to page 296 (see previous left-hand page). No matter how elegant the *Brontosaurus* and pterodactyls were, there was just no getting away from the *T. rex*. That thing was king. So I made a bunch of Xeroxes of it, and even tried drawing on the original page itself with ink and pencil. At first I started with the image of just the head/skull, for an emblematic look. That seemed to work, but I also wanted to try the full skeleton. I blew up the Xeroxes on our photostat machine, taped a sheet of vellum on top of it, and with my rapidograph pen, started filling it in.

What I quickly realized was that there were a lot more opportunities to create edges within the image of the entire skeleton rather than just the skull, and I could sharpen them. So yes, I did a good bit of *interpreting*. Even though the ribs and the neck bones would, of course, be covered with flesh on the living animal, here they could look just as menacing and dangerous as its teeth and claws. The key regarding my "coloring in" of the bones was figuring out when to stop. The result is what you see (opposite top).

I had always meant for the lettering to look very plain and workman-like, as you might encounter on wayfinding signs at an actual public park (though to this day I don't know why I put the black drop shadow under the red lettering of his name—it's totally unnecessary). If you look closely in good light at a copy of the original hardcover you'll also see that the skeleton image is printed in a very dark green, not black. I can't remember why I did that either (probably some sort of reference to primordial ooze).

Anyway, this finally made everyone happy (there were *many* false starts on this cover actually, which I am purposefully not boring you with here).

Crichton's book came out and was a mammoth bestseller, and then shortly thereafter my office phone rang—it was a representative from Universal, looking to buy the rights to the image. I did not own it, naturally, as I designed this as part of my salaried job. So I referred the rep to someone in Knopf's legal department to work things out.

And the rest, as they say, is history.

Chip Kidd is a graphic designer and writer, and editor at large for Pantheon. A three-time Eisner Award winner, he has written and designed over a dozen books on comics including *Peanuts: The Art of Charles M. Schulz*, *Only What's Necessary: Charles M. Schulz and the Art of Peanuts*, *Mythology: The DC Comics Art of Alex Ross*, *Marvelocity: The Marvel Comics Art of Alex Ross*, and *Fantastic Four No. 1: Panel by Panel*. His novels, *The Cheese Monkeys* and *The Learners*, were national bestsellers, as was *True Prep: It's a Whole New Old World* (with Lisa Birnbach). Other books include *Go: A Kidd's Guide to Graphic Design* and *Judge This*. He can be found online at chipkidd.com, @chip_kidd (Instagram), and @chipkidd (Twitter).

JURASSIC PARK
MICHAEL
CRICHTON

For Chip Kidd—
If only this book
were as good as its jacket!
With thanks and best
wishes—
Michael Crichton
AAK
11.30.90

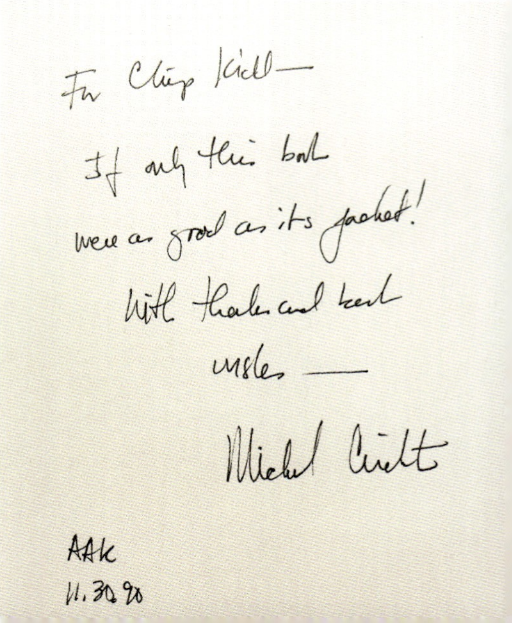

Above Right: Hardcover jacket for *Jurassic Park*, Knopf, 1990. Design and illustration by Chip Kidd.

Right: *Jurassic Park* book inscription from Michael Crichton to Chip Kidd, November 30, 1990

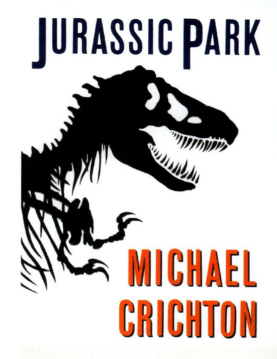

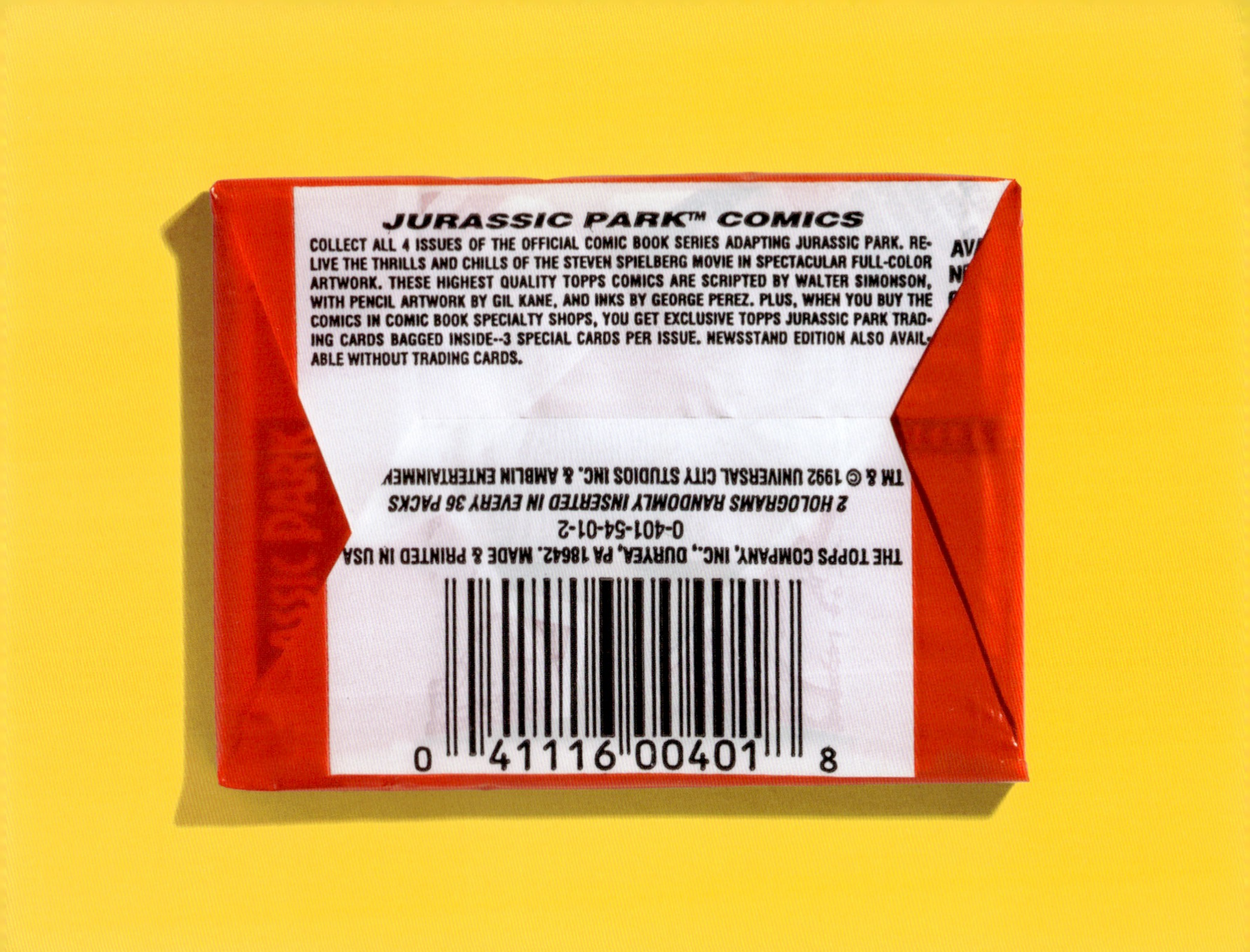
JURASSIC PARK™ COMICS
COLLECT ALL 4 ISSUES OF THE OFFICIAL COMIC BOOK SERIES ADAPTING JURASSIC PARK. RELIVE THE THRILLS AND CHILLS OF THE STEVEN SPIELBERG MOVIE IN SPECTACULAR FULL-COLOR ARTWORK. THESE HIGHEST QUALITY TOPPS COMICS ARE SCRIPTED BY WALTER SIMONSON, WITH PENCIL ARTWORK BY GIL KANE, AND INKS BY GEORGE PEREZ. PLUS, WHEN YOU BUY THE COMICS IN COMIC BOOK SPECIALTY SHOPS, YOU GET EXCLUSIVE TOPPS JURASSIC PARK TRADING CARDS BAGGED INSIDE--3 SPECIAL CARDS PER ISSUE. NEWSSTAND EDITION ALSO AVAILABLE WITHOUT TRADING CARDS.
THE TOPPS COMPANY, INC., DURYEA, PA 18642. MADE & PRINTED IN USA
0-401-54-01-2
2 HOLOGRAMS RANDOMLY INSERTED IN EVERY 36 PACKS
TM & © 1992 UNIVERSAL CITY STUDIOS INC. & AMBLIN ENTERTAINMEY
0 41116 00401 8

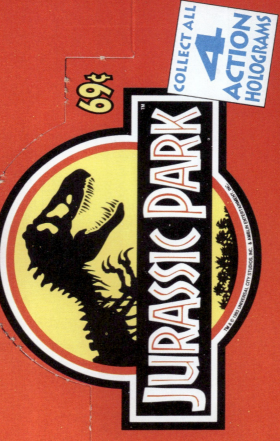

69¢

JURASSIC PARK™

COLLECT ALL **4** ACTION HOLOGRAMS

TM & © 1993 UNIVERSAL CITY STUDIOS, INC. & AMBLIN ENTERTAINMENT, INC.

MOVIE CARDS • STICKERS • HOLOGRAMS

2 HOLOGRAMS RANDOMLY INSERTED IN EVERY 36 PACKS

topps®

JP™